TEACHER'S MANUAL

FOCUS ON GRAMMAR

An **ADVANCED** Course for Reference and Practice

TEACHER'S MANUAL

Focus on Grammar

An **ADVANCED** Course for Reference and Practice

SECOND EDITION

Jay Maurer

Longman

Focus on Grammar: An Advanced Course for Reference and Practice, Teacher's Manual

Pearson Education, 10 Bank Street, White Plains, NY 10606

Vice president, director of publishing: Allen Ascher
Editorial director: Louisa Hellegers
Senior development manager: Penny Laporte
Development editors: Lise R. Minovitz and Paula H. Van Ells
Vice president, director of design and production: Rhea Banker
Executive managing editor: Linda Moser
Production manager: Alana Zdinak
Production editor: Robert Ruvo
Director of manufacturing: Patrice Fraccio
Senior manufacturing buyer: David Dickey
Cover design: Rhea Banker
Text design adaptation: Wendy Wolf and Steven Greydanus
Text composition: TSI Graphics

Tests by Lise R. Minovitz

ISBN: 0-201-38313-6

4 5 6 7 8 9 10–BAH–05 04

CONTENTS

INTRODUCTION

Focus on Grammar: An Advanced Course for Reference and Practice, Second Edition helps advanced students of English to understand and practice basic English grammar. However, teaching the rules is not the ultimate goal of the course. Rather, the aim is for students to use the language confidently and appropriately.

This Teacher's Manual provides suggestions for teaching the advanced level Student Book.

The first part of this Teacher's Manual contains general suggestions for every unit. The next part gives practical unit-by-unit teaching suggestions as well as Background Notes and Culture Notes to accompany specific exercises and grammar content in the Student Book. The Teacher's Manual also provides ready-to-use diagnostic and final tests for each part in the Student Book. In addition, the Teacher's Manual includes answer keys for the diagnostic and final tests as well as a tapescript for all the listening activities in the Student Book.

Focus on Grammar recognizes different styles of language learning and provides a variety of activities to accommodate these different styles. Some learners prefer an analytical, or rule-learning, approach. Others, especially younger learners, respond best to exposure to the language in meaningful contexts. Indeed, the same students may adopt different styles as they learn or may use different styles at different times. To complicate things further, some students respond better to visual instruction, and some better to auditory.

As teachers, we want to help the rule-learners in our classes become more able to take risks and to plunge into communicative activities. We also want to encourage the risk-takers to focus on accuracy. To this end, the ***Focus on Grammar*** series provides the variety, including listening activities, that students need. Each unit presents a balanced approach with a variety of activities so that all learners can benefit.

GENERAL SUGGESTIONS

GRAMMAR IN CONTEXT

Each unit in *Focus on Grammar: An Advanced Course for Reference and Practice, Second Edition*, begins with a reading to present the grammar in a realistic context. Students first focus on the meaning of the reading, thereby establishing a context for the language study before they focus on the target grammatical structure.

Questions to Consider: Before each reading, a drawing, cartoon, or picture and some warm-up questions get students familiar with the topic of the reading.

1. Have the class look at the reading and illustrations and identify the context.
2. Read the questions aloud to the class and ask students to respond.
3. Alternatively, have pairs of students read the questions, respond, and then share their ideas with the class.
4. Alternatively, give students two or three minutes to read the questions individually and jot down their own responses. Then invite students to share their ideas with the class.

Reading: The reading text presents language in various formats, including newspaper and magazine articles, essays, conversations, and stories. All of the readings are recorded on cassettes and CDs.

There are many ways to treat this text in the classroom. Here are several alternative suggestions:

If you have the cassette/CD:

1. Have students listen to the cassette/CD, books closed, first. Have students answer the comprehension questions provided in the unit teaching suggestions and then read the text to confirm their answers.
2. Play the cassette/CD a second time as students read along. For pronunciation practice, have students read the passage aloud in pairs as a final review.

If you don't have the cassette/CD:

1. Have students read the text silently. Then have them take turns reading the text aloud.
2. Read the passage aloud to the class. Have students read along in their books.

Comprehension questions are provided in the unit teaching suggestions. When the text is particularly challenging, you may want to supply the questions before the reading. When the text is easier, present the comprehension questions after the reading. Write the questions on the board or dictate them to the class. Have students respond in pairs and then share their ideas with the class.

The next step is to get students to identify the target grammatical structure(s) embedded in the reading.

1. Because this is an advanced-level text, target structures are not presented in boldface in the reading. Provide students with one example of each target structure. Then elicit other examples from the reading and write them on the board.
2. Ask inductive questions to get students to identify the forms of the grammatical structures and key grammar points.
3. List students' responses to these (inductive) questions on the board. As students continue on to the Grammar Presentation, they may compare these notes with the information presented in the grammar charts and grammar notes.

CULTURE NOTE: This Teacher's Manual includes Culture Notes relevant to the topic of the reading and theme of the unit.

Understanding Meaning from Context: This vocabulary comprehension exercise gets students to use context clues to define vocabulary from the reading. This exercise may be done in class (individually or in pairs) or as homework.

Developing vocabulary is especially important at the advanced level, as is taking responsibility for one's own learning. A systematic technique for achieving both these goals is to have students keep vocabulary notebooks. Encourage them to record each new expression they hear or read and the sentence in which they hear or read it. Also encourage them to guess its meaning before looking it up. You may want to make these notebooks a course requirement. If so, collect or check them at regular intervals during the course.

GRAMMAR PRESENTATION

At this point in the lesson, students should understand the structures in context and are now ready to study their forms in isolation. This section presents the target grammatical structures in a straightforward and comprehensive way. The grammar charts focus students on the form and mechanics of the grammatical structures. The grammar notes list the grammar points and exceptions in order to help students understand variations in the meaning, use, and forms of the structures.

The language presented in *Focus on Grammar: An Advanced Course for Reference and Practice*, *Second Edition* is the English of daily life in the United States and Canada. Contractions and short answers are often practiced, though more formal usage is also mentioned (and later practiced in the unit exercises) in the grammar notes.

Common grammatical terms are used throughout the book because they make grammar explanations clearer and because students have often learned them in previous language study. Students need to understand the terms as they are used and, in some cases to produce them—for example, by identifying nouns and verbs or writing certain types of clauses.

Grammar Charts: The grammar is presented visually in grammar charts. It is important to allow ample time for this part of the lesson so that students may begin to internalize the patterns.

1. Write key paradigms on the board and circle or underline important features, such as gerunds or noun clauses.
2. Give additional examples. Encourage students to supply their own examples.
3. Use magazine pictures or other cues for a drill so that students become accustomed to producing the form. See specific suggestions for classroom drills in each unit.

Grammar Notes: These notes pull together and make explicit the information about meaning, use, and form that students have encountered in the introductory reading and grammar charts. The grammar notes also offer information about degrees of formality. These will help students to use the forms appropriately as well as correctly.

1. Ask students to read each note. Write the examples on the board and highlight important features.
2. Give additional examples and ask students to supply their own.
3. For each note, check students' comprehension by asking them to complete a sentence or fill in the blank of a sentence.
4. For some units, this Teacher's Manual provides suggestions for teaching this section inductively. The inductive approach works especially well with advanced-level students who have enough language to intuit or explain a rule or a grammar point.

FOCUSED PRACTICE

This section gets students to practice using the target grammar structure in various contexts. Many of the exercises have straightforward and objective answers (and are cross-referenced to the grammar notes), so they can serve well as homework or for individual work in class. However, some of the exercises have more open-ended answers, in which students are challenged to come up with alternative ways of using the structures. Students can benefit from completing these exercises in pairs or small groups. Specific teaching suggestions for these exercises are provided in each unit.

All of the exercises develop the theme of the introductory reading, so they often provide cultural information as well as grammar practice. The completed exercises can be used as readings to develop students' reading skills and cultural knowledge. Comprehension questions for the longer and more substantial exercise passages are provided in the unit teaching suggestions.

Discover the Grammar: This is the opening activity for the Focused Practice section. It gets students to identify (and occasionally to manipulate) the target grammar structures in a realistic context. This exercise may be done by the whole class, in pairs, or individually as homework. Specific teaching suggestions are provided in each unit.

Editing: All of the units include an editing exercise to test students' sensitivity to incorrect usage of the target grammar structures. Students are required to identify and correct errors in a contextualized passage such as a letter, diary entry, or essay. The direction line indicates the number of errors in the passage. Remind students that the example error is included in the total number of errors.

1. Have students read through the passage quickly to understand its context and meaning.

2. Have students read the passage line by line, circling in pencil any incorrect structures and then writing in their corrections.

3. To review the material, have students take turns reading the passage line by line, including all sentences, even the correct ones. Alternatively, slowly read the passage aloud to the class and have students interrupt you with their corrections. There are usually correct usages of the target structures in each editing exercise. Be sure to ask students about these usages as well—i. e., why they are not errors.

COMMUNICATION PRACTICE

This section gets students to apply the target structures appropriately in realistic situations, as well as to develop their listening comprehension and speaking fluency. The types of exercises in this section range from listening comprehension to information gaps, games, and group discussions. Since there are many variations in the exercise types, specific instructions are provided in the unit teaching suggestions. The following are general instructions for each type of exercise you will encounter.

Listening:

1. Explain the situational context of the listening passage.

2. Before playing the cassette/CD, ask the students to read over the items in the exercise so that they know what to listen for.

3. You may or may not wish to explain unknown vocabulary before the students listen. Sometimes it is necessary to do so. However, students at an advanced level are often skilled enough to perceive unknown vocabulary words or expressions, and they may be helped more by simply being given the instruction to "listen for words you don't know and try to write them down."

4. Ask the students to listen the first time with their pencils down.

5. Play the cassette/CD, or read aloud the tapescript included in this Teacher's Manual. If you choose to read, speak with a lot of expression and at a natural pace. Change positions and tone of voice to indicate who the speaker is. You can also draw stick figures and label them with the characters' names, so that you can point to the appropriate character as you change roles. However, it may benefit your students more not to have this assistance.

6. Tell the students to listen again to complete the task. Play the cassette/CD again or read the tapescript.

7. Let the students listen as many times as necessary in order to complete the task.

8. Elicit answers and write them on the board. Answer any questions the students may have.

9. Go over any new words and expressions contained in the listening. Ask the students to write them in their vocabulary notebooks, along with the sentences in which they occur.

10. You may wish to play the cassette/CD a final time for students to review the passage, using the corrected answers.

Games:

Games occur in many of the units. They allow the students to use the target structures in a natural context without focusing too much on the grammar. Nonetheless, when students are instructed to use a certain grammatical structure as part of the game, be sure that they do so.

In some of the games, students construct the questions or items. Don't rush through this activity or short-circuit it. Much is to be gained by having students use their language skill in a creative way.

Information Gaps:

Information gap activities occur in at least half of the units. Most often, students work in pairs and ask each other questions in order to fill in the missing information, which often involves the grammatical structures taught in the units. Do not rush through this activity. Model the kinds of questions that students will need to ask to get the correct information.

Make sure that each partner has the correct information in the information gap. Go around the room and check for this.

Many of the information gap activities are followed by a discussion of the issues involved in the text they have been working with. Make sure that the information gap activity goes beyond the level of a task to complete. Stress this part of the activity.

Pair and Group Discussions:

These are intended to be realistic activities in which students communicate in a real way about issues stemming from the unit theme. Many students do not always take discussion activities seriously, regarding them as opportunities to slack off or take a break. It is important that this not happen. Each discussion should have an outcome produced by the students, so it is a good idea to require the students to do something concrete with each discussion. You might ask them to share their opinions with the class. Appoint a class scribe to summarize the main points made. Alternatively, you may wish students to write a paragraph or even an essay about points or insights that came out of the discussions.

Essays:

Every unit in *Focus on Grammar: An Advanced Course for Reference and Practice, Second Edition* includes an essay writing activity. Essays earlier in the book are shorter—two to three paragraphs. As students progress through the text, the essays become longer so that by the end of the course they are writing compositions of four or five paragraphs. Essay writing activities should be coordinated as carefully as possible with the *From Grammar to Writing* sections that end each Part. Essays are always based in some way on the theme of the unit and originate from material covered in previous exercises, so that students are well prepared to complete the writing task. Specific teaching instructions are provided in the unit's teaching suggestions. The following are general suggestions for the teaching of writing.

Prewriting: Be sure students understand the requirements of the assignment. Have students brainstorm ideas for the writing in pairs or larger groups. It may be helpful to have students begin with a focused freewriting activity in which they write for ten or fifteen minutes on a topic they have selected without stopping or worrying about correctness.

Composing and Correcting:

1. Have students compose a draft of the essay as homework. Ask them to submit it to you or share it with a partner in class. You or the students may correct this draft for meaning—i.e., has the student made his or her point and supported it fully? Are the topic sentences adequate? If students do peer corrections, have them submit the writing to you for final review.

2. Return the first draft and have students revise it and submit a second draft. Read the second draft for accuracy of grammatical expression and appropriateness of vocabulary.

3. When correcting students' writing, circle the grammatical errors studied in the current and / or previous units and have students work in small groups to correct the errors. Have them submit the corrections to you for final review.

Presentation: When you and the students are satisfied with the quality of their writing, have them share it with the class in small groups or in pairs. In some instances, essays may be posted on the classroom bulletin board or published in a series of students' writings.

Picture Discussion:
This is the culminating activity in the unit. Every unit ends with a picture: a cartoon, an illustration, a painting, or a photograph. Follow the specific suggestions given in the teaching notes for each unit. However, here are general suggestions:

1. First have students work in pairs or, alternatively, in groups of three or four. Have them simply describe everything they see happening in the picture.

2. Have them answer the questions given in the Picture Discussion direction line. Follow the suggestions given in the teaching notes for each unit for ways in which to get the students to use the target structures as much as possible.

Expansion: An Expansion exercise can be found at the end of every unit in this Teacher's Manual. This exercise offers further writing practice with the target structure(s) of the unit.

REVIEW OR SELFTEST

The units in the Student Book are grouped into ten parts. At the end of each part there is a *Review or SelfTest* section and a *From Grammar to Writing* section. The *Review or SelfTest* section gives students a chance to check their knowledge of the part's grammar and review any weak areas before moving on to the next chapter. There are various ways to use this section. The following is a list of alternative suggestions.

1. Have students complete the exercises at home and check their answers in the *Answer Key*, bringing to class any remaining questions. Alternatively, have students compare answers in pairs or go over them as a class when they return.

2. Have students complete the exercises in class so that you can circulate to see how individual students are coping.

3. Use appropriate exercises as extra practice for students who need them as you progress through the units.

FROM GRAMMAR TO WRITING

The *From Grammar to Writing* section focuses on the following writing issues: the sentence; subject-verb and pronoun-antecedent agreement; topic sentences; parallelism; fragments, run-on sentences, and comma splices; punctuation in adjective clauses; direct and indirect speech; and unity, support, and coherence. Each section has several exercises designed to familiarize students with a specific issue. These exercises are suitable for homework or class activity, including pair work.

The most important feature of each *From Grammar to Writing* section is a final writing exercise called *Apply It to Your Writing*. In this activity, students apply the principles they have just learned. They write short compositions and then work with partners to edit each other's work. This exercise should be done carefully and thoroughly. Ask your students to submit both their original and revised writing to you. These *Apply It to Your Writing* activities can be coordinated with the essays in each unit of the Student Book.

TEACHING SUGGESTIONS

PART I TENSE AND TIME

 UNIT 1 PRESENT AND FUTURE TIME

GRAMMAR **IN CONTEXT** (pages 2–3)

See the General Suggestions for Grammar in Context on page 2.

ESTABLISH THE CONTEXT: The theme of the unit is travel. The unit reading deals with one aspect of travel, bargaining. Ask your students what experiences they have had with bargaining and what they think of the process.

Questions to Consider, page 2: Read the questions aloud or have students read them. Give the class one minute to look at the cartoon and jot down a response. Briefly discuss the students' ideas.

Reading, pages 2–3: See the General Suggestions for Reading on page 2.

CULTURE NOTE: Some Americans are quite willing to bargain, but others are inhibited by the prospect. Bargaining is probably less common in North America than in many other places in the world.

Understanding Meaning from Context, page 2
See the General Suggestions for Understanding Meaning from Context on page 2.

You may want to point out the following vocabulary: *landmarks* (important natural geographical features or prominent buildings that identify a location); *souvenirs* (remembrances; items bought, usually while traveling, that remind the buyer of the trip); *not too big a deal* (not very important or common); *yard* or *garage sale* (in North America, an informal sale of household items, usually at greatly reduced prices, held in a person's yard or garage); *intimidated* (literally, "made timid"; afraid, anxious).

GRAMMAR **PRESENTATION:** Present and Future Time (pages 4–7)

See the General Suggestions for Grammar Presentation on page 3.

Much of Unit 1 will be review. It seems, however, that even advanced students can always benefit from extra work on the tenses, particularly the contrast between the simple present and the present progressive. Begin with a simple review of this contrast. Bring some pictures to class showing actions. Have students work in pairs, making as many statements as possible about what can be seen happening in the picture (present progressive) and what can be generalized about the picture (simple present).

NOTE 1: Simple present: The use of the simple present to narrate actions in sequence may be new to your students. Have them practice it by writing a paragraph of ten sentences or so that narrates a happening. The first time they write this, they should write it in the past. Then have them change it to the present, placing the verbs in the simple present to show the sequence of events.

NOTE 2: Present progressive: Read the note in the Student Book with your class. Answer any questions.

NOTE 3: Present perfect and present perfect progressive: Remind your students that the use of these structures is to connect the past and the present. They will be dealt with again in Unit 3; for now, have your students review them by asking them to construct sentences such as these:

I've been married for five years.
I've been studying English since March.

Note 4: *Will* in the progressive: This structure may be used to describe an action that will be in progress at some future time, but it is more commonly used in conversation to show a future intention that is close in time to the present.

Note 5: *Be going to*: Read the note in the Student Book with your class. Answer any questions.

Note 6: *Will* and *be going to*: Students commonly use these interchangeably, but the two structures are used distinctly. Stress that if the action or event has already been planned, *be going to* should be used. If it is decided at the moment of speaking, *will* should be used. Point out that when native speakers use *will*, they often use it in its other sense—to show willingness, not to indicate the future.

Note 7: Present progressive as future: Students often have difficulty with this structure, perhaps thinking that the future must be expressed only with *will* or *be going to*. However, the use of the present progressive to show already-arranged future actions is extremely common. Stress the difference between the progressive and *be going to*. *Be going to* shows future intention but not necessarily any prior arrangement. Have students write a number of sentences using present progressive about their future actions that have already been arranged.

Note 8: Simple present as future: A common error is to use the simple present to talk about near future actions, but this is only correct in English if there is a timetable or schedule.

Note 9: Two actions in the future: This is one of the most difficult aspects of English grammar for students to master. Practice is the key. Demonstrate that when two future actions are described in two clauses, one independent and one dependent, the one in the dependent clause shows the earlier of the two actions. *Will* and *be going* with a future meaning are not used in the dependent clause. Have students practice this by asking them to construct sentences such as these:

As soon as class is over, I'm going to go home.
When I get home, I'll call my friend Alicia.
I'm going to watch TV after I finish dinner.

Another way to practice this is to take paragraphs from newspapers or magazines and delete the future verbs. Ask students to restore the verbs.

Note 10: Future perfect: Read the note in the Student Book with your class. Answer any questions.

FOCUSED PRACTICE (pages 8–13)

See the General Suggestions for Focused Practice on page 3.

1. Discover the Grammar, page 8
See the General Suggestions for Discover the Grammar on page 4.

2. A Postcard Home, page 9
Point out that in informal English, the subject *I* is often deleted:

Went to the British Museum. Also went to the Tower of London.

3. Did You Do Any Bargaining?, page 9
The second part of the exercise, questions 4–6, can be used as prompts for a role play.

4. The Flea Market, page 10
You may want to point out the following vocabulary: *flea market* (a market, usually held outdoors, where antiques and household items are sold, often at reduced prices); *splitting headache* (a very bad headache); *excuse me for living* (a common phrase said to indicate that another person has made an unreasonable and overly critical statement).

5. A World Traveler, page 10
This is an authentic reading. You may want to point out the following vocabulary: *dog-eared* (worn or tattered, the result of much use); *sovereign* (independent); *roaming* (wandering, usually without much prior planning); *remote* (in faraway, difficult-to-get-to places); *finagle* (obtain or achieve by indirect methods, sometimes deceitful ones); *frostbite* (injury to the skin and tissue underneath it, usually through excessive exposure to cold temperatures); *like father, like son* (a saying indicating that a son often imitates his father's behavior); *mental baggage* (unnecessary and often inaccurate

information in the mind); *preconceived* (refers to impressions or beliefs, often inaccurate, reached before actually experiencing something); *go with the flow* (follow the easy, logical course of action).

Discussion: Ask students what they think of this article and Clouse's attempt to visit every country and place. Is it worthwhile? It might be interesting to take a map to class and locate the three places Clouse has not yet visited: the Paracel Islands, Bouvet, and Clipperton. Ask students if they agree with Clouse's statement about the basic goodness and hospitality of the majority of people. This will prepare them to write the essay in Exercise 11.

6. Understanding Meaning From Context, page 12
Allow students plenty of time to complete the exercise. Encourage them to discuss the reasons for their choices.

7. By This Time Next Year . . . , page 12
Students always seem to need practice with the future perfect. The tense is not greatly used in English, but it is not rare either. Have students practice making sentences in the future perfect, both in the affirmative and the negative. Extend the activity by asking the class to make predictions about the future of the Earth. For example:

By 2020, colonies will have been established on Mars.

8. Editing, page 13
You may want to point out that *mugged* means "robbed, usually on the street, or threatened with robbery."

COMMUNICATION PRACTICE, (pages 14–15)

See the General Suggestions for Communication Practice on page 4.

9. Listening, page 14
After students have finished the listening exercise, ask them to discuss their experiences regarding guided tours versus traveling on their own.

10. Group Guessing Game: A Vacation Spot, page 14
Have students take the time to prepare good questions. This activity provides a good opportunity to use the future progressive in a natural, conversational way.

11. Essay, page 14
The students should be well-prepared to write this essay using information from the reading and discussion of the article about Clouse in Exercises 5 and 6.

12. Picture Discussion, page 15
Have your students work in pairs and make statements about the picture, using as many of the structures presented in the unit as possible. For example:

It's raining. It's been raining for hours. The father is trying to fix the car. The man in the other car is going to stop.

Expansion

Travel Pictures: Have your students bring in travel pictures (for example, postcards, magazine pictures, or photographs). Have them write essays about what is happening in their pictures and what they think will happen next. Encourage them to use correct verb tenses.

UNIT 2 · PAST TIME

GRAMMAR IN CONTEXT (pages 16–18)

See the General Suggestions for Grammar in Context on page 2.

ESTABLISH THE CONTEXT: The theme of the unit is marriage, and the reading is about a recent marriage in which the groom advertised for a bride and his friends and relatives voted on the best one. This amounts to an "arranged marriage."

Questions to Consider, page 16: Read the questions aloud or have your students read them. What do they think is the ideal way for a couple to get to know each other? Are there any arranged marriages in their culture?

Reading, pages 16–17: After your students have finished the reading, discuss it. What do the students think? Is this marriage likely to last?

Understanding Meaning From Context, page 18
See the General Suggestions for Understanding Meaning from Context on page 2.

You may want to point out the following vocabulary: *mixer* (an informal party where people can get acquainted); *rolled around* (finally arrived); *looked on* (watched).

GRAMMAR **PRESENTATION:** Past Time (pages 19–21)

See the General Suggestions for Grammar Presentation on page 3.

NOTES 1 AND 2: Some of Unit 2 will be review. Although your students will probably have a good understanding of the difference between the simple past and the past continuous, they will benefit from some drill.

NOTE 3: A key contrast in Unit 2 is between the simple past and the present perfect. Even at an advanced level, many students make mistakes, using the present perfect where the simple past should be used and vice versa. Stress that the present perfect is the indefinite past. No specific past time is mentioned or implied. The simple past is the definite past; a specific past time is stated or implied.

Another key point about the present perfect is that it shows relevance of the action to the present moment. At 7 P.M., the question *Have you eaten dinner yet?* is likely to be asked—not *Did you eat dinner yet?* At the same time, the question *Have you had breakfast yet?* will not be asked.

One of the best ways to practice the contrast is to have students ask *Have you ever . . . ?* questions. When the answer is *yes*, the question "when" can be asked. That question, of course, will be answered in the simple past.

NOTE 4: The contrast between the simple past and the past perfect is an important one. One good way to present the contrast is to ask students to describe their actions on a particular day in chronological order: "At 6:30, I got up. I took a shower. Then I had breakfast." After this, show them how the usage changes when you use "by" or "by the time." This is a point in the past, so all actions before it will use the past perfect: "By 8:30 A.M., I had gotten up, taken a shower, eaten breakfast, walked the dog, read the newspaper, and left for work."

Another good way to practice the past perfect is to ask students historical questions like these:
Had television been invented by 1900?
Had Columbus traveled to the New World by 1500?

NOTES 5 AND 6: The principal difference between *used to* and *would* is that *would* is used to express regularly-occurring actions in the past, while *used to* can be used to refer to past states or actions. *Would* is neutral about whether the action still takes place. *Used to*, in contrast, has the added implication that the situation or action is no longer true. Thus, *would* is not used in the past with the verbs *have*, *be*, and so forth, because these verbs are stative and do not suggest actions. Practice this contrast by having students work in groups and list past actions, describing them with *would*. Then, have them make sentences with past states or actions that are no longer true, using *used to*.

NOTE 7: The term *future in the past* may be a bit difficult to understand; it simply refers to past states and actions seen from a present point of view. Remind students that *be going to* is used to show future of intention. Have them construct affirmative sentences about things they intended to do but didn't, along with things that they didn't intend that happened.

FOCUSED PRACTICE (pages 22–28)

See the General Suggestions for Focused Practice on page 3.

1. Discover The Grammar, page 22
See the General Suggestions for Discover the Grammar on page 4.

2. Do Opposites Attract?, page 23
You may want to point out the following vocabulary: *blind date* (an arranged date between two people who have not met each other before); *opinionated* (having excessively strong opinions).

Discussion: When your students have completed this exercise, discuss the question of opposites attracting. Is a relationship more likely to succeed if the partners are similar or dissimilar?

3. The Rest Is History, page 24
Find out whether the students feel that events happen in this fashion, by chance.

4. Before and After, page 24
You may want to point out the following vocabulary: *That's a trip* (That's really an amazing experience); *been there, done that* (an expression people use to suggest that they are no longer interested in doing or repeating the experience).

5. Plans and Expectations, pages 25–26
What do your students think about expectations? Do things usually turn out as they have planned?

6. Dear Ann, page 27
This is an authentic reading. You may want to point out the following vocabulary: *No-shows* (people who don't come to something they said they were going to attend); *caterers* (professionals who provide food for parties and weddings); *RSVP* (Please respond as to whether or not you are going to attend—from the French expression *répondez s'il vous plaît*); *slobs* (untidy, rude, obnoxious people).

Culture Note: In the United States, it is not uncommon to discuss personal problems with relative strangers. People may seek the advice of acquaintances, psychiatrists, or advice columnists.

7. Editing, page 28
See the General Suggestions for Editing on page 4.

COMMUNICATION PRACTICE (pages 29–32)

See the General Suggestions for Communication Practice on page 4.

8. Listening, page 29
You may want to point out the following vocabulary: *souls* (people); *conventional* (normal, usual); *takes the cake* (is the most outrageous or disappointing example); *one for the scrapbook* (an experience important enough to be documented—for example, a picture placed in a scrapbook).

Discussion: Have your students heard of other unusual wedding ceremonies? If so, have them describe them.

9. Information Gap: Better Than It Used to Be, pages 30 and 32
What do the students think of the underlying ideas here? Do marriages suffer when the partners do not spend much time with each other?

10. Essay, page 31
Make sure that your students interview older people who can tell them about the way things used to be. You might ask your students to comment on whether they think customs have improved.

11. Picture Discussion, page 31
Have the students carefully describe what is happening here. Do they think the artist intended to make a statement? If so, what was it? Does this picture show a negative view of marital relationships, or is this portrayal just usual in situations where the people know each other well?

EXPANSION

Courtship and Marriage: Have your students write short stories describing the courtship and marriage of couples they know well (for example, their parents, their grandparents, themselves). Encourage them to use the simple past, past perfect, *would*, and *used to* correctly.

 UNIT 3 PAST, PRESENT, AND FUTURE

GRAMMAR **IN CONTEXT** (pages 33–35)

See the General Suggestions for Grammar in Context on page 2.

ESTABLISH THE CONTEXT: The theme of the unit is technological development in general and robots in particular. Begin by asking students what they know about robots—either from fact or fiction. They will probably mention such robot figures as C-3PO and R2-D2 from *Star Wars*. The existence of such robots may be closer than we think. Are the students aware that robots already exist, particularly in industry?

Questions to Consider, page 33: See the General Suggestions for Questions to Consider on page 2.

Reading, pages 33–34: After your students have finished the reading, have your students discuss the pros and cons of robots. Do they think that it would be good to have personal robots in the home? What are the potential disadvantages?

Understanding Meaning from Context, page 35
See the General Suggestions for Understanding Meaning from Context on page 2.

You may want to point out the following vocabulary: *humanoid* (looking vaguely like humans); *drudgery* (tasks performed by a "drudge," a person who does unpleasant, repetitive work).

GRAMMAR **PRESENTATION:** Contrasting Tenses: Past, Present, and Future (pages 36–39)

See the General Suggestions for Grammar Presentation on page 3.

NOTES 1 AND 2: Much of Unit 3 will be review. However, four major points are intended to deepen students' knowledge of grammar. One of the key contrasts in the unit is that between the present perfect and the present perfect progressive. Two points need to be made clearly. First, the two tenses are not interchangeable in reference to finished or unfinished actions. The verb *write* provides a good illustration. Consider these sentences:

Novelist Frank Garcia has written six novels.
He's been writing his seventh novel since last January and expects to finish it soon.

Verbs that lend themselves to this difference include *visit*, *read*, *take a trip*, and *build*. Second, the two structures have slightly different meanings with regard to actions in progress. For example:

Carrie has been living in Salamanca since last February. (The suggestion is that the situation is temporary and a change may occur.)
Sam has lived in Salamanca for five years. (The suggestion is that the situation is permanent and not likely to change.)

To practice these points, have your students ask each other questions such as:

How long have you been attending this school?
How many courses have you taken?

Also have the class make sentences with the word *always*, reminding them that only the present perfect can be used when *always* is present in the sentence. For example:

I've always lived here. (NOT: *I've always been living here.*)

NOTE 3: Many verbs are inherently stative but can be used in active ways, generally taking on different meanings. Have students practice using these verbs actively. For example:

He's been <u>seeing</u> a psychiatrist. (visiting)
Joe and Mary have been <u>seeing each other</u> for months. (dating)
I thought I was <u>seeing things</u>. (hallucinating)
I thought I was <u>hearing things</u>. (having auditory hallucinations)
I'm really <u>being a jerk</u> today. Sorry. (behaving like a jerk)

NOTE 4: Even advanced students have difficulty with the use of *there*. Have your students practice making sentences with *there* in more complex structures—*there used to be, there didn't use to be, there ought to be, there wouldn't be, there must have been, there has been, there had been*, and the like.

NOTE 5: To practice sequence of tenses, have students write a number of sentences in the present and future. Then ask them to change them to the past. Note the changes that occur. For example:

I <u>think</u> I <u>can</u> come	→	*I <u>thought</u> I <u>could</u> come.*
She <u>says</u> it <u>will</u> rain.	→	*She <u>said</u> it <u>would</u> rain.*
I'm sure there <u>won't</u> be time.	→	*He <u>was</u> sure there <u>wouldn't</u> be time.*

FOCUSED PRACTICE (pages 40–43)

See the General Suggestions for Focused Practice on page 3.

1. Discover the Grammar, page 40
See the General Suggestions for Discover the Grammar on page 4.

2. In the Year 2012, pages 41–42
When the students have finished doing this exercise, ask them to imagine a time when personal robots are common in the household. What tasks would students want robots to perform? What tasks would they want to reserve for themselves?

3. We've Come a Long Way, pages 42–43
Allow your students plenty of time to complete this exercise. Make sure that they interview people who grew up some time ago.

4. Editing, page 43
See the General Suggestions for Editing on page 4.

COMMUNICATION PRACTICE (pages 44–46)

See the General Suggestions for Communication Practice on page 4.

5. Listening, page 44
This newscast is hypothetical. You may want to point out that *affordable* means "reasonably priced."

6. Information Gap: Renegade Robots, pages 44–45 and 46
This is an authentic reading. You may want to point out the following vocabulary: *renegade* (runaway; rebellious); *summons* (a command to report to some location); *the Twilight Zone* (a place where nothing seems normal—if your students are not familiar with the science fiction TV program by this name, tell them that it dramatized situations involving strange occurrences and supernatural experiences); *shuffling* (a movement or noise as of feet being dragged slowly); *heading* (coming or going in the direction of); *intruder* (someone who enters a place wrongly or illegally); *eerie* (very strange, supernatural); *den* (a room in a house for study or relaxation). Point out that the last sentence, "So who are you going to call when a robot comes to life?" is reminiscent of lines from the movie *Ghostbusters*: "Who are ya gonna call?" "Ghostbusters."

7. Essay, page 45
If the students don't want to write serious essays, give them the option of writing humorous essays, using the Information Gap or Listening for ideas.

8. Picture Discussion, page 45
You may want to point out the following vocabulary: *fluke* (something, often positive, that happens abnormally); *bizarre* (very strange); *aberration* (a departure from normality); *you're goin' down* (you're going to be defeated).

Discussion: Are humans doomed to lose to computers in game situations? Will humans lose their capacity to think if they depend too much on machines? Is this already happening?

EXPANSION

A Major Invention in Our Lives: Have your students write essays about a modern technological invention (for example, the cell phone, the Internet, DVD players). Encourage them to use correct verb tenses to answer the following questions:

- *What did people use before this was invented?*
- *How has the invention impacted our lives today?*
- *How do you think the invention will change in the future?*

REVIEW OR SELFTEST
See the General Suggestions for Review or SelfTest on page 6.

FROM GRAMMAR TO WRITING: THE SENTENCE
See the General Suggestions for From Grammar to Writing on page 6.

This section deals with the sentence, so you might wish to teach it along with the first essay assignment in Unit 1.

Introduction, page 52
Begin by asking the students what a sentence is. They will probably have heard the statement that a sentence is a complete thought. Tell them that this is true at some level. However, it is not a very useful tool for figuring out what a sentence is because different people may not agree on the definition of a complete thought. Give the students a grammatical definition of the sentence: *A sentence contains a subject, a verb, at least one independent clause, initial capitalization and end punctuation.* Elicit examples of sentences from the class, writing them on the board.

Make sure that the students understand the difference between dependent and independent clauses. An enjoyable activity for teaching the difference is to write the dependent and independent clauses of a number of complex sentences on separate file cards. Distribute them to class members. Have each student read his or her clause. Each student then finds the person with the other half of his or her sentence and puts the sentence together. Then, have them write the complex sentences on the board. For example:

unless you pay your bill immediately (dependent clause) +
your telephone service will be cut off (independent clause) =
Unless you pay your bill immediately, your telephone service will be cut off. (complex sentence)

Remind students that the order of the clauses can be changed:
Your telephone service will be cut off unless you pay your bill immediately.

The next step is to determine why certain word groups are not sentences. Carefully go over the examples on page 52 of the Student Book. Make sure that your students understand why the last five examples are not sentences. Elicit more examples of non-sentences, writing these on the board. Then ask the students to add words to make them sentences.

Demonstrate that one way to determine whether a word group is a sentence or not is to read it aloud. Our internal language sense will often tell us whether or not a word group is a sentence. Advise the students to pay close attention to the rise and fall of their voices. This sort of activity is particularly important when reading a piece of discourse. Advise your students to always read their compositions aloud to catch errors, particularly sentence fragments.

Exercise 1, page 53
Assign students to complete the exercise in pairs. Go over the exercise as a class when they have finished.

Exercise 2, pages 53–54

Divide students into small groups to complete the exercise. Have them read the sentences aloud. This will help them to decide which word groups are not sentences. When they have finished, go over the exercise as a class. Ask which phrases or dependent clauses can be combined with independent clauses to make the paragraph completely correct. You may want to have the class rewrite the entire passage using correct punctuation.

Teach your students the difference between the period and the semicolon. Explain that the two marks do essentially the same thing, but that the semicolon connects two independent clauses that have a close connection in meaning. Stress that the word after a semicolon is not capitalized. Give examples of incorrect sentences consisting of two independent clauses with no end punctuation or initial capitalization. Ask your students how they can be punctuated using the period and the semicolon. For example:

we finally went to South America last year we had been planning the trip for years →
We finally went to South America last year. We had been planning the trip for years. OR
We finally went to South America last year; we had been planning the trip for years.

Have the students work in groups to create pairs of sentences that are separated by periods and others that are separated by semicolons. Go over their examples as a class.

A day or two after you have taught the semicolon, bring in example sentences with colons. Explain that the colon introduces a list or an explanation. For example:

We went to five places on our vacation: Buenos Aires, Lima, Machu Picchu, Rio de Janeiro, and Cuzco. (list)
This is what I told Jim when he asked to borrow my book: You didn't return the last book I lent you. (explanation)

Have the students work in groups to construct sentences using the colon. Go over them as a class.

Exercise 3, page 55

Divide the students into groups to work on the exercise. Encourage them to read the sentences aloud to determine the sentence breaks. Go over the entire paragraph as a class.

Exercise 4: Apply It to Your Writing, page 55

Ask your students to complete the assignment at home or individually in class. Be sure to stress the step of reading their paragraphs aloud to themselves. Then have the students work in pairs to read each other's compositions aloud, pointing out possible sentence fragments. Then have the students revise their compositions if necessary before submitting them to you.

PART II MODALS

 ## UNIT 4 MODALS: NECESSITY

GRAMMAR **IN CONTEXT** (pages 58–60)

See the General Suggestions for Grammar in Context on page 2.

ESTABLISH THE CONTEXT: The theme of the unit is cross-cultural differences. Begin with the illustration. In your students' culture, are people supposed to take off their shoes when entering someone's house? Are there other practices expected in their culture but not in certain others?

Questions to Consider, page 58: See the General Suggestions for Questions to Consider on page 2.

Reading, pages 59–60: Play the tape. Ask the students to tell about any similar personal cross-cultural experiences they have had.

Understanding Meaning from Context, page 60

See the General Suggestions for Understanding Meaning from Context on page 2.

You may want to point out the following vocabulary: *gracious* (kind, courteous, and warm); *chuckled* (laughed quietly or gently); *get going* (leave).

GRAMMAR **PRESENTATION**: Modals: Necessity (pages 61–65)

See the General Suggestions for Grammar Presentation on page 3.

Unit 4 will be partly review and consolidation. Focus on those modals or uses of modals that are likely to be new to your class. After the students have read the opener, ask them to identify each modal that expresses necessity. Take one example of each modal and ask the students to paraphrase what the modal means.

NOTES 1–3: Read the note in the Student Book with your class. Answer any questions.

NOTE 4: Review the difference between *must, have to,* and *have got to. Have to* is the all-purpose expression that can be used in all kinds of situations. Also review the difference between *don't have to* and *mustn't.* While *mustn't* is often replaced in conversation by *shouldn't* or *had better not,* it is still used enough that students need to be familiar with it.

NOTE 5: Read the note in the Student Book with your class. Answer any questions.

NOTE 6: Even though students are expected to have learned most modals and modal-like expressions by now, it is a good idea to review them. Review the difference between *should* and *must.* A good context for illustrating the difference is travel to foreign countries. For example:

You must have a passport. (There's no escaping it.)
You should take several different kinds of clothing. (It's a good idea but not a requirement.)

NOTE 7: Point out the forms of *had better.* It is sometimes used in the past:

You'd better not have scratched my car. (You're in trouble if you did.)

The question form is also worth mentioning:

Hadn't we better get going soon?

As the grammar note points out, students need to exercise care in using *had better.* It is not interchangeable with *should* and, inappropriately used, can sound rude.

NOTE 8: Compare *have to* and *be supposed to.* A good illustration is this:

You have to have a license to drive. (It's a requirement.)
You're supposed to obey the speed limit. (This is the expectation, but many people don't obey it.)

NOTE 9: Give your students plenty of practice with *should have* and *shouldn't have.* Ask them to work in groups and write down things they regret, using *should* and *shouldn't have.*

NOTE 10: Read the note in the Student Book with your class. Answer any questions.

NOTE 11: Point out that *could have* and *might have* referring to past opportunity are close in meaning. The form with *might have* is a little more polite, less direct.

It is worth spending some time using *had to* in combination with the modals *must have* and *might have.* Your students may not be very familiar with the use of the perfect modals to express past obligation. If they need more preparation, create situations that elicit these structures and present them to the class in a handout. For example:

John said that he didn't have to go to work today and that he would be here by 2:30, and it's already 3:00. He might have had to go to work after all.

Point out that the form *hadn't to* is incorrect; *didn't have to* must be used.

NOTE 12: As the grammar note says, *shall* is rare in American English except in questions about somebody else's advice as to a course of action. In this case, *shall* means "Do you want me / us to . . . ? Or "Is it your opinion that I should . . . ?" North Americans occasionally use *shall* for the future, but when they do, they are being very formal or trying to sound funny or different.

NOTE 13: To practice the difference between *could* and *was / were able to,* have the students write down five things that they could do (had the ability to do) five years ago that they can't do now.

Questions to Consider, page 77: Discuss the questions. Elicit as many answers to the questions as possible. Then play the tape or read the opener. Ask students to confirm their previous answers.

Reading, pages 77–79: See the General Suggestions for Reading on page 2.

Understanding Meaning From Context, page 79
See the General Suggestions for Understanding Meaning from Context on page 2.

You may want to point out the following vocabulary: *groaned* (complained loudly but not too seriously); *tolerantly* (allowing something in a good-natured manner); *chorused* (said together in a group); *fanatics* (people who are excessively enthusiastic about something); *mused* (said while being absorbed in one's own thoughts).

GRAMMAR **PRESENTATION:** Modals: Certainty (pages 80–82)

See the General Suggestions for Grammar Presentation on page 3.

Unit 4 deals with one of the major uses of modals: expressing degrees of necessity. Unit 5 deals with the other major use: expressing degrees of certainty. Your students will already be familiar with the forms and sentence patterns of modals, so the main thrust of Unit 5 should be semantic.

NOTE 1: Your students will probably already have a reasonably good mastery of the use of modals to show certainty, but you might nonetheless begin with a continuum drawn on the board showing the range of modal use. For example:

0 %		*50 %*				*100 %*
is not	*could*	*might*	*may*	*should*	*must*	*is*

This diagram represents one way of conceptualizing degrees of certainty. There are no mathematical equivalents, of course, but this shows the general range. Regarding the use of *may* and *might*, many speakers seem to feel that *might* is strictly a 50/50 situation and that *may* suggests more likelihood. Not all speakers agree, however.

One good way to practice the use of modals to show certainty is to take a number of magazine pictures to class. Ask students to speculate about what is happening in the pictures. Have students work in groups and write as many sentences as they can. It is suggested that you focus on practicing the past forms (*must have, might have,* etc.) even more than the present forms. These are the forms that students have more difficulty using or are reluctant to use.

NOTE 2: The meaning of *must* to show probability is essentially this: "It's true, or almost certainly true, but I have no direct evidence to prove it." *Have got to,* as in its use to express necessity, is more informal than *must* and *have to. Must have* + past participle and *had to have* + past participle are similar in meaning, but *had to have* shows a greater certainty: It's almost impossible that the situation is otherwise. For example:
John must have gone home. (I'm almost certain that he did.)
John had to have gone home. (It's almost impossible that he didn't, but I have no direct evidence to prove it.)

Point out that *must not* is contracted only when the meaning is obligation not to do something—not to mean "it's probable that it didn't happen."

NOTE 3: Read the note in the Student Book with your class. Answer any questions.

NOTE 4: Point out that *may not* and *might not* are not normally contracted.

NOTE 5: Point out that *should* and *ought to* show a degree of certainty that can be termed "expectancy." The situation is not as certain as with *must. Should* and *ought to* are normally used to show future probability.

NOTE 6: Point out and practice the two meanings of *could have* + past participle:
Mary could have gone home. (It's possible that she went home.)
Mary could have gone home. (She didn't go home, but she should have.)

FOCUSED PRACTICE (pages 83–87)

See the General Suggestions for Focused Practice on page 3.

1. Discover the Grammar, page 83
See the General Suggestions for Discover the Grammar on page 4.

2. Where's Harry?, pages 84–85
You may want to point out the following vocabulary, as appropriate: *cherchez la femme* (French expression for "look for the woman," meaning that a woman is somehow involved in the underlying situation); *retirement center* (a home where older people go to live in their retirement; people living in retirement centers usually do not have the same kinds of medical needs as those living in nursing homes).

3. The Tunguska Event, pages 85–86
You may want to point out the following vocabulary: *plowed* (moved with some difficulty, as when a farmer uses heavy machinery to move soil before planting crops); *erratically* (with no clearly directed or consistent motion or direction); *obliterated* (destroyed completely, without leaving any trace); *ascertained* (established with certainty; note the connection with *certain* and the difference in pronunciation); *wrought* (caused, done); *errant* (wandering; moving from a proper or expected course).

Discussion: A discussion of the content of this essay is featured in Exercise 7 on page 89.

4. Editing, pages 86–87
See the General Suggestions for Editing on page 4.

You may want to point out the following vocabulary: *hives* (a skin condition characterized by itching, sometimes caused by a reaction or infection); *rash* (a skin eruption, usually red in color); *receptors* (neurological structures in the body that receive and transmit physical stimuli); *vermin* (small animals or insects, often harmful to the health); *Hodgkin's disease* (a type of cancer, sometimes fatal, characterized by enlargement of the lymph nodes, liver, or spleen); *tolerable* (something that one can bear or accept).

Discussion: When your students have completed this exercise, ask them whether they agree that itching is more difficult to bear than pain.

COMMUNICATION PRACTICE (pages 88–90)

See the General Suggestions for Communication Practice on page 4.

5. Listening, page 88
You may want to point out the following vocabulary: *I'd venture to say* (I would assume); *Let me see a show of hands* (Raise your hands if you agree.); *fidelity* (faithfulness, accuracy).

Discussion: Ask your students about their experiences hearing their own voices. Do they agree with Professor Stevens' ideas?

6. Solve the Puzzle, page 89
Ask the students to write as many possible explanations as they can, using a variety of modals.

7. Small Group Discussion, page 89
This discussion involves the reading "The Tunguska Event." Focus on students' ideas as to the cause of the event. Do your students know of other unsolved mysteries regarding natural phenomena?

8. Essay, page 89
If none of these topics suits some of your students, ask them to create similar topics about everyday mysteries.

9. Picture Discussion, page 90
Before your students speculate about what must be happening, what might be the case, etc., have them describe the picture in as much detail as possible.

An Unsolved Mystery: Have your students research an unsolved mystery (for example, the Bermuda Triangle) in the library or on the Internet. Have them summarize what is known about the mystery and speculate about possible causes. Encourage them to use different modals of certainty correctly.

REVIEW OR SELFTEST

See the General Suggestions for Review or SelfTest on page 6.

FROM GRAMMAR TO WRITING: TOPIC SENTENCES

See the General Suggestions for From Grammar to Writing on page 6.

In this section, students practice writing topic sentences for paragraphs. They share their writing with a partner and evaluate each other's topic sentences.

Introduction, page 96

Understanding and mastering the use of topic sentences is key to the development of one's writing. Often, a paragraph is difficult to understand simply because no topic sentence is present. Therefore, it is important to stress the importance of using topic sentences. Begin by asking your students if they have ever listened to a speech in which they could not figure out the speaker's main point. This may be because the speaker did not state it. Point out that writing is similar. Like a speech, a piece of writing needs a topic sentence to let the reader know where the writer is going and what point he or she is making.

Exercise 1, pages 96–97

Have the students do the exercise individually. Then, as a class, discuss the choices. Ask them why **c.** is the best topic sentence and what is wrong with **a.**, **b.**, and **d.** Elicit that **a.** is off target because the paragraph doesn't mention enjoyment, **b.** is off target because it is too narrow (taking a gift is only one of three recommendations), and **d.** is off target because the paragraph doesn't mention not eating too much.

Exercise 2, page 97

Have the students do the exercise individually. Then, as a class, discuss why **b.** is the best topic sentence and why **a.**, **c.**, and **d.** are inadequate. Elicit that **a.** is not a sentence, **c.** is not a sentence and is too general (but might be good as a title), and **d.** is wrong because the paragraph doesn't really say that men are still prejudiced about women's capabilities.

Exercise 3, pages 97–98

Have the students work in pairs to write a topic sentence for each set of details. Then write some of their sentences on the board and discuss them as a class. Ask the students whether they feel the sentences summarize each paragraph effectively.

Exercise 4, Apply It to Your Writing, page 98

Before doing this exercise, you may wish to give your students additional practice in writing topic sentences by doing one or more of the following activities:

1. Find writing samples that contain good topic sentences. Bring them to class and have the students identify the topic sentences. The topic sentence of a paragraph is often the first sentence, but not always.
2. Find well-written paragraphs. Delete the topic sentences. Bring them to class and have the students work in groups to write good topic sentences. Discuss the sentences.
3. Divide the students into pairs. Each pair of students writes a topic sentence and several supporting details to support that topic. They then show the supporting details to another group, but they do not show the topic sentence. The other pair writes an appropriate topic sentence. They then discuss each other's topic sentences.

Once you are satisfied that your students understand the basics of topic sentences, ask them to write a paragraph (either in class or outside class) on one of the topics presented. Then have them share their work in small groups. Have them point out strengths and weaknesses and make constructive suggestions. You may want to have your students rewrite their paragraphs using their peers' suggestions.

PART III NOUNS

UNIT 6 — COUNT AND NON-COUNT NOUNS

GRAMMAR **IN CONTEXT** (pages 102–104)

See the General Suggestions for Grammar in Context on page 2.

ESTABLISH THE CONTEXT: The theme of the unit is food.

CULTURE NOTE: Some American children are finicky, not wanting to eat what their parents consider appropriate and healthful food.

Questions to Consider, page 102: Have the students jot down their answers. Write their answers on the board and discuss them.

Reading, pages 102–103: See the General Suggestions for Reading on page 2.

DISCUSSION: Discuss the cartoon. Ask the students to what extent children are finicky eaters in their culture. Have their parents ever forced them to eat food they didn't like? How should parents deal with this situation? Are there ways, such as cooking more interesting and differently prepared meals, to get children to eat what they should? Discuss whether it is important or even possible to make food preparation a priority, especially at a time when people are increasingly busy.

Understanding Meaning from Context, page 104
See the General Suggestions for Understanding Meaning from Context on page 2.

Make sure that the students know what each food mentioned in the article is: *enchilada*, *curry*, etc. Ask how many class members have eaten these foods. You may want to point out the following vocabulary: *stomach* (to stand, to bear); *bland* (tasteless, uninteresting); *Pacific Rim* (the countries bordering on the Pacific Ocean, from South America through North America through Asia); *exotic* (intriguingly unusual or different); *culinary* (related to cooking); *seismic* (related to an earthquake); *gotten into* (begun to do or practice); *synthesis* (a putting together); *eatery* (informal: restaurant); *pidgin* (a simplified form of a language containing elements of two or more languages, used for cross-cultural communication); *monotony* (sameness); *advent* (beginning).

DISCUSSION: Discuss the prevalence of fast food all over the world. What do students think of it? Can it be nutritious? Do they like it? What are the potentially negative consequences of the fast food revolution? Discuss the ideas in the last paragraph of the reading. Do the students think that we are really developing a world culture? Is this a good thing, or will it eliminate too many individual cultural differences? What examples of this phenomenon can they point to in their own culture?

GRAMMAR **PRESENTATION:** Count and Non-Count Nouns (pages 105–108)

See the General Suggestions for Grammar Presentation on page 3.

The main new grammar in this unit is the use of non-count nouns in a count sense.

NOTES 1–3: Begin your treatment of this point by asking questions to elicit a few examples, such as *television*, *radio*, and *coffee*:

What do you watch in the evenings? (television)
What do you watch it on? (a television—a TV set)
Which do you like better, television or radio? How many radios do you have?
Do you drink coffee? What is a common way of asking for three orders of coffee?

Write them on the board. Discuss whether each noun is count or non-count.

Notes 4–6: Write non-count nouns on the board. Elicit sentences with non-count and count uses of each noun.

Note 7: Elicit sentences of singular and plural use of *criterion*, *phenomenon*, *nucleus*.

Ask students to come up with other nouns ending in *-s* that are usually singular (for example, *means*, *sports*, *linguistics*). Elicit a sentence or two using the word *cattle*.

Note 8: The use of the word *people* is usually a particularly difficult thing to master. Elicit a number of sentences from the class in which the word is used both in the plural (as they are used to) and in the singular (which they may not be used to).

FOCUSED PRACTICE (page 109–113)

See the General Suggestions for Focused Practice on page 3.

1. Discover the Grammar, page 109
See the General Suggestions for Discover the Grammar on page 4.

2. Blending, pages 109–110
Pay particular attention to Part B of the exercise. Ask students to defend their answers.

3. Community Bulletin Board, page 111
When the students have completed this exercise, go over it. Ask them to explain why they chose each answer.

4. A Work of Art, page 112
Devote considerable time and effort to doing this exercise. Make sure that each student writes a sentence for each item. You may wish to collect these sentences.

5. Editing, page 113
See the General Suggestions for Editing on page 4.

It might be helpful to have students write or tell about cross-cultural experiences they have had that are similar to those in the letter. What countries or cities have they visited? What struck them as different, interesting, or unusual? How was the food?

COMMUNICATION PRACTICE (pages 114–117)

See the General Suggestions for Communication Practice on page 4.

6. Listening, page 114
In groups, students could create listening exercises similar to that in the listening. They could then present them to the class and ask follow-up comprehension questions.

7. Information Gap: A Grain Of Sand, pages 115 and 117
Take the time to play this game and make it work in class. Make sure that the A and B groups do not look at each other's pages. When students have learned the meaning of *bovine*, you might choose to also teach them the related words describing other animals: *equine* (horses), *porcine* (pigs), *feline* (cats), *canine* (dogs), *lupine* (wolves), *ovine* (sheep), *ursine* (bears). You can also have students construct a similar game with other non-count nouns and the phrases used to make them countable. To prepare for this, write each phrase used to make a noun countable on the board: *a game of, a piece of, an article of*, etc. Elicit as many variations as possible.

8. Essay, page 115
One way to make this task more enjoyable is to encourage students to write about a humorous meal experience. Have they ever been in an embarrassing meal situation that involved spilling something, knocking over a platter of food, etc.? Have they ever been in a situation in which they were expected to eat something they didn't like or felt they couldn't eat? What did they do?

9. Picture Discussion, page 116
The key to this activity is for students to look carefully and then remember as many details as possible. If you wish, you may ask them to jot down the names of foods they see. The goal in

describing the table with books closed is to use as many count and non-count nouns correctly as possible.

EXPANSION

Favorite Recipes: Have your students write recipes for favorite dishes from their country. Encourage them to use count and non-count nouns correctly. If you wish, you could put the recipes together in a class recipe book. You could also have a party in which students prepare or bring the dishes.

UNIT 7 DEFINITE AND INDEFINITE ARTICLES

GRAMMAR **IN CONTEXT** (pages 118–120)

See the General Suggestions for Grammar in Context on page 2.

ESTABLISH THE CONTEXT: The theme of the unit is the environment.

Questions to Consider, page 118: Have the students jot down answers to the questions and discuss them. Pay particular attention to question 1. There are many environmental problems, ranging from momentous issues like dealing with nuclear waste to more everyday questions like how we can get rid of garbage. What environmental problems do they see in their country? Regarding question 2, ask the students if they think environmentalists really have something to say. Are there areas where environmentalists have gone too far?

Reading, page 118: See the General Suggestions for Reading on page 2.

Understanding Meaning From Context, page 120
See the General Suggestions for Understanding Meaning from Context on page 2.

You may want to point out the following vocabulary: *stellar* (related to the word for star); *yellowish* (having the general quality of something yellow, but not exactly—compare with *bluish, reddish, two-ish*, etc.); *toxic* (poisonous).

DISCUSSION: What did the students think of the story? Did they think that it was about Earth? Do they think the story is too pessimistic? Can morality (in this case, the "proper" attitude toward and treatment of the environment) be legislated, controlled by governments?

GRAMMAR **PRESENTATION:** Articles (page 121–124)

See the General Suggestions for Grammar Presentation on page 3.

To teach the various uses of definite and indefinite articles, you might want to do one or more of the activities below.

NOTE 1: Definiteness: The key to understanding the difference between the definite and indefinite article mastery is the concept of definiteness. If students are weak in their understanding of this concept, you may wish to use the cuisenaire rods or other similar objects of different colors and lengths. Place a number of rods on a table, making sure that you have more than one of certain colors. Once a rod has been picked up (or if there is only one of its color), it is definite. Give students commands like these: *Pick up a yellow rod and a red rod. Give the yellow rod to Juan, and give the red rod to Anh.*

NOTE 2: Uniqueness: Write examples of unique things on the board—for example, the sun, the sky, the moon, the Earth, the ozone layer, the atmosphere. Elicit other examples from the class.

NOTE 3: Read the note in the Student Book with your class. Answer any questions.

NOTE 4: Definiteness by context: Use items in the classroom and pictures of objects. Ask students to make sentences about things in the classroom and the objects in the pictures, using the definite article.

Notes 5 and 6: Read the notes in the Student Book with your class. Answer any questions.

Note 7: Zero article (for plural count nouns and non-specific non-count nouns): Make flashcards with single words on them such as *environmentalists*, *pollution*, *smoke*, *whales*, or *gold*. Ask the students to construct sentences with them. Make sure they understand the indefinite nature of these nouns.

Note 8: Read the note in the Student Book with your class. Answer any questions.

Note 9: Generic Nouns: Write a number of these on the board and ask students to make sentences using *a / an* or zero article. Then introduce the concept of the use of *the* with the three main types of generic nouns: inventions, musical instruments, and animal species. Have the students work in groups to produce sentences with *the*. For example:

The wheel was invented thousands of years ago.
Jack plays the piano.
The blue whale is an endangered species.

Then have them produce sentences such as these:

An orangutan is a primate.
The orangutan is a primate.

The orangutans are primates.
Orangutans are primates.

Explain that these sentence pairs have approximately the same meaning when one is classifying or defining something. However, this is a generic use [of a noun], not a specific use.

Note 10: Caution the students that a sentence like "We demonstrated to save a whale" is not a correct sentence if the speaker is classifying or defining.

Note 11: Geographical terms: Bring in copies of a world or regional map. Practice the structures, eliciting sentences which specify the names of oceans, mountain ranges, seas, and the like.

FOCUSED PRACTICE (pages 125–129)

See the General Suggestions for Focused Practice on page 4.

1. Discover the Grammar, page 125
Go over this exercise carefully with the students, asking them to explain the reasons for their choices.

2. July Breaks Record, pages 126–127
For Part A, you may want to point out the following vocabulary: *pet causes* (favorite causes); *slammed* (hit forcefully; compare with *slam the door*); *toiling* (working hard); *El Niño* (an ocean current thought to influence weather; compare it with its counterpart, *La Niña*); *greenhouse gases* (carbon dioxide and other gases that are trapped in the atmosphere and create conditions resembling those in a greenhouse); *droughts* (periods of extreme dry weather); *inundate* (flood).

For Part B, it might be worth pointing out the correspondences between the Fahrenheit and Celsius scales. The most important part of this exercise is not for students to get the right answer as much as it is to focus their attention on the reasons for their choices. Take the time to do this exercise carefully.

Discussion: Discuss the issue of global warming with the students. Do they understand what it is? Do they think this is a significant problem? What might be done about it?

3. Disasters, page 128
You may want to point out the following vocabulary: *meltdown* (disaster in which the radioactive material in a nuclear power plant becomes so hot that it melts out of its containers and affects the surrounding environment); *vicinity* (immediate surrounding area).

Here is a categorization of the rules governing the use of each item in this exercise:
1. The *Titanic* (uniqueness) 2. a British steamer (first mention of a count noun) 3. the North Atlantic (uniqueness) 4. an iceberg (first mention of a count noun) 5. the worst nuclear accident

(uniqueness)   6. the United States (uniqueness)   7. the causes (context)   8. equipment failure (unspecified non-count noun)   9. human error (unspecified non-count noun)   10. the reactor (previous mention)   11. a partial meltdown (first mention of a count noun)   12. the reactor's nuclear core (previous mention)   13. the meltdown (previous mention)   14. the nuclear core (previous mention)   15. coolant (unspecified non-count noun)   16. the accident (previous mention) 17. fires (unspecified plural count noun)   18. an unauthorized experiment (first mention of a count noun)   19. the worst accident (uniqueness)   20. the history of nuclear power (uniqueness)   21. the disaster (context)   22. radioactive material (unspecified non-count noun)   23. the vicinity (context) 24. possible future cancer . . . deaths and defects (unspecified plural count nouns)   25. the accident (previous mention)   26. the oil tanker *Exxon Valdez* (uniqueness)   27. the worst oil spill (uniqueness)   28. U.S. history (unspecified non-count noun)   29. oil (unspecified non-count noun) 30. many animals (unspecified plural count noun)   31. great environmental damage (unspecified non-count noun)   32. the captain (uniqueness)   33. the *Valdez* (uniqueness)   34. the time (context) 35. the accident (context)   36. the ship (context *or* previous mention)   37. the first mate (uniqueness)   38. the cost (uniqueness)   39. the spill (previous mention)   40. the captain (uniqueness)   41. the first mate (uniqueness)   42. the vessel (context *or* previous mention)

4. Editing, page 129
See the General Suggestions for Editing on page 4.

You may want to point out that *tamper* means "interfere in a harmful manner."

Discussion: After the students have completed the exercise, have them discuss the content of the student essay. Do they basically agree or disagree with the writer? Why? Do they think genetic engineering is potentially a good thing or a dangerous thing?

COMMUNICATION PRACTICE (pages 130–134)

See the General Suggestions for Communication Practice on page 4.

5. Listening, page 130
See the General Suggestions for Listening on page 4.

Culture Note: This passage is based on recent events involving the Makah Indian tribe in northwest Washington. United States courts have ruled that, based on treaties between the Makah and the United States government, the Makah have the right to hunt a limited number of whales each year.

Discussion: Ask your students what they think about this issue. Do they agree more with the wife or the husband? Should limited whaling be allowed anywhere in the world?

6. Information Gap: Your Environmental Quotient, pages 131 and 134
Compare the term *EQ* (Environmental Quotient) with the term *IQ* (Intelligence Quotient), on which *EQ* is based. You may want to point out the following vocabulary: *fluorocarbons* (chemical compounds used in making aerosol propellants, refrigerants, plastics, and resins); *marsupial* (a mammal having a pouch on the abdomen); *anthropoid* (resembling humans); *Mesozoic* (the third era of geologic time, during which the dinosaurs appeared and disappeared); *Jurassic* (the second part of the Mesozoic era, when the dinosaurs and the first mammals co-existed); *Milky Way* (the galaxy in which the solar system is located); *cetacean* (an order of marine mammals which includes whales and dolphins); *primate* (an order of mammals which includes apes and humans).

7. Essay, page 132
The key consideration here is to allow students to write on topics that interest them. The topics given are only suggestions; it may be better for students to concentrate on local environmental issues touching their lives.

8. Picture Discussion, pages 132–133
It is strongly suggested that students visit one of the listed websites if they have access to the Internet. This exercise could serve as the basis of a major term project. A creative variation on the assignment might involve allowing the students to present the information in story or dramatized form.

EXPANSION

An Endangered Animal: Have your students research an endangered animal in the library or on the Internet. Have them write about where the animal is found and why it is endangered. Encourage them to use definite and indefinite articles correctly.

 UNIT 8 MODIFICATION OF NOUNS

GRAMMAR **IN CONTEXT** (pages 135–137)

See the General Suggestions for Grammar in Context on page 2.

ESTABLISH THE CONTEXT: The theme of the unit is the mind and its powers, particularly regarding the fulfillment of expectations. You might begin by asking the students to freewrite for five minutes or so about an experience they or someone else had that did not turn out as expected. Ask students to summarize briefly the situations they have written about.

Questions to Consider, page 135: Have the students discuss the questions.

Reading, pages 135–136: See the General Suggestions for Reading on page 2.

DISCUSSION: When the students have read or heard the reading twice, discuss it. Have they had similar experiences with expectations? Have they experienced *focal dystonia* or something similar to it? How do they react to a situation in which one is "supposed to" feel a certain way? What is the difference between hoping and expecting?

Understanding Meaning from Context, page 137
See the General Suggestions for Understanding Meaning from Context on page 2.

You may want to point out the following vocabulary: *syndrome* (a pattern of characteristics indicating an unpleasant or undesirable condition, quality, or behavior. To clarify the meaning, elicit other syndromes—for example, *chronic fatigue syndrome*, the film *The China Syndrome*); *written him off* (decided he has little or no chance of success); *film buff* (someone fond of and knowledgeable about movies); *focal dystonia* (physiological condition influenced by the mind); *short circuit* (to harm or impede the success of something).

GRAMMAR **PRESENTATION:** Modification of Nouns (pages 138–141)

See the General Suggestions for Grammar Presentation on page 3.

The principal grammatical focus of the unit involves the order of modifiers before nouns. While we can prescribe the order to a considerable degree, there are areas where a speaker has considerable freedom in ordering modifiers, particularly among descriptive adjectives.

NOTE 1: Read the note in the Student Book with your class. Answer any questions.

NOTES 2 AND 3: Go over the list of the order of modifiers presented in the text. For your reference, here is a more complete list adapted from Thomas Lee Crowell, Jr., *Index to Modern English* (McGraw-Hill, 1964):

a. *all, any, both, double, each, every, half, no, triple, twice, which, what*
b. Determiners: articles (*a, an, the*), demonstratives (*this, that, these, those*), possessives (*my, Mary's,* etc.)
c. The word *own* (occurs only after possessives)
d. The word *whole*
e. Sequence words: ordinal numbers (*first, second,* etc.), *next, last, preceding, following, present, past*
f. Quantifiers: cardinal numbers (*one, two,* etc.), count or quantity words (*most, much, several, some, few, little,* etc.)
g. The words *additional, more, other*
h. The word *such* (preceding *a / an*)
i. Opinion modifiers: *wonderful, interesting, gorgeous,* etc.
j. Size, height, or length: *big, short, enormous,* etc.

k. Age or temperature: *young, cool,* etc.
l. Shape: *round, rectangular,* etc.
m. Color: *red, blue, purple,* etc.
n. Nationality, origin, or location: *Canadian, northwestern,* etc.
o. Material or composition: *wood, copper,* etc. (noun modifiers)
p. Operation: *mechanical, automatic,* etc.
q. Power: *gas, vacuum,* etc. (noun modifiers)
r. Purpose or destination: *party, study,* etc. (noun modifiers)

Another category is adjectives derived from present or past participles: boiled, boiling, carved, written, rolling, processed, and so forth. This category is not included above because adjectives within it can be variably placed. Their usual position is between the color and origin groups. For example:

We bought a knife with a large, beautiful old carved wooden handle.

You may or may not want to teach your students the full list. If so, do it over a considerable period of time, working on a few modifiers at a time.

NOTE 4: Write this sentence on the board:

Dan Jansen is a famous American speed skater.

Ask the students to identify the modifiers of *skater*, and then point out to them that *famous* and *American* are adjective modifiers and *speed* is a noun modifier.

You may wish to give some attention to practicing noun adjuncts, (sequences of two nouns together). Bring to class a list of noun adjuncts such as *teamwork, work team, milk chocolate, chocolate milk, traffic light,* and *light traffic* (adjective plus noun). At this level, students should be able to construct defining sentences with adjective clauses like these:

What's milk chocolate?   It's chocolate that is made with milk.
What's chocolate milk?   It's milk that contains chocolate.

NOTE 5: Devote considerable time and effort to practicing the use of compound modifiers. Students may be relatively unfamiliar with them. Provide sentences containing phrases and ask students to convert them to modifiers that precede the noun. For example:

She has a daughter who is twelve years old.   →   *She has a twelve-year-old-daughter.*
It's a program controlled by the government.   →   *It's a government-controlled program.*
It's a bag that weighs forty pounds.   →   *It's a forty-pound bag.*

Be sure to emphasize to the students that when a plural noun modifier is moved before a noun, the *-s* disappears. Point out this sort of error:

I have a ten-year-old daughter. (NOT: ~~*I have a ten-years-old daughter.*~~)

NOTE 6: Explain that two adjectives that modify a noun separately are called coordinate adjectives. Adjectives within the opinion category are often coordinate. They can be joined by a conjunction such as *and.* For example:

This is an interesting and challenging course.

Without the conjunction, the two modifiers are separated by a comma. This comma is reflected in speech by a pause between the adjectives. For example:

This is an interesting, challenging course.

NOTE 7: Writers of college composition and technical writing texts commonly ask students to avoid "stacking noun modifiers." Sentences with more than two noun modifiers together are often difficult to understand. Create a number of sentences with stacked noun modifiers and have the students unstack them so that no more than two nouns occur in succession. For example:

I bought a student party idea book.

can be rearranged as

I bought a book containing ideas for student parties. OR
I bought a book containing ideas for parties. The book was written by a student.

FOCUSED PRACTICE (pages 142–145)

See the General Suggestions for Focused Practice on page 4.

1. Discover the Grammar, page 142
See the General Suggestions for Discover the Grammar on page 4.

2. Reading Aloud, pages 142–144
You may want to point out the following vocabulary: *lisped* (pronounced *s* like *th*); *gunslinger* (a person armed with a gun, especially in the American West in the nineteenth century).

DISCUSSION: Ask students if they have ever had a problem like Joshua's or known someone who did. If so, was the problem solved?

3. Party Expectations, pages 144–145
You may want to point out that *humor me* means "do what I ask as a favor to me."

DISCUSSION: This exercise is intended to be humorous. Ask the students if they find it so. What is the intended humor?

4. Editing, page 145
See the General Suggestions for Editing on page 4. You may want to point out that *exhilarated* means "invigorated, happily or joyfully refreshed."

COMMUNICATION PRACTICE (pages 146–151)

See the General Suggestions for Communication Practice on page 4.

5. Listening, pages 146–147
You may want to point out the following vocabulary: *growth spurt* (a period of rapid physical growth often experienced by adolescents).

DISCUSSION: Ask the students what they think of the idea of distracting oneself or others to keep from excessive focus on goals. Have they had any experience with this sort of thing? Does it work?

6. Tape Discussion, page 147
Take time to have a good discussion here. Most people have had some sort of problem similar to Joshua's. Encourage students to share their experiences or describe situations they are familiar with.

7. Information Gap: Baseball, pages 147–148 and 151
The Information Gap is intended to prepare the students to understand the poem "Casey at the Bat" that follows. If you live in an area where baseball is popular or at least known, this exercise may be quite easy for the students. If you do not, some extra preparation may be necessary. Taking pictures to class of a baseball diamond, a ball, a bat, a glove, and the like might be a good idea.

8. A Poem, pages 148–149
The Information Gap will help prepare the students to understand Ernest Thayer's poem to some degree. However, there is much potentially unknown vocabulary here. Before beginning the study of the poem, ask the class to imagine a soccer match in which the hometown team is expected to win the game and a particular player is certain to score the winning goal if necessary. However, a referee (= umpire in a baseball game) makes a call which the crowd doesn't like, and the result is that the team doesn't win. Play the tape a couple of times and try to get the students to articulate the general idea of the poem: that Casey was sure he was going to hit the ball and be a hero, that all the fans expected this, and that these expectations led to his failure. Once the students understand the basic idea, they should be able to handle the Discussion questions.

You may want to point out the following vocabulary: *Mudville nine* (the team of nine baseball players in the town of Mudville); *Cooney died at first* (Cooney was thrown out before he reached first base); *pall-like silence* (silence like that at a funeral); *a straggling few* (remaining few); *whack* (a hit); *a hoodoo* (something / someone that brings bad luck); *stricken multitude* (a shocked or troubled crowd); *tore the cover off the ball* (hit the ball very hard); *safe at second* (on second base); *hugging third* (on third base); *lusty yell* (a powerful shout); *dell* (a small wooded valley); *doffed his hat* (took off his hat and bowed to the crowd); *'twas* (it was); *writhing* (moving in a twisting fashion); *the leather-covered sphere* (the baseball); *hurtling* (flying almost uncontrollably); *haughty* (arrogant); *ain't* (is not); *muffled roar* (a low roar); *Kill the umpire* (Remove the referee); *visage* (face); *stilled the rising tumult* (made the crowd be quiet); *bade the game go on* (said the game had to continue); *spheroid* (a round object, such as a ball); *Fraud!* (Dishonesty! Wrongness!); *awed* (deeply impressed—compare with *awesome*); *clenched* (held together painfully); *struck out* (struck three times and was ineligible to continue batting).

9. Essay, page 150
It should be fairly easy for students to recall a time when things didn't turn out as they had expected. Stress to the students the importance of including plenty of supporting details to explain their situation.

10. Picture Discussion, page 150
There will probably be one or more students in your class who are capable of re-drawing the picture according to the instructions of the other students. This exercise should work well if (1) the student who draws has not looked at the picture, or not looked at it recently; (2) the students giving instructions use adjective and noun modifiers in as many of their statements as possible. At the minimum, they should include the following: a tailless, black-pawed Siamese cat; a three-legged oval glass table; a braided, multi-colored, diamond-shaped rug; four upside-down soup bowls; four misplaced table settings; a large, sleeping dog (probably a golden retriever); a large, oval, four-footed soup tureen. If possible, they should make statements like:

The cat is standing on his hind legs, pawing at the soup tureen. The tureen's lid is askew, and there is a soup ladle in the tureen.

The more detail the students can provide, the more they will benefit from the exercise.

EXPANSION

Expectation and Experience: Have your students write essays about experiences that did not turn out as well as expected based on their freewriting from Establish the Context on page 27. Encourage them to use adjectives and noun modifiers to describe the experience in detail.

 UNIT 9 QUANTIFIERS

GRAMMAR IN CONTEXT (pages 152–153)

See the General Suggestions for Grammar in Context on page 2.

ESTABLISH THE CONTEXT: The theme of the unit is money. Begin with the cartoon. Ask the students to describe what is happening. Is it possible to buy items on the street with a credit card?

Questions to Consider, page 152: Use the cartoon to lead into the questions. In discussing them, try to get students to think objectively. Elicit advantages and disadvantages of living in a cashless society and write them on the board. Ask the students how they or others they know pay for items. Are checks commonly used? Do they think the trend toward a cashless society or world is irreversible?

Reading, pages 152–153: See the General Suggestions for Reading on page 2.

Understanding Meaning from Context, page 154
See the General Suggestions for Understanding Meaning from Context on page 2.

You may want to point out the following vocabulary: *accelerate the trend* (speed up the current momentum); *take plastic* (accept credit or debit cards for purchases); *cold, hard cash* (actual physical money); *a bit of a pain* (a little difficult and unpleasant). It may be worthwhile to spend some time on synonyms. Ask students to provide synonyms or alternate ways of saying each of the following:

A major event <u>took place</u> on January 1, 1999. (happened)
<u>for the time being</u>, at least (for the present)
<u>maintaining</u> their own currencies (keeping)

Are there any <u>advantages to</u> cash? (benefits of using)
It wouldn't be <u>that</u> easy without cash. (so)
<u>Now, however</u> . . . (But now)
<u>Mistakes</u> are easily made. (Errors)

GRAMMAR **PRESENTATION:** Quantifiers Of Nouns (pages 155–159)

See the General Suggestions for Grammar Presentation on page 3.

NOTE 1: Ask the students what they think quantifiers are and elicit several examples. Write a few examples of sentences with quantifiers in them: *some, any, a few, a lot, much, many,* and so on.

NOTE 2: Remind students of the distinction between count and non-count nouns. Point out that certain quantifiers are used with count nouns, certain ones with non-count nouns, and others with both types. Practice the difference between quantifiers used generally (for example, *most students*) and those used specifically (for example, *most of the students*). Have students work in pairs or groups to write illustrating sentences with *most / most of, many / many of, few / few of,* and *all / all of.*

NOTES 3 AND 4: Point out to the students that the quantifiers fall loosely into a formal / informal continuum. Some quantifiers are clearly used in more formal English: *a great deal, a great many,* and *much* used in affirmative sentences. Even the word *many* used in an affirmative sentence has a somewhat formal feel to it. Other quantifiers are clearly on the informal side: *a bunch of, a couple of, plenty of,* and the like. Most others are neutral as to formality.

NOTES 5 AND 6: Remind students of the distinction between *some* and *any*: Both can be used in questions, though *any* is preferred in negative questions (for example, *Don't you have any friends you can ask to help you?*). If *any* is used in an affirmative question, there is a greater expectation of a negative answer than with *some*: *Do you want any coffee?* may mean that the speaker expects a negative answer.

Remind students that *any* is used with negatives and that *some* is used in affirmative sentences. If *any* is used in an affirmative sentence, it takes on the meaning "any one particular person, place or thing." Thus, it is not a quantifier.

NOTE 7: Read the note in the Student Book with your class. Answer any questions.

NOTE 8: For the distinction between *few* and *a few, little* and *a little,* provide many examples of your own and ask students to work in groups to create situations where each form is used correctly. In general terms, we may say that *few* and *little* are negative in meaning, while *a few* and *a little* are positive, but the sense of negative or positive depends on the context. A sentence in the president's speech in Exercise 4, Editing, on page 163, illustrates this concept:

Third, we have no money to finance health-care reform, <u>and</u> we've made <u>little</u> progress in reducing pollution and meeting clean-air standards.

The president is essentially making a negative statement, so *little* in the second half of the sentence must match *no* in the first half. However, if we change the conjunction connecting the two clauses from *and* to *but, little* will be replaced by *a little*:

Third, we have no money to finance health-care reform, <u>but</u> we've made <u>a little</u> progress in reducing pollution and meeting clean-air standards.

NOTE 9: You might point out that in sentences containing *none* + count noun, a plural verb is generally used in conversation, though in formal English a singular verb is generally correct:

None of us <u>are</u> experts. (conversational)
None of us <u>is</u> an expert. (formal)

FOCUSED **PRACTICE** (pages 160–163)

See the General Suggestions for Focused Practice on page 3.

1. Discover the Grammar, page 160
See the General Suggestions for Discover the Grammar on page 4.

2. Saving for a Trip, pages 160–161

You may want to point out the following vocabulary: *left over* (remaining); *premium cable channels* (extra channels); *brownbag lunch* (a lunch prepared at home and taken elsewhere in a brown paper bag).

Discussion: Are there things in your students' lives they could get by without? You might want to have the class discuss how they could save money if they feel it is important to do so. This is also a good way to practice *less* and *fewer*. For example:

I could save money by seeing <u>fewer</u> movies and eating out less.

3. The Euro, pages 162–163

This is an authentic reading. The purpose of the exercise is not so much to get the students to fill in the correct quantifier as to heighten their awareness as to what quantifiers *could* correctly and logically go in the blanks. Focus on having the students discuss their answers in pairs. You may want to point out the following vocabulary: *keep track of* (remain aware of); *get fleeced like a Shetland sheep* (lose your money as a sheep loses its wool when it is shorn); *short-term headaches* (temporary problems); *stem from* (come from, originate from—related to the stem of a plant); *math mayhem* (confusion from having to do complicated mathematical calculations); *the mathematically challenged* (those who have difficulty with mathematics); *a snap* (something very easy—relate this to snapping one's fingers).

4. Editing, page 163

See the General Suggestions for Editing on page 4.

You may want to point out the following vocabulary: *pledges* (promises); *shouldering* (carrying—relate this to carrying things on the shoulders); *income tax brackets* (levels of payment—the higher the income, the more tax one has to pay).

Discussion: Ask the students what they think of this speech and of political speeches in general. Should the very wealthy be asked to shoulder more of the tax burden? Or should there be a *flat tax* (a system in which all income levels pay the same tax rate)?

COMMUNICATION PRACTICE (pages 164–167)

See the General Suggestions for Communication Practice on page 4.

5. Listening, pages 164–165

Ask your students what they know about or what experience they have with repaying loans and getting behind in the payments. What would they do if they were in Andrews's position? What would they do if they were in Grant's?

6. The Numbers Game, pages 165–166

Take the time to allow the students to play this as an actual game. It is not as difficult as it looks. Insist that students use the correct quantifiers in their questions and responses.

7. Essay, page 166

If the students do not have any experience using the currency of another country, allow them to write on another money-related topic (for example, a time they saved up for something, a time they spent their money foolishly, or the importance of having a personal budget).

8. Picture Discussion, pages 166–167

Ask students to describe situations in which they or someone they knew did not have enough money to pay for something. Were they embarrassed? What are the options in a situation like this? You will probably get a range of responses, including the possibility of washing dishes at a restaurant. Encourage students to use quantifiers such as *a few*, *a little*, *less*, *more*, and *enough* in their discussion.

EXPANSION

If I Won the Lottery . . . : Have your students write essays on the topic "What would you do if you won the lottery?" Encourage them to use quantifiers of nouns correctly to answer questions such as the following:

What would you do with the money? Would you spend all of it? Invest most of it? Give a little to charity?

REVIEW OR SELFTEST

See the General Suggestions for Review or SelfTest on page 6.

FROM GRAMMAR TO WRITING: AGREEMENT

See the General Suggestions for From Grammar to Writing on page 6.

In this section, students learn to make their writing more understandable by using correct subject-verb and pronoun-antecedent agreement. They edit a piece of writing, share their writing with a partner, and evaluate each other's work.

Introduction, page 174
Students first need to understand the notions of subject and predicate. Write a few sentences of varying lengths on the board. Ask students to separate each sentence into its two basic parts. For example:

Sherry / smokes.
Water / boils at zero degrees Celsius.
That strange old man wearing green tennis shoes / is actually the president of the university.

The students will probably be able to divide each sentence into subject and predicate. If they have difficulty, asking a *who* or *what* question will help:

Who smokes? (Sherry.)
What boils at zero degrees Celsius? (Water.)
Who is the president of the university? (That strange old man wearing green tennis shoes.)

Exercise 1, page 175
Have the students work in pairs to complete this exercise. They should ask a *who* or *what* question about each sentence. Doing so will enable them to determine the complete subject in each sentence. For example:

What guests are coming over tonight to play volleyball? (Five of my best friends.)

Exercise 2, pages 175–176
Before students do this exercise, make sure that they understand the meaning of "simple subject"—the one word in each complete subject that controls subject-verb agreement. Review the examples from Exercise 1. Also write additional sentences on the board. For example:

Only one of my brothers is married.
The choice of the voters was Tony Blair.
The woman in the middle of all those men is the prime minister.

Ask students to find the simple subject in these sentences using the method described in Exercise 1:

Who is married? (Only one of my brothers.)
Who was the choice of the voters? (Tony Blair.)
Who is the prime minister? (The woman in the middle of all those men.)

Ask the students to underline the prepositional phrases in the sentences. Emphasize the point that the simple subject is never within a prepositional phrase.

After the students are familiar with the concept of the simple subject, have them do the exercise in pairs. Go over the answers as a class.

Exercise 3, page 176
Before having your students complete the exercise, review the use of *there*. Write several example sentences in different tenses containing the word *there* on the board. Ask which word *there* refers to in each sentence. Have the students underline the word or words in each sentence that *there* refers to. This will help them to determine correct subject-verb agreement. For example:

There have been <u>many great scientific developments</u> in the last 100 years.
There were <u>three hurricanes</u> in the Caribbean last month.
There is <u>a lot of oil</u> in the Middle East.

Then have students make up their own sentences using *there*. Check subject-verb agreement. Then ask the students to do the exercise, either individually or in pairs. Go over the answers as a class.

Exercise 4, page 177

Make sure students understand the concept of unity. That is, is something considered one thing or several separate things? For example:

The United States lies north of Mexico and south of Canada. (one thing)
Bacon and eggs is a nourishing meal. (one thing)
Bacon and eggs both contain a lot of cholesterol. (two things)
My family is important to me. (one thing)
My family are living in a lot of different places. (several separate individuals)

Have students complete the exercise in pairs. Go over the answers as a class.

Exercise 5, page 178

The key to pronoun-antecedent agreement involves the recognition of formal versus informal language. In many varieties of formal English, it is still considered correct and desirable to use singular masculine forms to agree with such words as *everybody*, *anyone*, *nobody*, or *a person*, etc. For example:

Everybody brought <u>his</u> own food to the picnic.

Today many people, however, feel this usage is sexist or inaccurate. It is possible to replace *his* with *his or her* and *him* with *him or her*, but these phrases become very awkward when repeated several times. In informal writing and conversation, native speakers often make gender-neutral statements using plural forms to avoid such awkward constructions. For example:

Everybody brought <u>their</u> own food to the picnic.

Point out that this type of usage is acceptable in informal spoken English. In formal English, however, the traditional masculine forms (or the newly developed phrases such as *his or her*) are considered necessary. Also point out that words such as *anybody* and *everyone* take singular verbs in formal English but can take plural pronouns when used informally. For example:

Does everyone have <u>their</u> homework? (informal)

Once your students are familiar with this concept, have them complete the exercise individually. Go over the answers as a class.

Exercise 6, pages 178–179

The use of the connectors *or, either or, neither nor*, and *not only . . . but also* to join a singular subject and a plural subject is a difficult concept. It is primarily a written rather than a spoken feature. Nonetheless, certain speakers and writers, particularly in the academic world, object to the conversational tendency to use a plural verb. Before dealing with this exercise, create a series of such sentences. Have students change the order of the subjects connected by the connectors and change the verb if appropriate. For example:

Neither <u>the twins</u> nor <u>Sarah is</u> here today.   →   *Neither <u>Sarah</u> nor <u>the twins are</u> here today.*

Drill this until the students have mastered it. Then have them complete the exercise in pairs. Go over the answers as a class.

Exercise 7, page 179

Have the students edit the letter in pairs or small groups. Then go over the answers as a class.

Exercise 8: Apply It to Your Writing, page 179

Give your students enough time and encouragement to complete the exercise. In writing their paragraphs, they should make sure that they have included sentences that incorporate both singular and plural subjects. Stress the importance of peer review and editing.

PART IV ADJECTIVE CLAUSES AND PHRASES

GRAMMAR **IN CONTEXT** (pages 182–184)

See the General Suggestions for Grammar in Context on page 2.

ESTABLISH THE CONTEXT: The theme of the unit is personality types. An interesting way to begin the unit might be to ask students to write down a number of characteristics that they feel describe them (for example, *shy*, *outgoing*, *generous*, *conservative*, *wild*). Point out that the reading is not the Myers-Briggs test; it merely describes some of its major elements.

CULTURE NOTE: It is common in North America to classify people according to such criteria as their perceived personality type, their birth order, and so on.

Questions to Consider, page 182: Ask students what they understand by the terms *extrovert* and *introvert*. Many people are under the misconception that an introvert is shy and an extrovert not shy. Point out that this is not true.

Reading, pages 182–184: See the General Suggestions for Reading on page 2.

DISCUSSION: Ask the students whether they feel the categories of *introvert* and *extrovert* (and the related term *ambivert*, a person who has elements of both introversion and extroversion) have validity and whether they fit into one of these categories. Then ask them to provide examples of people (possibly themselves) who fit in the remaining categories: *sensor / intuitive*, *thinker / feeler*, and *judger / perceiver*.

Understanding Meaning from Context, page 184
See the General Suggestions for Understanding Meaning from Context on page 2.

This is a good exercise for students to work together to write guesses as to the meanings of the italicized words and phrases from the reading. You may want to point out the following vocabulary: *four o'clock* (a flower that blooms in the late afternoon each day and then later closes up again); *validated* (proved through actual experimentation to be valid); *extrovert / introvert* (Point out that *extro-* means "outward" and *intro-* means "inward."); *keeping their options open* (keeping a wide range of choices available).

GRAMMAR **PRESENTATION:** Adjective Clauses: Review and Expansion (pages 185–189)

See the General Suggestions for Grammar Presentation on page 3.

Before the students read or listen to the opener or look at the grammar chart, you might write all of the relative pronouns on the chalkboard and elicit an example sentence with an adjective clause for each one. Then ask students to identify the adjective clauses in the opening reading and circle the relative pronoun in each one.

NOTES 1–3: An effective way of teaching the distinction between identifying and nonidentifying material is to ask students to construct two different types of sentences about other people in the class. Working individually, they create sentences with identifying adjective clauses containing no names. For example:
The person (whom) I'm thinking of has dark brown hair, blue eyes, and . . .
One of the people who sits in the back row has . . .
A person in class (whom) I would like to know better has . . .

Other students guess who each student has written about. Then, working in pairs, students create nonidentifying adjective clauses, using names. For example:
Luis, who is originally from Venezuela, has lived in this city for eleven months.

For practice with formal versus informal sentences, students can omit or include the relative pronoun (e.g., *whom*) in their sentences. If desired, you can return to the opening reading and ask students to identify the subject and verb of each adjective clause.

Note 4: Write three sentences containing relative clauses on the board. Include an extra pronoun subject. Ask students if the sentences are correct and what must be removed to make them correct.

Notes 5–9: Read the notes in the Student Book with your class. Answer any questions.

Note 10: Have students practice writing adjective clauses with *when* and *where* by completing these sentences. The class guesses what they are talking about. For example:

I have in mind a place <u>where</u> you can get your hair cut. (a barbershop or a hair salon)
I'm thinking of a time <u>when</u> people gave me a lot of presents. (a birthday party)

Note 11: It is relatively easy to practice the use of a *which*-clause that modifies an entire preceding idea. Ask students to make comments about their classmates, adding a *which*-clause. For example:

Roberto has a nice smile, <u>which</u> is what I like about him.

It is important to emphasize that this structure is informal and thus best avoided in nonconversational writing.

FOCUSED PRACTICE (pages 190–192)

See the General Suggestions for Focused Practice on page 4.

1. Discover the Grammar, page 190
See the General Suggestions for Discover the Grammar on page 4.

This is a good exercise for pair work. Ask students to discuss and then report to the class why the suggested rewritten sentences in Part A would be correct or incorrect.

2. People in the Office, page 191
You may want to point out the following vocabulary: *team player* (a person who works well with a group and contributes to its overall success and harmony); *recruited* (through research, found a potentially good employee and asked that person to work for the firm); *congenial* (friendly, easy to get along with).

3. Formal and Informal, pages 191–192
Stress the distinction between formal and informal regarding the use of *who / whom*, the deletion of the relative pronoun, and the placing of prepositions and the end of the sentence in informal usage. You may want to point out the following vocabulary: *even-tempered* (emotionally steady; not losing one's temper often).

Discussion: Do the students believe that someone who has been in prison can be rehabilitated, reenter society, and be a good citizen?

4. Editing, page 192
See the General Suggestions for Editing on page 4.

You may want to point out the following vocabulary: *hectic* (characterized by much activity and confusion, often at a very fast pace); *dormitory* (a place provided by a university where students live).

Culture Note: North American parents often accompany their children the first time they go to a university.

COMMUNICATION PRACTICE (pages 193–195)

See the General Suggestions for Communication Practice on page 4.

5. Listening 1, page 193
You may want to point out the following vocabulary: *grim* (uninviting, negative); *slave driver* (an authority figure who makes those under him / her work unreasonably hard); *paper pusher* (someone whose job involves completing paperwork); *passive-aggressive* (a person who does not express his or

her anger about something or someone openly but does it indirectly, in a disguised fashion); *disgruntled* (discontented, unhappy); *impulsive* (acting without thinking something through beforehand).

6. Tape Discussion, page 193

Listening 1 provides material for a good discussion about getting along with others, either in a work situation or with friends. Take the time to work through this activity carefully. Allow the students to report their views to the class.

7. Listening 2, pages 193–194

To reinforce the identifying / nonidentifying distinction, you might dictate the repeated sentences from the listening. Ask students whether or not they hear a pause. Apply this to the items in the exercise.

8. Interaction, page 194

Emphasize that this is not a copyrighted personality test. It is merely a made-up test similar to the kinds of personality tests that are often given. Give the students ample time to work with a partner and compare their perceptions of themselves and their partner with their partner's perceptions.

9. Essay, page 195

It should be relatively easy for your students to write this essay. If they have Internet access, encourage them to visit the Keirsey website and take the test.

10. Picture Discussion, page 195

Have students try to produce as many sentences with adjective clauses as they can. For example:

Most of the people who are in the picture are quite elegantly dressed.
One of the men who are in the lower-left corner of the picture is wearing a black top hat.

When the students have described the picture as fully as possible, ask them what they think Georges Seurat was trying to show in this picture. Try to elicit the idea that this sort of society seems to be characterized by wealth, formality in relationships, and rigidity in posture and perhaps attitude toward life.

EXPANSION

Tell Me About Yourself: Have your students interview each other. Encourage them to ask questions about their likes, dislikes, personality, etc. Have them write essays describing their partners. Encourage them to use a variety of adjective clauses correctly.

UNIT 11 · ADJECTIVE CLAUSES WITH QUANTIFIERS; ADJECTIVE PHRASES

GRAMMAR **IN CONTEXT** (pages 196–198)

See the General Suggestions for Grammar in Context on page 2.

ESTABLISH THE CONTEXT: The theme of the unit is movies. To begin this unit, you might ask your students about the last movie they saw. Find a movie that many students have seen. Ask them to try to be objective about it, to list strong points and weak points about the movie. Write these on the board.

Questions to Consider, page 196: Many of the students will probably have seen *Titanic*.

Reading, pages 197–198: See the General Suggestions for Reading on page 2.

DISCUSSION: Ask the students if they basically agree or disagree with the reviewer. On what points do they agree or disagree?

CULTURE NOTE: You might want to inform your students that movie reviews, both in newspapers and on television, are common in the United States and Canada. A lot of people depend on reviewers to provide them with information that will help them decide whether or not to see a particular movie. Films are often given ratings on the basis of stars (four stars normally being the top), numbers (ten usually being the best), or grades (A or A+ being the best grade).

Understanding Meaning from Context, page 198

See the General Suggestions for Understanding Meaning from Context on page 2.

You may want to point out the following vocabulary: *blockbuster* (a major success, particularly of a movie or other performance); *jotted down* (wrote down quickly); *dragged me to* (made me go to); *grossing* (earning money); *mounted* (put together); *flashbacks* (switches in a storyline to an earlier time); *impending* (threatening to happen); *come down on the side of* (prefer); *the former* (the first mentioned of two items; opposite of *the latter*); *downer* (something that makes people unhappy); *divulging* (revealing, giving away).

GRAMMAR **PRESENTATION:** Adjective Clauses with Quantifiers; Adjective Phrases (pages 199–200)

See the General Suggestions for Grammar Presentation on page 3.

NOTE 1: Read the note in the Student Book with your class. Answer any questions.

NOTE 2: Write some sentences with adjective phrases on the chalkboard. Ask students to expand them by adding a subject and verb that will make them clauses. For example:

The woman sitting in the back row and wearing a red dress is Rosa. =
The woman <u>who</u> is sitting in the back row and wearing a red dress is Rosa.

Also write two sentences containing adjective clauses with quantifiers on the board (for example, *of whom* and *of which*). Ask students to expand the information into two sentences with independent clauses. For example:

The students in this class, most of <u>whom</u> are present today, are advanced students. =
The students in this class are advanced students. Most of them are present today.

NOTE 3: Point out the difference between *in which case* and the parallel phrases *in this case*, *in that case*, etc. *In this case / In that case* are found in independent clauses. *In which case* is found only in dependent clauses. Therefore, a sentence may not correctly begin with *in which case*. It must follow a comma, not a period, semicolon, or colon.

NOTE 4: Remind students of the difference between a clause and a phrase: A clause is a group of related words having a subject and a verb. A phrase is a group of related words that may have a subject or a verb (in present or past participle form) but does not have both.

NOTE 5: Divide your class into two teams. Teams A and B each prepare a number of statements containing adjective clauses about members of the other team. The opposing team converts each statement to a sentence containing an adjective phrase. For example:

A: *The woman <u>who is wearing tennis shoes</u> is from Venezuela.*
B: *The woman <u>wearing tennis shoes</u> is from Venezuela.*

An alternate way of performing this activity is to use pictures, flashcards, or cued sentences. Divide the class into pairs, each member of which has a card. Student A has to convert two single sentences into one sentence with an adjective clause with a quantifier. Student B has to do the opposite: convert a clause with a quantifier into two sentences. For example:

A: *Ella and Halina are from Poland. They are both excellent students.* → *Ella and Halina, both of whom are from Poland, are excellent students.*
B: *Cozumel and Ixtapa, both of which are popular tourist destinations, are located in Mexico.* → *Cozumel and Ixtapa are located in Mexico. Both of them are popular tourist destinations.*

EXTENSION: You may wish to teach students about the punctuation of titles. Students will have noted the use of italics to show names of movies. You may wish to teach your students that in handwriting, titles of long works (movies, books, plays, etc.) are normally underlined instead of italicized. Titles of short works (poems, individual essays, etc.) are set in quotation marks. If a word processor is used, they can be italicized.

FOCUSED PRACTICE (page 201–204)

See the General Suggestions for Focused Practice on page 4.

1. Discover The Grammar, page 201
See the General Suggestions for Discover the Grammar on page 4.

2. Film Trivia, page 202
You may want to point out the following vocabulary: *trivia* (Point out that things which are labeled "trivia" are not trivial. The word in its newest sense refers to "single facts."); *critical successes* (successes according to the critics).

3. Popular Movies, pages 202–203
Have students work in pairs or groups to create sentences with quantifiers about other movies that they are familiar with.

4. Movie Genres, page 203
Have students work together to construct and combine sentences about other movies.

5. Editing, page 204
See the General Suggestions for Editing on page 4.

DISCUSSION: After the students have completed the exercise, it might be worthwhile to ask them if they understand the comparison between amusement park rides and the structure of many of today's movies. Ask them to give examples. Then ask what students think about movies ending happily. Should this always be the case? What movies have they seen which did not end happily, and was the unhappy ending justified?

COMMUNICATION PRACTICE (pages 205–208)

See the General Suggestions for Communication Practice on page 4.

6. Listening, page 205
You may want to point out that the word *junkies* refers to drug addiction, but its use here is joking and simply means people who are very fond of an activity.

DISCUSSION: If students have seen any of the movies mentioned by the reviewer, ask them whether they agree or disagree. You might then discuss the issue suggested in question 10: black and white versus color movies. Some critics and movie fans feel that many of the world's greatest movies are in black and white, that movies in color make life look too pretty. How do they feel about this?

7. A Review of *The Lion King*, page 205
You may want to point out the following vocabulary: *sabotaged* (deliberately destroyed by an enemy); *dazzling* (extremely impressive, especially visually); *hip* (sophisticated).

DISCUSSION: It's possible that students will have seen this film. If so, do they agree or disagree with the reviewer? Would they give it a higher or lower rating, or the same rating? What do they think about the violence in literature question? Do students think violence seen in films or on television desensitizes people or even causes some to commit crimes?

8. Information Gap: A Movie Review, pages 206 and 208
This exercise should provide a kind of model for the review that the students are asked to write later in the Essay on page 207. You may want to point out the following vocabulary: *staggering* (stunning; extremely impressive—so good that it causes the viewer to "stagger"); *flourished* (did well financially); *sucking up to* (flattering someone for self-serving reasons, a slang expression that should be used with care if at all); *went broke* (lost all of one's money); *crockery* (dishes, especially pottery); *gritty* (looking like it is composed of small pieces of rock or gravel—refers to the composition of the screen image); *b & w* (black and white); *frenzied* (wildly excited); *towering* ("like a tower"—extremely good and impressive); *odious* (hateful, terrible).

DISCUSSION: If your students have seen *Schindler's List*, ask them to what degree they agree with the reviewer. Do they consider it an important film? This question provides a link with one of the

Questions to Consider at the beginning of the unit: Should movies be about serious things? Or are they just for entertainment? What is their value to society?

9. Group Discussion, page 207
The rating system that the students find might be one used in North America. Are they familiar with other rating systems? If these exist, are the ratings enforced? Should they be? Should children be prohibited from seeing certain movies? Are some of today's movies too violent or sexually explicit? If so, what might be done about the problem?

10. Essay, page 207
Encourage students to look at the three reviews in the unit and to listen again to the spoken reviews. You may wish to return to the question of objectivity suggested for treating the opener of this unit. Tell students that their review should be critical. This does not mean they have to find fault with the movie they are reviewing; it simply means they should objectively point out strengths and weaknesses. When they have completed the assignment, ask some of them to read their reviews in class.

11. Picture Discussion, page 207
First have students write a short dialogue between the TV reporter and the person she is interviewing. Then ask students to explain what *censorship* means. Is restricting admission to movies an example of censorship? Ask the class to say whether they agree with the sign "TEENAGERS ARE NOT CHILDREN!" Have they had any similar experiences? Can they get into any film, or are they sometimes asked for I.D.?

EXPANSION

Performer Biography: Have your students research a favorite actor, actress, or director on the Internet. Have them write a biography of that person. Encourage them to use adjective clauses with quantifiers and adjective phrases correctly.

REVIEW OR SELFTEST
See the General Suggestions for Review or SelfTest on page 6.

FROM GRAMMAR TO WRITING: PUNCTUATION OF ADJECTIVE CLAUSES
See the General Suggestions for From Grammar to Writing on page 6.

In this section, students practice using adjective clauses and phrases with correct punctuation, particularly in the writing of a descriptive paragraph. They share their writing with a partner and evaluate each other's work.

Introduction, page 214
Before doing the exercises, bring a short descriptive paragraph to class. Make sure that the paragraph has examples of identifying and nonidentifying clauses. Write the paragraph on the board without any punctuation. Ask the students to practice reading the paragraph aloud in pairs. Then elicit suggestions for punctuation. Point out that reading one's work aloud will often help determine the natural pauses that correspond to written punctuation.

Exercise 1, page 215
Before doing the exercise, review the distinction between identifying and nonidentifying clauses by writing sentences such as the following on the board:
People who live in glass houses shouldn't throw stones.
Students who live close to the college save money on gas.
The French chefs, who are wearing long aprons, are from Marseilles.
The French chefs who are wearing long aprons are from Nice.
Cats, which make good pets, are independent creatures.
Cats that make good pets have been declawed.

Teaching Suggestions

For each sentence, ask the students whether the sentence refers to all members of the subject of the sentence or only to some of them. The first sentence above, for example, refers only to those people who live in glass houses, not to all people. In contrast, the fifth sentence refers to all cats. Ask the students to work in pairs to write similar sentences of both types. Remind them that, in an identifying clause, the adjective clause distinguishes one person, thing, or group from another; however, in a nonidentifying clause, the clause simply adds information.

After this activity, the students should have a clear idea of the correct punctuation of adjective clauses. Have them complete the exercise in pairs. Then go over the answers as a class.

Exercise 2, page 215
Students will probably have no difficulty applying the concepts of adjective clause punctuation to adjective phrase punctuation. Before doing this exercise, however, you may wish to have them work in pairs to convert each adjective phrase into a clause, and then punctuate the sentences correctly. For example:

A film produced by George Lucas is almost a guaranteed success. (phrase) →
A film that is produced by George Lucas is almost a guaranteed success. (clause)

After they complete this activity, have the students complete the exercise in pairs. Then go over the answers as a class.

Exercise 3, page 216
Have the students complete the exercise individually, either at home or in class. Then have them work in pairs, reading the letter aloud and comparing their answers. Go over the answers as a class.

Exercise 4: Apply It to Your Writing, page 216
Give the students sufficient time to write the paragraph in class and to punctuate their partner's paragraphs. Make sure that the students include at least one identifying and one nonidentifying clause in their paragraphs. After the students have submitted their paragraphs, read a few good ones aloud in class. Write some correctly punctuated adjective clauses on the board.

PART V PASSIVE VOICE

UNIT 12 THE PASSIVE: REVIEW AND EXPANSION

GRAMMAR IN CONTEXT (pages 220–222)
See the General Suggestions for Grammar in Context on page 2.

ESTABLISH THE CONTEXT: The theme of the unit is mystery. You might begin by asking students how they feel about mystery. Do they like mystery stories or movies? Are they familiar with the TV show *Unsolved Mysteries*?

Questions to Consider, page 220: Take time to work carefully on these questions.

Reading, pages 220–221: The story of "Dan Cooper" is an intriguing one. Begin by asking the students if they have heard of this situation. If they haven't, ask them if they know of any famous criminals or crimes that have never been solved. Then follow the General Suggestions for Reading on page 2.

DISCUSSION: You might ask the following discussion questions: Do you think that Cooper escaped or that he was killed? What are some possible indications that he survived? What are some possible indications that he didn't survive? If he survived, do you think most people do or do not want him to be caught?

Understanding Meaning from Context, page 222
See the General Suggestions for Understanding Meaning from Context on page 2.

You may want to point out the following vocabulary: *proceeded* (continued); *cockpit* (place where the pilots fly the plane); *loafers* (light shoes resembling moccasins or slippers); *accomplice* (a helper, especially in a crime); *patrons* (customers).

See the General Suggestions for Grammar Presentation on page 3.

Remind the students that we commonly use the passive when we don't know or care who performed an action. Four features of the passive presented in this unit may be somewhat unfamiliar to students. They are the passive with *get*, the use of progressive passives with both *be* and *get*, the choice of the active or the passive, and the passive sentence with an indirect object as subject.

NOTE 1: Read the note in the student book with your class. Answer any questions.

NOTE 2: Stress that, other than in these three types of statements, the active voice is generally preferred. Have the students work together to construct example sentences for each of these three types of statements. Perhaps the most interesting of the three uses is the "psychological avoidance" use—to avoid mentioning the performer when inappropriate (e.g., "politically incorrect") to do so. For example:

My son was given some erroneous information about his health care policy. (The speaker feels it is best not to say who gave the advice.)

We were told not to use the photocopy machine for personal use. (The speaker doesn't want to say who told them this.)

NOTE 3: Read the note in the Student Book with your class. Answer any questions.

NOTE 4: Students are sometimes not used to using an indirect object as a subject in a passive sentence. To practice this, place an object on several students' desks when the class is out of the room. When they return, have the students make two types of sentences:

A set of keys was given to Maria.
Maria was given a set of keys.

To practice constructing passive sentences emphasizing the recipient of the action, you might create a type of quiz game in which students produce questions such as:

Who was Don Quixote *written by?* (Cervantes)
Who was the telephone invented by? (Alexander Graham Bell)
Who were the Pyramids built by? (the ancient Egyptians)

In teams, they ask and answer these questions using complete sentences. Award points for correct answers with correct grammar.

NOTE 5: The *get*-passive seems to be increasing in use. Stress that it is used frequently in conversation and less commonly in writing. Also point out that it seems to emphasize action and to suggest that someone or something is subjected to another force. Write two sentences like these on the board:

The boy <u>was hit</u> by a car.
The boy <u>got hit</u> by a car.

Point out that the first sentence is a relatively neutral factual statement, while the second emphasizes the action and takes on a more dramatic connotation. Bring in pictures to practice the *get*-passive.

NOTE 6: Students can always use practice with the passive causative. Review this by asking students (and having them ask each other) questions like these:

Where do you get your photographs developed?
Do you cut your own hair or have it cut?
Who would you go to if you wanted to get your teeth straightened?

NOTE 7: Read the note in the Student Book with your class. Answer any questions.

FOCUSED PRACTICE (pages 226–229)

See the General Suggestions for Focused Practice on page 3.

1. Discover the Grammar, page 226
See the General Suggestions for Discover the Grammar on page 4.

For Part B, you may want to point out the following vocabulary: *blanketed* (covered, as by a blanket); *pelted* (hit repeatedly, especially painfully); *No one is about* (No one is around); *ajar* (slightly open); *crumpled* (crushed or pressed together, like a piece of paper); *perpetrator* (person who committed a crime); *whereabouts* (location). Part C gives your students the chance to use the passive creatively.

2. Three Famous Mysteries, pages 227–228
You may want to point out the following vocabulary: *teem* (to be abundant with); *brigantine* (two-masted sailing ship); *erratically* (wanderingly, without direction); *impending* (about to happen); *quintessential* (best and most typical example); *rugged* (strong and tough); *beast* (creature, especially a large one).

DISCUSSION: When the students have completed the exercise, ask them what they think is the most likely explanation for each case.

3. Joyce's Diary, page 228
As an extension, have students talk or write about a strange personal experience that they have never been able to explain.

4. Editing, page 229
See the General Suggestions for Editing on page 4.

There seems to be considerable prejudice against using the passive voice among English teachers and others in the humanities who believe that the passive voice is wordy and "deadening." Make sure that your students understand when the passive is actually used in real writing. You may wish to bring in passages from newspapers and magazines and have students identify the active and passive constructions and explain why they are used.

COMMUNICATION PRACTICE (pages 230–233)

See the General Suggestions for Communication Practice on page 4.

5. Listening, page 230
You may want to point out the following vocabulary: *janitor* (custodian; one who supervises and / or takes care of the cleaning of offices, etc.); *underworld* (the world of organized crime).

6. Information Gap: A Mystery Entity, pages 230–231 and 233
Make sure that students don't look at each other's prompts when they do this exercise. If you have time, you might want to ask your class to divide into groups and construct a similar exercise about another "mystery entity."

7. "Raffles" Gang Hits Palaces of Venice, pages 231–232
This is an authentic reading. You may want to point out the following vocabulary: *stripping* (taking away, stealing); *heists* (robberies); *spirited away* (taken quickly away); *cost his family dearly* (cost his family much); *Sotheby* (a famous London art dealership that conducts auctions of pieces of art); *bludgeoned* (killed with a heavy object). Take the time to do the Small Group Discussion questions.

8. Essay, page 232
Some students might elect to choose a genealogical question as their unsolved mystery. Whatever topic your students choose, the essay seems to fall naturally into a three-paragraph treatment. Describe the basic mystery in paragraph 1, discuss its causes in paragraph 2, and offer solutions in paragraph 3.

9. Picture Discussion, page 233
Point out that there is no officially accepted explanation of the cause of the crop circles. Two British painters, David Chorley and Douglas Bower, have claimed that they made the circles by using wooden planks and wire. However, these two may merely be seeking notoriety. What do your students think? Have them create as many passive sentences as possible to describe possible solutions. For example:
I think they were made by spirit creatures such as fairies.
Maybe they were placed there by alien visitors.

Encourage them to create sentences using the passive with modals of certainty. (Note: You may want to first review the Grammar Presentation in Unit 5.) For example:

They may have been formed by forces involved in weapons testing.
They could have been caused by the actions of air currents.

EXPANSION

My Diary: Using the diary entry on page 228 as a model, have your students write diary entries for one week. Encourage them to use the passive correctly.

 # UNIT 13 REPORTING IDEAS AND FACTS WITH PASSIVES

GRAMMAR **IN CONTEXT** (pages 234–236)

See the General Suggestions for Grammar in Context on page 2.

ESTABLISH THE CONTEXT: The theme of the unit is mystery, particularly as it regards myth and legend. Although there is no crystal clear line separating the concepts of myth and legend, myths are generally regarded as attempts to explain certain natural phenomena and usually recount stories of heroes and gods. Legends are thought to be more verifiable, perhaps because they often deal with more recent events.

DISCUSSION: You might want to begin by asking your students to define and give examples of myths and legends that they are familiar with. Once they are familiar with the concepts of myth and legend, ask them what they understand by the term *primitive*. In the twentieth century, anthropologists have gone to great lengths to stress that there really are no primitive cultures and that attempts to label groups as such are merely examples of arrogance and self-centeredness. Do your students think there are really any primitive cultures?

Questions to Consider, page 234: Discuss the questions, paying particular attention to the cartoon.

Reading, pages 234–235: Ask the students to close their books and listen carefully to the reading on tape. If they listen carefully, they may be able to figure out the joke. Anthropologist Horace Miner presumably wrote this tongue-in-cheek essay to parody the many attempts of supposedly "civilized" westerners to put down so-called primitive groups. When students have heard the article once, ask them who they think the Nacirema are. Have them listen a second time if necessary.

Understanding Meaning from Context, page 236
See the General Suggestions for Understanding Meaning from Context on page 2.

You may want to point out the following vocabulary: *focal point* (main point, point which captures attention); *font* (related to the word "fountain"). You may want to point out the following correspondences: *shrine room* (bathroom); *magic cream* (shaving cream); *magical paste* (toothpaste); *women baking their heads in ovens* (women sitting under hair dryers); *animal hairs in the mouth* (refers to the fact that toothbrushes were once made of hog bristles); *supernatural substance* (dental amalgam for filling a tooth); *listener* (psychiatrist).

Comprehension, page 236: Once the students understand Miner's joke, they should be able to respond well to the questions. Ask them where they think Miner got the term *Nacirema*.

DISCUSSION: You may now want to revisit the question posed at the beginning: Are there really any primitive cultures? Miner points out in his essay that North Americans (and by extension other First World peoples) can be regarded as just as "primitive" in their own way as any "indigenous" tribes found in underdeveloped areas.

GRAMMAR **PRESENTATION:** Reporting Ideas and Facts with Passives (pages 237–238)

See the General Suggestions for Grammar Presentation on page 3.

NOTE 1: Write a few sentences on the board showing the passive used to report facts and ideas. For example:

Pollution is considered a serious problem.
The danger of nuclear war is thought to have lessened in recent years.

Ask students for examples of similar sentences. Ask them to convert the passive sentence in the first box of the Grammar Chart into the active voice. Then explain the difference between active passives (as in sentences like "The bank was robbed." or "A new store is being built.") and these new passive uses.

NOTES 2–4: Read the notes in the Student Book with your class. Answer any questions.

NOTES 5 AND 6: The passive for reporting ideas uses verbs that suggest mental states but denote no action. These verbs suggest opinions, positions, thoughts, and beliefs. To practice this usage, you might write three columns on the board, one with subjects such as *Greece*, *Egypt*, *Britain*, and *Japan*; the second with passive phrases such as *is regarded*, *is considered*, *is believed*, *was thought*, *was felt*, and *is found*, and a third with complements such as *an economic superpower* or *a major colonial power*. Have students make logical sentences using the items in the three columns.

NOTE 7: The passive for reporting facts uses verbs that are sometimes called stative passives. They include *is located*, *are known*, *is found*, and the like. It is difficult to convert these types of passives into corresponding active constructions. Thus, we do not normally encounter pairs like these:

Turkey is located in Asia Minor. / Mapmakers locate Turkey in Asia Minor.

It is probably best to teach students that these stative passives are simply phrases or formulas to be learned and memorized. To practice these, bring in a map of any part of the world and ask students to make sentences with stative passives about the locations of countries, cities, rivers, and so on. (See the Picture Discussion on page 246.)

NOTE 8: Read the note in the Student Book with your class. Answer any questions.

FOCUSED **PRACTICE** (pages 239–242)

See the General Suggestions for Focused Practice on page 4.

1. Discover the Grammar, page 239
See the General Suggestions for Discover the Grammar on page 4.

2. Myth, Legend, or Reality?, page 240
Before students do this exercise, you may want to bring in a map of or pictures from the Four Corners region of the American Southwest (Arizona, Utah, Colorado, New Mexico) to kindle student interest. You may want to point out the following vocabulary: *subsistence agriculture* (growing of crops to support local or family needs); *dwellings* (places where people live, houses); *forebears* (ancestors); *flourishing* (very successful, flowering); *tale-spinners* (storytellers); *wisps* (foggy traces).

DISCUSSION: You might want to discuss whether the explosion on the island of Thira in the Mediterranean could be the source of the Atlantis legend. Have students speculate about what happened to the Anasazi.

3. Editing, page 242
See the General Suggestions for Editing on page 4.

You may want to point out the following vocabulary, as appropriate: *abominable* (terrible); *sherpas* (people of Tibetan descent living on the southern side of the Himalayas).

DISCUSSION: Some of your students may have heard of the yeti and his supposed relatives such as Bigfoot. What do they think? Is there any truth to the stories?

COMMUNICATION **PRACTICE** (page 243–246)

See the General Suggestions for Communication Practice on page 4.

4. Listening 1, page 243

Play the tape enough times for students to realize that this newscast is fictional and about Atlantis.

5. Listening 2, pages 243–244

After students have played the game and completed the dictation, you may want to have a discussion about Anastasia Romanov. Some students may have seen the Disney film, and some may even have seen the 1954 film with Ingrid Bergman and Helen Hayes. Most Russian citizens seem to think that Anastasia's having escaped assassination is completely impossible. Recent DNA evidence seems to corroborate this belief. Nonetheless, the story has been featured on *Unsolved Mysteries* and continues to have considerable appeal. What do your students think? Are there any similar mysteries or legends in their own country?

6. Group Guessing Game, pages 244–245

Take the time to do this activity, for students are likely to learn to use the passive structures if they have to make up questions using them.

7. The Nacirema, page 245

This is an authentic reading quoted directly from Miner's original essay. Miner is humorously poking fun at the tendency of Americans not to remove old medicines from their medicine chests. The ancient and secret language used by the herbalists is Latin. You may want to point out the following vocabulary: *maladies* (ailments). You may want to point out the following correspondences: *charm-box* (a medicine chest); *medicine men* (doctors); *herbalists* (pharmacists); *magical packets* (boxes or bottles of medicine).

8. Essay, page 245

Encourage your students to have fun with this writing assignment. Ask them to make a list of characteristics of people in their own culture that could be considered amusing. Then have them make up similar explanations for these practices in the way that Miner did.

9. Picture Discussion, page 246

A good way to begin this activity is to do one example on the board with the class. Taking Thailand as an example, you might elicit sentences like these:

Thailand is located in southeastern Asia between Myanmar on the west, Laos and Cambodia on the east, China on the north, and Malaysia on the south.
Thailand is known as the land of smiles.
Thailand is considered one of the most stable countries in the Far East.

Since the map covers the entire Far East area, there are multiple possibilities for discussion of both present time (for example, *Java is considered an ideal vacation spot.*) and past time (for example, *The Taj Mahal was built by an ancient Indian rajah in memory of his wife.*), and for review of names of countries and nationalities.

EXPANSION

Mythical Creatures and Folk Heroes: Have your students write essays about a mythical creature or folk hero from their culture. Encourage them to use passives, stative passives, and reduced passives correctly.

REVIEW OR SELFTEST

See the General Suggestions for Review or SelfTest on page 6.

FROM GRAMMAR TO WRITING: PARALLELISM

See the General Suggestions for From Grammar to Writing on page 6.

In this section, students practice making their writing more cohesive through parallelism with nouns and articles and with active or passive voice. They share their writing with a partner and evaluate each other's work.

Introduction, page 252
The concept of parallelism (also called parallel structure) may not be familiar to your students, but it is mastered relatively easily. You might wish to teach this section together with the essay in Unit 12 so that students begin writing and editing their essays with an eye toward parallel structure.

A good way to begin teaching parallelism is to bring in pictures, flashcards, or sets of sentences that show series of items (nouns). Alternatively, you might bring in a collection of objects. Ask the students to describe them in sentences including the article (definite or indefinite) before each noun *or* before the first noun only. For example:

I see a wallet, a purse, a key ring, an apple, a banana, and a handkerchief. OR
I see a wallet, purse, key ring, apple, banana, and handkerchief.

Exercise 1, page 253
Have the students work in pairs or small groups to complete the exercise. Then go over the answers as a class.

Exercise 2, page 254
Before doing the exercise, have the students practice using parallelism with active and passive voice. Write some example sentences that do not demonstrate parallel structure on the board. Ask students to improve them. For example:

The principle of gravity was formulated by Newton, Faraday formulated the principle of electromagnetism, and the principle of relativity was formulated by Einstein.

Students will probably easily recognize that the second item is nonparallel. Ask them to change it:

The principle of gravity was formulated by Newton, the principle of electromagnetism was formulated by Faraday, and the principle of relativity was formulated by Einstein.

Students will probably sense that this sentence is wordy. Ask them to reduce it to its most concise form while maintaining parallel structure:

The principle of gravity was formulated by Newton, the principle of electromagnetism by Faraday, and the principle of relativity by Einstein.

Once the students understand the principle of parallelism with active or passive voice, have them complete the exercise in pairs. Go over the answers as a class.

Exercise 3, pages 254–255
Have the students do the exercise individually. Then go over the answers as a class.

Exercise 4: Apply It to Your Writing, page 255
It might be worthwhile to have a brief discussion about the fate of Judge Crater or about another mystery that the students are familiar with. They might then write their paragraph about one of these mysteries. Alternatively, you might ask your students to write a creative ending to the Judge Crater mystery. Insist that they include sentences with items in parallel structure.

PART VI AUXILIARIES AND PHRASAL VERBS

UNIT 14 AUXILIARIES: CONTRAST AND EMPHASIS

GRAMMAR **IN CONTEXT** (pages 258–260)

See the General Suggestions for Grammar in Context on page 2.

ESTABLISH THE CONTEXT: The theme of the unit is families and family dynamics, and the reading deals with a much-discussed current issue: the theory of birth order. It certainly has not been proved that the effects of birth order actually exist, but it does seem that the theory has some validity. Ask students if they have heard of it and, if so, what they think of the theory.

Questions to Consider, page 258: Ask students to apply the concept to their own families.

Reading, pages 258–260: See the General Suggestions for Reading on page 2.

Understanding Meaning from Context, page 260
See the General Suggestions for Understanding Meaning from Context on page 2. You may want to point out the following vocabulary: *perfectionist* (a person who always wants to do things perfectly and has difficulty accepting anything less than perfect, particularly in himself / herself); *high achiever* (a person who does well in things and is generally quite successful); *enterprises* (projects, things a person does); *outlandish* (unconventional, bizarre); *conscientious* (guided by one's conscience, principled); *sibling* (brother or sister).

Discussion: Once students understand the article well, ask them how valid they think the birth-order theory is.

GRAMMAR **PRESENTATION:** *Be* and Auxiliaries (pages 261–263)

See the General Suggestions for Grammar Presentation on page 3.

Note 1: It may be helpful to suggest that students think of an auxiliary as being potentially present in every complete sentence in English (except those with *be*). The auxiliaries *do*, *does*, and *did* can be thought of as "ghost" auxiliaries which appear when one wants to ask a question, make a negation, establish a contrast with a preceding statement, or place emphasis on a verb. This auxiliary may appear on the surface, or it may be triggered only in certain situations, such as negatives and questions, as is the case with *do*, *did*, and *does*.

Sam likes (does like) pizza.
Those men work (do work) hard in their jobs.
Shakespeare wrote (did write) thirty-three plays.

Note 2: Review contractions and contrast them with noncontracted forms. Remind students that we do not have sentences in English such as *Yes, I'm*. If your students still don't use contractions naturally and normally, this is a good place to move them forward. Many students assume that contractions are somehow less correct, even sloppy forms of the language. This is not the case, however. Point out that in the spoken language, contractions are the norm except in contrast and emphasis sentences. Give some attention to the use of auxiliaries to refer to previous verb or adjective phrases without having to repeat those phrases. Bring in some paragraphs containing auxiliaries that do this. Have the students identify what the auxiliaries refer to.

Note 3: This is a good time to review and practice tag questions. You might point out some of the unusual ones. For example:

I'm right, aren't I?

Since it is difficult to say *amn't*, the form *aren't* has developed in the first person singular negative tag question. Other tag questions your students may not be familiar with are those in which the sentence contains the *–one* or *–body* words: *everyone, everybody, anyone, anybody*, etc. The normal tag question for sentences containing these items has *they*, not *he* or *she*:

Everybody came to the picnic, didn't they?
Anyone could do that, couldn't they?

Note 4: Advanced-level students are often quite conversant with *too* and *either* but not with *so* and *neither*. Give your class plenty of practice on the latter two. Point out that *neither* is merely a compressed form of *not either*. We use *so* and *neither* when we want to emphasize the subject, which comes last in the sentence.

Note 5: Compare the emphasis on the following sentence:

*I love **JANE**.* (It's Jane I love, no one else.)
*I **LOVE** Jane.* (I don't just like her.)
I love Jane (I'm the one who loves Jane; it's not someone else.)

Write example sentences of your own on the board, making sure that they contain both emphatic and contracted forms. Ask the students why contracted forms are used in certain places and full forms elsewhere. Pay particular attention to the use of *do, does,* and *did*; the use of these auxiliaries in affirmative sentences may be new to them. Point out that in sentences in the simple present or simple past, we make sentences emphatic by using *do, does,* or *did*. In other sentences, we use full forms instead of contractions (*have* instead of *'ve, had* instead of *'d, am* instead of *'m, is* instead of *'s,* and the like).

FOCUSED PRACTICE (pages 264–265)

See the General Suggestions for Focused Practice on page 3.

1. Discover the Grammar, pages 264–265
See the General Suggestions for Discover the Grammar on page 4.

2. You'd Better Tell Them, page 265
For Part A, you may want to point out the following vocabulary: *the way to go* (the right thing to do); *gorgeous* (extremely beautiful or good-looking). For Part B, take some time to have a short discussion. Relate Jeremy and Sara's situation to the birth-order theory. Students should be able to understand that Sara is probably the older child, since she is telling Jeremy what to do and is in some way connected to the parents' point of view.

3. Let's Talk It Over, page 266
The key activity here is the students' hearing the stressed words on the tape. When the students have completed the exercise, you may wish to ask them how parents can keep their children from falling victim to distractions which prevent them from learning what they should be learning.

4. Family Dynamics, pages 267–268
Do not give your students any help with this exercise. They should be able to fill in the auxiliaries on their own without hearing the conversation.

5. Editing, pages 268–269
See the General Suggestions for Editing on page 4.

You may want to point out that *monitor* means "watch, supervise." Point out that the contracted forms in this letter are not wrong per se, but that emphatic forms are more natural and make for a stronger style.

COMMUNICATION PRACTICE (pages 270–275)

See the General Suggestions for Communication Practice on page 4.

6. Listening, page 270
If the students are not familiar with TV and radio talk shows, you may wish to record one to play in class. Ask the students if they ever listen to or watch such programs and why they think some Americans and Canadians like to listen to talk shows and to call in to them.

You may want to point out the following vocabulary: *jitters* (feelings of nervousness); *level with him* (be open and honest with him); *inheritance* (money or possessions passed on by people, usually after they die); *down payment* (initial large payment on a piece of property—a percentage of the total cost, perhaps 20%); *ethical* (morally correct, right).

EXTENSION: After the students have completed the written questions, ask them to summarize the conversations between the talk show host and the two people who call. Have them discuss whether or not they feel that the host's advice is correct and what advice they would have given.

7. Information Gap: Childrearing, pages 270–273 and 274–275
This is an authentic reading. You may want to point out the following vocabulary: *childrearing* (raising children); *pandemonium* (a situation of chaos and disorder, literally "all the devils"); *decibels* (units for measuring the loudness of sound); *an incessant state of yell* (they were continually yelling); *trinket* (small ornament or trivial thing); *hauls* (the things their parents bought them); *mayhem* (destruction; extreme disorder); *arrived to these shores* (arrived here); *appalled* (horrified, dismayed); *180 degrees removed* (the opposite); *bribe* (to give something to someone in order to achieve a certain result or behavior).

Culture Note: There has been much criticism in the last two or three decades about how permissive many American parents are regarding the raising of their children.

Discussion: Be sure that your students understand Mr. Rosemond's point of view. Do they basically agree or disagree? What is the situation in the students' cultures?

8. Essay, page 273
A thorough discussion of John Rosemond's article should prepare the students to write a good essay.

9. Picture Discussion, page 273
See the General Suggestions for Pair and Group Discussion on page 5.

Culture Note: Most states in the United States require the use of seatbelts by law, though drivers and passengers don't always wear them. Also, drivers who receive too many speeding tickets (or tickets for more serious infractions) are penalized by their insurance companies with higher rates.

Discussion: What is the situation regarding seat belts and speeding in your students' area? Is it as it should be?

EXPANSION

In My Family: Have your students write essays describing their families. Encourage them to focus on similarities and differences between family members, and to use auxiliaries of contrast and emphasis correctly.

 UNIT 15 PHRASAL VERBS

GRAMMAR **IN CONTEXT** (pages 276–278)

See the General Suggestions for Grammar in Context on page 2.

Establish the Context: The theme of the unit is gift giving, especially from the viewpoint of different cultures. Begin by asking your students their ideas about this practice. On what occasions do they give gifts? To whom? Do they consider gift giving important?

Questions to Consider, page 276: See the General Suggestions for Questions to Consider on page 2.

Reading, pages 276–277: See the General Suggestions for Reading on page 2.

Discussion: Ask the students if they've had any similar experiences in which there was cross-cultural misunderstanding.

Understanding Meaning from Context, page 278
See the General Suggestions for Understanding Meaning from Context on page 2.

You may want to point out the following vocabulary: *perplexed* (puzzled); *take on* (opinion of, treatment of); *a big deal* (something important); *figurine* (a small molded, sculpted, or carved figure).

GRAMMAR **PRESENTATION:** Phrasal Verbs (pages 279–280)

See the General Suggestions for Grammar Presentation on page 3.

The concept of phrasal verbs will not be new to your students, and they will know many commonly used ones. It seems, however, that students can always use more practice in phrasal verbs, for there are so many of them in English and they are one of the most characteristic features of the language. This unit reviews the grammar of phrasal verbs, particularly with regard to separable and inseparable, and familiarizes students with some of the most important and common phrasal verbs in the language. As recommended in the Understanding Meaning from Context section of the General Suggestions on page 2, students should keep a vocabulary notebook and record a new phrasal verb every time they hear or read one. This recording should include the sentence (or an approximation of it) in which the new phrasal verb was used. The keeping of such a book could be a class assignment.

NOTE 1: Begin by writing a few easy phrasal verbs on the board: *listen to, wait for, look at, talk about,* and the like. Elicit examples of other phrasal verbs.

NOTES 2 AND 3: Ask the students to put the verbs on the board in sentences or phrases with nouns and pronouns following. Remind them of the separable / inseparable distinction. Classify the verbs on the board into two lists.

NOTES 4: Ask the students to use the phrasal verbs on the board in new sentences as gerunds, infinitives, and participles. For example:

give up: *Bob needs <u>to give up</u> smoking.* (infinitive)
put up with: *<u>Putting up with</u> barking dogs is difficult.* (gerund)
put away: *<u>Putting away</u> the book, Mom told the children it was bedtime.* (participle)

NOTE 5: Spend some time changing phrasal verbs to nouns. Not every phrasal verb has a noun associated with it, but many do. Here are some examples:

break down / a breakdown
brush off / a brushoff
brush up / a brushup
clean up / a cleanup
come down / a comedown
change over / a changeover
check up / a checkup
crack down / a crackdown
get together / a get-together
hold over / a holdover
hold up / a holdup
hook up / a hookup
let down / a letdown
let up / a letup
pay back / a payback
run away / a runaway
sell out / a sellout
take over / a takeover
try out / a tryout
turn off / a turnoff
turn on / a turn-on
turn out / a turnout
work out / a workout

FOCUSED PRACTICE (pages 281–285)

See the General Suggestions for Focused Practice on page 3

1. Discover the Grammar, pages 281–282
See the General Suggestions for Discover the Grammar on page 4.

2. Meanings, pages 282–283
When the students have finished this exercise, ask them to work in groups to prepare other similar examples with phrasal verbs.

3. Figuring Out the Meanings, pages 283–284
When the students do this exercise, it is beneficial if they try to write a definition for each phrasal verb.

4. Editing, page 285
See the General Suggestions for Editing on page 4.

CULTURE NOTE: The surprise party, particularly to celebrate birthdays, is common in North America, so common in fact that sometimes people have to go to great lengths to hide the fact that they are planning a surprise party because such a party is expected.

DISCUSSION: Are surprise parties common in your students' culture? What do they think of this kind of party?

COMMUNICATION PRACTICE (pages 286–289)

See the General Suggestions for Communication Practice on page 4.

5. Listening, page 286
You may want to point out the following vocabulary: *subdued* (conservative, not flashy); *will do* (I'll do it.).

6. Information Gap: Gift Giving Practices, pages 286–287 and 289
You may want to point out the following vocabulary: *adamant* (insistent); *crushed* (severely hurt feelings); *prevalent* (common, widespread); *replicas (*exact copies); *ironic* (contrary to expectation).

DISCUSSION: Ask your students if they know of any similar situations in which gift giving practices are sharply different from their own culture's practices.

7. Charades, page 287
If your students haven't played charades before, remind them of a few basic rules: No words can be used by the actor. It is acceptable to give one's team clues by holding up the number of fingers corresponding to the number of words in the phrasal verb.

8. Essay, page 288
In order to allow your students' ideas to come out freely, you might ask them to freewrite their essay before they begin to write the actual essay.

9. Picture Discussion, page 288
See the General Suggestions for Pair and Group Discussion on page 5.

CULTURE NOTE: North American parents sometimes are chagrined by their children's gift expectations; at times it seems that, the more they receive, the more they want and expect.

DISCUSSION: What is the situation in the culture of your students? Is the value of a gift important, or is the thought primary? You might discuss the Hallmark Company's greeting card advertising slogan: "When you care enough to send the very best." What does it mean? Is the value of a gift in proportion to the amount the giver spends? Can a person's feelings toward another person be measured quantitatively?

EXPANSION

A Letter to a Friend: Using the letter on page 285 of the Student Book as a model, have your students write letters to friends. Encourage them to use phrasal verbs correctly.

REVIEW OR SELFTEST

See the General Suggestions for Review or SelfTest on page 6.

FROM GRAMMAR TO WRITING: UNITY, SUPPORT, AND COHERENCE

See the General Suggestions for From Grammar to Writing on page 6.

In this section, students practice improving unity, support, and coherence in their writing. They share their writing with a partner and evaluate each other's work.

Introduction, page 295
Have the students read the introductory text. Answer any questions.

Exercise 1, pages 295–296
Before dealing with the exercise, find a well-written paragraph and revise it, adding one or two irrelevant or off-target sentences. Ask the students to identify the off-target sentence or sentences. Elicit the problem or problems. Explain that the principle of unity in writing requires that every sentence in a paragraph be related to the topic sentence. When the students appear to understand this principle, have them complete the exercise in pairs. Go over the answers as a class.

Exercise 2, pages 296–297
Bring two or three well-written paragraphs of eight or more sentences to class. Read the paragraphs aloud, but omit one or two key supporting details. Ask the students to identify where necessary supporting details are needed. Read the paragraphs more than once if necessary. Then have the students complete the exercise in pairs. Write some of their examples of supporting details on the board. Discuss them as a class.

Exercise 3, page 297
Find a well-written paragraph. Rewrite the sentences in a different (i.e., ineffective) order. Ask the students to rewrite the paragraph with the sentences in an effective order. Compare their suggestions with the original. Then have them work in pairs to complete the exercise. Go over the answers as a class and discuss them. Stress that the most effective ordering of supporting details in a paragraph may vary according to the writer's perception of their importance.

Exercise 4: Apply It to Your Writing, page 297
Spend a sufficient amount of time on this exercise. Your students' paragraphs don't have to be particularly long, but they do need to have two or more sentences in the wrong order and at least one off-target sentence. Your students will probably need to rewrite their paragraphs before submitting them to you.

PART VII GERUNDS AND INFINITIVES

 GERUNDS

GRAMMAR **IN CONTEXT** (pages 300–302)

See the General Suggestions for Grammar in Context on page 2.

ESTABLISH THE CONTEXT: The theme of the unit is the use of leisure time, particularly regarding hobbies and pastimes. You might want to begin by eliciting from the students a list of hobbies and pastimes that they are aware of and / or participate in. Write them on the board. Take a vote to decide the top three in terms of interest.

Questions to Consider, page 300: See the General Suggestions for Questions to Consider on page 2.

Reading, pages 300–302: Have your students look at the picture. Ask them what they think "couch potato" means. Then see the General Suggestions for Reading on page 2.

DISCUSSION: Have your students heard of any of the hobbies mentioned in the reading? Ask them what the underlying viewpoint expressed by the writer is toward excessive TV watching. Do they agree or not? Do they think that roller coasting, orienteering, and letterboxing sound like interesting hobbies? Do they feel that there is indeed more stress in people's lives today?

Understanding Meaning from Context, page 302
See the General Suggestions for Understanding Meaning from Context on page 2.

You may want to point out the following vocabulary: *stressed out* (excessively nervous and tired because of overwork); *pop* (to put quickly); *mesmerized* (hypnotized); *stumble* (to move in an awkward, perhaps tired manner); *grab a bite* (to get something to eat quickly); *vegetate* (passively do nothing; act like a vegetable); *channel surfing* (flipping quickly through TV channels by using a remote control); *fall out of fashion* (become less and less popular); *breakneck* (extremely fast); *sprang up* (suddenly came into being); *R.I.P.* (Rest in Peace—letters often found on a tombstone).

GRAMMAR **PRESENTATION:** Gerunds (pages 303–306)

See the General Suggestions for Grammar Presentation on page 3.

NOTE 1: Gerunds used as complements, particularly appositives, may be new to your class. Elicit similar examples of gerunds acting as subjects, direct objects, objects of prepositions, subject complements, and appositives. If the students have difficulty understanding the difference between appositives and complements, you can explain to them that the appositive is simply a complement moved next to the subject and enclosed in commas. Appositives, being phrases, do not normally have verbs within them.

NOTE 2: To teach the perfect gerund, remind students that perfect constructions, those with *have / has / had*, are used to show which of two actions is earlier in time. Tell the students that *having* + a past participle shows an earlier action. A good way to practice this structure is to have students create their own sentences with the verb *remember*. For example:

I remember <u>having heard</u> that . . .

NOTE 3: To teach gerunds in passive constructions, you might write structures such as these on the board and elicit others from the students:

I hate / dislike being . . . / I hate getting . . .
I like / enjoy being . . . / I like getting . . .
Having been + (<u>past participle</u>) is one of the best things that ever happened to me.

Then have students create sentences based on their experience.

NOTE 4: To review the use of the possessive before a gerund, use the following examples:

<u>My snoring</u> irritates my wife.
<u>My wife's talking</u> on the telephone for hours annoys me.

Point out that in conversation, native speakers often use an object pronoun instead of a possessive:

<u>My wife talking</u> on the telephone for hours annoys me.

NOTE 5: Learning which verbs and verb phrases are followed by gerunds and which by infinitives takes considerable practice. In particular, the verb phrases *spend time, have trouble / difficulty, be worth* (+ gerund) are often difficult. Give students plenty of practice with them. For example, have them make sentences using the following prompts:

I spend a lot of time (<u>gerund</u>).
(<u>Gerund</u>) is / is not worth doing.
I have trouble (<u>gerund</u>).

For Part **d.** of Note 5, ask students to construct example sentences with gerunds and infinitives for each verb: *forget, quit, regret, remember, stop,* and *try*.

NOTE 6: Make sure that your students remember what present and past participles are. Present participles are verbs in the *–ing* form that are not gerunds. Past participles are verbs in the *–ed* form used with *have, has, had* and with *be* and *get* in the passive.

To help students distinguish between gerunds and progressives, use the following formula: If you can replace the *-ing* word or phrase with a single noun, it is a gerund. If you can't, it is a progressive. For example:

Mr. Ramos loves <u>singing</u>. = Mr. Ramos loves <u>music</u>.

The word *singing* can be replaced with the noun *music*, so *singing* is a gerund. Similarly:

<u>Sitting and doing nothing</u> can be healthful. = <u>Relaxation</u> can be healthful.

The phrase *sitting and doing nothing* can be replaced by the single noun *relaxation*, so *sitting* and *doing* are gerunds. However:

Sitting and doing nothing, Joan took stock of her life. ≠ *Relaxation*, Joan took stock of her life.

The phrase *sitting and doing nothing* cannot be replaced by a single noun such as *relaxation*, so it is not a gerund phrase.

FOCUSED PRACTICE (pages 307–312)

See the General Suggestions for Focused Practice on page 3.

1. Discover the Grammar, page 307
See the General Suggestions for Discover the Grammar on page 4.

2. All Work and No Play, page 307
You may want to point out the following vocabulary: *rat race* (a stressful situation brought on by too much work and too little leisure—people become like rats racing in cages); *punching a time clock* (inserting a card into a machine which stamps the time of beginning and ending work).

DISCUSSION: Do your students know any people who claim their work situation is a rat race? How can one deal with this problem?

3. Togetherness, page 309
In your students' culture, is family mealtime a common occurrence? Do they feel that family activities are beneficial? Why or why not?

4. A Lifestyle Survey, page 311
Verb prompts have been deliberately left out of this exercise in order to give advanced students a chance to be creative. If your class has difficulty, you can give them these prompts:

Picture 2: *be / tell / what to do*	or	*tell / others what to do*
Picture 3: *get / surprise / on your birthday*	or	*plan / your own birthday party*
Picture 4: *be / entertain / by others*	or	*entertain others / yourself*
Picture 5: *be / wait on / by others*	or	*serve yourself*
Picture 6: *have things / explain / to you*	or	*figure things out / yourself*

5. Editing, page 312
See the General Suggestions for Editing on page 4.

You may want to point out the following vocabulary: *chauffeured* (driven); *two-step* (a country-western dance, especially popular in the U.S. Southwest); *kicking up our heels* (enjoying ourselves, particularly in a physical activity like dancing); *weaving* (making cloth by hand).

COMMUNICATION PRACTICE (pages 313–316)

See the General Suggestions for Communication Practice on page 4.

6. Listening, page 313
See the General Suggestions for Listening on page 4.

7. Information Gap: Letterboxing, pages 313–315 and 316
For Part A, you may want to point out the following vocabulary: *whereabouts* (location); *modest* (unpretentious, not extreme). For Part B, ask your students how they would vary the activity.

8. Essay, page 315
The students will probably write better, more interesting essays if they write about unusual hobbies or pastimes.

9. Picture Discussion: A Day in the Life of Ted, page 315
Guide the students into creating as many sentences with gerunds as possible, using different verbs for *like* and *dislike*. For example:

He <u>hates</u> sitting through meetings.
He <u>can't stand</u> going to meetings.
He <u>loves</u> playing cards.

The Pros and Cons of Watching TV: Have your students review the article "Do You Really Enjoy Being a Couch Potato" on pages 300–302. Do they agree or disagree with the author's opinion about TV watching? Have them write essays about the advantages and disadvantages of watching TV. Encourage them to use gerunds correctly.

UNIT 17 INFINITIVES

GRAMMAR **IN CONTEXT** (pages 317–319)

See the General Suggestions for Grammar in Context on page 2.

ESTABLISH THE CONTEXT: The theme of the unit is procrastination. You might begin by asking the students whether they think time can be controlled or whether we are essentially at its mercy. You could then introduce the concepts of procrastination and "seizing the moment." Ask the students what they understand by the concepts. Ask them to give examples of procrastination and whether they think that procrastination is always a bad thing.

Questions to Consider, page 317: See the General Suggestions for Questions to Consider on page 2.

CULTURE NOTE: It is relatively common in the United States and Canada for elderly people to move to nursing homes when they can no longer care for themselves. Nursing homes are of varying quality, ranging from excellent to terrible. You may wish to ask students what they think of this practice.

Reading, pages 317–318: Since the reading is a story with something of a surprise ending, it might be most effective to have the students listen to it before they read it.

Understanding Meaning from Context, page 319
See the General Suggestions for Understanding Meaning from Context on page 2.

You may want to point out the following vocabulary: *boomed on* (came on suddenly and loudly); *jarred* (affected in a harsh, jolting, fashion); *distemper and feline leukemia* (diseases that commonly affect cats); *lap* (the front part of the body of a seated person from the waist to the knees); *leaky* (with a small amount of water coming out of it); *racing* (beating rapidly).

Comprehension, page 319: Have the students discuss the questions in pairs or small groups.

DISCUSSION: How do the students feel about the actions of Steve, the man in the story? Is he an uncaring person, a good person, or something in between? What are the responsibilities of an adult child toward an elderly parent? Have they had any similar experiences in which they waited too long to attend to something important?

GRAMMAR **PRESENTATION:** Infinitives (pages 320–323)

See the General Suggestions for Grammar Presentation on page 3.

NOTE 1: Have students work in groups to create their own sentences with infinitives as subjects, direct objects, and adjective complements.

NOTE 2: Have the students practice infinitives in the perfect form by completing prompts such as these:
When I started high school, I was expected to have . . .
By the time people are twenty-one years old, they are supposed to have . . .

NOTE 3: As a way of practicing infinitives in the passive form, ask students to recall things that were supposed to have been completed or established in their neighborhood or city by a certain time but weren't. For example:
The new highway was supposed to have been finished by April, but it's not finished yet.

You may provide more practice by giving a series of prompts such as the following. Have students work in pairs or groups to complete them:

Customers expect <u>(to be treated fairly)</u>.
Elderly people often need <u>(to be taken care of)</u>.
Students' progress in school needs <u>(to be monitored)</u>.
The environment needs <u>(to be protected)</u>.

NOTE 4: Have students practice the infinitive of purpose with prompts such as these:

I'm studying English (in order) to . . .
(In order) to get a good job, you need . . .
(In order) to be happy in life, you need . . .
(In order) to be successful in life, . . .

NOTE 5: An effective way to practice ellipsis is to create questions that will elicit answers that use it. For example:

A: *Are you going to the party?*
B: *I'm planning to.*
A: *Why did you take a second job?*
B: *I had to. I've got a lot of expenses.*

NOTE 6: Students need practice in using verbs followed by infinitives and those followed by gerunds. Have a class activity, perhaps a game, in which you write many of the verbs in Note 6 on the board without classifying them as requiring infinitives or gerunds. Teams score points by using each verb correctly in a sentence.

FOCUSED PRACTICE (pages 324–331)

See the General Suggestions for Focused Practice on page 4.

1. Discover the Grammar, pages 324–325
See the General Suggestions for Discover the Grammar on page 4.

2. What Would You Expect?, pages 325–326
When students have completed this exercise, have the students discuss what a reasonable expectation would be in each case.

3. Seize the Day, pages 326–327
You may want to point out the following vocabulary: *syndrome* (refer to the explanation of *the expectation syndrome* presented in Unit 8); *live up to other people's expectations* (meet other people's expectations).

DISCUSSION: After you have gone over this exercise, you might have a discussion on the content of the interview. You could give an explanation of the Latin phrase *carpe diem* ("seize the day") and ask the students to provide their own examples of it. Do the students agree or disagree that much procrastination is caused by fear, not laziness?

4. Editing, page 328
See the General Suggestions for Editing on page 4.

When the students have finished this exercise, point out that it is supposed to be humorous. Ask them to identify statements that they find funny.

5. Helping Procrastinators Get to It, pages 329–331
This is an authentic reading. For Part A, you may want to point out the following vocabulary: *are cut from the same cloth* (are the same type of person—as if they were made as clothing is made); *hobble* (to prevent from moving freely and naturally, as a horse or other animal is hobbled by a device attached to its legs); *chronically* (regularly); *predominant* (strongest, most characteristic); *grandiose* (too big or grand in scope or intention); *comfort zone* (within a pattern of behavior that feels comfortable and does not offer much challenge); *adrenaline rush* (sudden feeling of great energy); *life on the edge* (life lived in an extreme fashion, characterized by the taking of many risks); *threshold* (lowest point; beginning point—here, the point at which one begins to be bored); *sulky* (withdrawn, gloomy); *delegating* (asking someone else to complete a task); *burnout* (feeling of physical or emotional exhaustion, usually caused by excessive stress); *finicky* (hard to please; being overly

selective); *peer* (someone who has equal standing or position with others). For Part B, spend considerable time having the students discuss their responses to gain insight about themselves.

COMMUNICATION PRACTICE (pages 332–335)

See the General Suggestions for Communication Practice on page 4.

6. Listening, page 332

You may want to point out the following vocabulary: *term paper* (in North American schools, a major written project done by the students); *kicked out* (removed, asked to leave); *bail you out* (help you out of a difficult circumstance, from the idea of paying bail to get someone out of jail after an arrest and before a trial); *my mind is made up* (I'm not going to change my mind). After the students have completed the listening task, ask them to talk about similar situations they know about.

7. Information Gap: On the Loose, pages 333 and 335

You may want to point out the following vocabulary: *maximum security facility* (a prison where the most dangerous prisoners are kept); *smuggled* (moved into or out of somewhere illegally or wrongly—for example, drugs or goods brought illegally into a country); *noncommittal* (not giving or wanting to give a clear, straightforward answer to a question); *bureaucratic* (characterized by rigid, perhaps unnecessary, attention to details—often used negatively).

8. Essay, page 333

Stress to the students that the quality of their essays will depend largely on the inclusion of enough supporting details. Have them describe their procrastinating experiences completely.

9. Picture Discussion, page 334

This activity is a good place to have students write extended conversations between the mother and daughter. After they have done that with present-tense forms, they can rewrite the conversations in the past.

EXPANSION

Me? Procrastinate?: Have your students discuss whether they usually do things right away or procrastinate. Do they fit into one or more of the six procrastination styles described in the article "Helping Procrastinators Get To It" on pages 329–330? If they procrastinate, have them write essays about which of the six procrastination styles they think they fit into. If they don't procrastinate, have them write essays on how they manage to meet deadlines. Encourage them to support their ideas with examples and to use gerunds and infinitives correctly.

REVIEW OR SELFTEST

See the General Suggestions for Review or SelfTest on page 6.

FROM GRAMMAR TO WRITING: PARALLELISM OF GERUNDS AND INFINITIVES

See the General Suggestions for From Grammar to Writing on page 6.

In this section, students continue the study of parallel structure introduced in Part V through using parallelism with gerunds and infinitives. They share their writing with a partner and evaluate each other's work.

Introduction, pages 342–343

Here are three techniques for getting your students to practice parallelism with gerunds and infinitives before they work on the exercises.

1. Create a series of flashcards containing cues. Have the students make sentences with items in parallel structure. For example:

My favorite hobbies are reading, skiing, and rock climbing. (cues: *hobby, read, ski,* and *climb rocks*)

Since I have been studying English, I have learned to understand TV newscasts, (to) *converse with people, and* (to) *read the newspaper.* (cues: *study English, understand TV newscasts, converse with people, read the newspaper*)

2. Bring in a series of pictures from magazines or other sources. Have the students make sentences with items in parallel structure. For example:

The people in the picture like swimming, sleeping on the beach, and playing volleyball. (from a beach picture)

3. Find short articles (one or two paragraphs) in newspapers or magazines. Rewrite some of the sentences so that items are not in parallel structure. Have the students edit the articles for parallel structure. Then show them the originals.

Have the students read the introductory text. Answer any questions.

Exercise 1, page 343
Have the students do the exercise in pairs. Go over the answers as a class.
For extra practice, have them rewrite sentences 1, 2, 3, and 5 with *I* (*My life* in sentence 5) as the subject, using their own ideas or experiences. For example:

I love swimming, canoeing, and traveling. (rewritten sentence 1)

Exercise 2, page 343
Have the students do the exercise in pairs. Go over the answers as a class.
For extra practice, have them rewrite sentences 1 and 2 from their own points of view. For example:

On my vacation this year, I want to cruise to Alaska, take pictures of wildlife, and meet some new people. (rewritten sentence 1)

Exercise 3, page 344
Have the students complete the exercise individually. Then go over it as a class. You may want to point out the following vocabulary: *scorned* (treated critically); *desensitization* (the process of reducing one's sensitivity).

Exercise 4: Apply It to Your Writing, page 344
Have the students write their paragraphs individually. Insist that they include examples of parallelism of gerunds and infinitives. Then have them edit each others' paragraphs in pairs, focusing on correct use of parallel structure.

PART VIII ADVERBS

UNIT 18 ADVERB CLAUSES

GRAMMAR IN CONTEXT (pages 348–350)

See the General Suggestions for Grammar in Context on page 2.

ESTABLISH THE CONTEXT: The theme of this unit is sports. Before dealing with the reading, you might have your students discuss sports and sporting events. Do they like them? What sports do they participate in? Then ask if they have heard of "extreme sports" and, if they have, what their opinion is.

Questions to Consider, page 348: See the General Suggestions for Questions to Consider on page 2.

Reading, pages 348–349: Before your students read or listen to the reading, have them look at the cartoons. Make sure they are familiar with these extreme sports.

Understanding Meaning from Context, page 350
See the General Suggestions for Understanding Meaning from Context on page 2.

You may want to point out the following vocabulary: *thirty-something, twenty-something* (somewhere in the thirties and twenties—the word "something" can be attached to any of the "decades," so we hear "forty-something," etc.); *deserted* (with no one there, connected to the noun *desert*); *bungee* (connected to the word *bungee cord*, a short, elastic cord used for fastening things); *the masses* (the vast majority of citizens); *globalized* (part of the "world culture").

GRAMMAR **PRESENTATION**: Adverb Clauses (pages 351–354)

See the General Suggestions for Grammar Presentation page 3.

Elicit an original example of each of the seven types of adverb clauses presented in the grammar chart.

NOTE 1: You may wish to ask students to identify the subject, verbs, and subordinating words for each adverb clause in the opening reading. Point out that it is normally the presence of the subordinating word that makes the clause dependent. If one removes the subordinating word, the clause becomes independent. Knowledge of the principles of subordination should help students learn to combine sentences effectively.

The two types of adverb clauses that may cause your students some difficulty are the clauses of comparison and result. This is because an element linked to the dependent clause (for example, *so, such, as much, as many*) is contained in the independent clause. If you feel it would be productive, have your students practice clauses with *as much as, as many as, more than, less than, so . . . that,* and *such . . . that* with magazine pictures and / or written prompts. For example:

Movies are so expensive today that . . .
There is less . . . today than . . .
It's such a beautiful day today that . . .

In particular, give your students plenty of practice in using *so* and *such*. Students often have difficulty using *such* before noun phrases.

NOTE 2: Remind your students that *will* and *be going to* are not used in future-time adverb clauses; they are used only in the result clause. In sentences such as

If you'll help me with my math, I'll help you with your English essay.
will indicates volition (i.e., willingness), not future.

NOTE 3: Read the note in the Student Book with your class. Answer any questions.

NOTE 4: On the board, write the subordinating conjunctions that your students are less familiar with. These might include *in spite of the fact that, once, even though, as soon as,* and *even if*. Ask them to construct complex sentences with adverb clauses. For example:

I'm sleepy <u>when</u> I get up in the morning. Once I've had breakfast, <u>though</u>, I'm completely awake.
<u>In spite of the fact that</u> cigarettes are not good for you, many people continue to smoke.

Point out the difference between *in spite of* and *in spite of the fact that, because of* and *because (of the fact that), on account of* and *on account of the fact that*. The phrases without *the fact that* are compound prepositions, not subordinating conjunctions, and have to be changed to other forms to be used as sentence connectors.

NOTES 5 AND 6: Read the notes in the Student Book with your class. Answer any questions.

FOCUSED **PRACTICE** (pages 355–359)

See the General Suggestions for Focused Practice on page 3.

1. Discover the Grammar, page 355
See the General Suggestions for Discover the Grammar on page 4.

2. Key Moments in Sports, page 356
Remind students of the correspondences between *if* and *unless, more than* and *fewer than*. For item 6, ask students to write an equivalent sentence with *such*. For example:

There was such a lot of ice on the slope that the competition had to be canceled.

3. When Sports Become Too Extreme, pages 357–358

Part A is an authentic reading. You may want to point out the following vocabulary: *launching out into* (going out into); *ultimate* (most perfect or satisfying); *unleashed* (set free); *egos* (overly prideful self-concepts); *anecdotal evidence* (evidence coming from particular incidents and not from a situation in general); *strides* (progress); *skyrocketing* (rapidly increasing and becoming very high). The discussion in Part B is important. Give your students plenty of time to complete it.

CULTURE NOTE: In the United States, there have been increasing numbers of lawsuits in the past twenty to thirty years as to whether or not a person's "constitutional rights" are being violated.

4. Editing, page 359

You may want to point out the following vocabulary: *winning a few and losing a few* (being successful sometimes and unsuccessful at other times); *ironed out* (compensated for, repaired).

CULTURE NOTE: It is common in North America to offer college scholarships to outstanding athletes. Theoretically, these students are expected to perform both scholastically and athletically. In reality, however, some of them do not measure up in the academic arena, and there have been a number of scandals involving the falsifying of grades and the paying of money to athletes at universities around the United States.

DISCUSSION: When the students have finished the exercise, have them discuss whether they think that recruitment of star athletes is fundamentally positive or negative. Do they agree with Jamal Jefferson's viewpoint in his essay? Discussion of this issue will help prepare your students for the essay later in the unit.

COMMUNICATION PRACTICE (pages 360–362)

See the General Suggestions for Communication Practice on page 4.

5. Listening, page 360

You may want to point out the following vocabulary: *a charmed athletic career* (an athletic career that seems to have involved a charm or magical intervention; that is, a very fortunate experience); *stuck to it* (did not quit; stayed on the task until it was completed).

DISCUSSION: After the students have completed the exercise, discuss Lillian Swanson's reasons for her success. How important is family support? How important are discipline and dealing with adversity?

6. The Name of the Game, pages 360–361

This game may look difficult at first, but students should be able to do well if they work in groups. For further practice, you might ask your students to write down and turn in the sentences they write.

7. Essay, page 361

Since students will have mastered adverb clauses in studying this unit, the essay for the unit is a good activity for beginning work on sentence combining. A worthwhile activity would involve having students combine sentences with adverb clauses in their revisions.

8. Picture Discussion, page 362

Sports-related violence happens often enough in the United States and Canada, but it also happens elsewhere. Ask the students to tell about other examples they've heard about. Pay particular attention to discussing the saying "It's not whether you win or lose that's important; it's how you play the game." Do they feel this is true or attainable?

EXPANSION

Opinions About Violence in Sports: Have your students write summaries of the students' opinions expressed from the Picture Discussion on page 362. Encourage them to include examples and use adverb clauses correctly.

GRAMMAR **IN CONTEXT** (pages 363–365)

See the General Suggestions for Grammar in Context on page 2.

ESTABLISH THE CONTEXT: The theme of the unit is cloning and genetic engineering. Begin by asking students what they know about cloning. Write their statements on the board. They may have heard about Dolly, the sheep that was cloned by a team of scientists in Scotland, and they may know of other examples. You might tell your class that, while the process of cloning may seem entirely modern, the concept has been around for millennia. *Clone* comes from the Greek word *klon*, meaning "twig." A rudimentary form of cloning has long been practiced through the use of twigs grafted on to fruit trees.

Questions to Consider, page 363: See the General Suggestions for Questions to Consider on page 2.

Reading, pages 363–365: Since the reading is the script of a radio talk show, have the students listen to the tape at least twice before they read the script.

DISCUSSION: Ask the class which caller they agree with more. What are their reasons?

Understanding Meaning from Context, page 365
See the General Suggestions for Understanding Meaning from Context on page 2.

Point out that the expressions *down the tube* and *off the wall* are common colloquial expressions. You might also tell them the origin of the term *Pandora's box*: In Greek mythology, Pandora, the first woman, was given a box. She was told not to open the box because it contained all of humankind's ills, but out of curiosity she opened it anyway. Out flew all of our ills, and they've been with us ever since. You may want to point out the following vocabulary: *keep your language clean* (not use swear or taboo words); *debilitating* (taking away the strength and energy of something); *playing God* (trying to be like God, taking God's role); *Give me a break!* (Don't bother me with ridiculous or tiresome statements!); *dread disease* (terrible disease); *doomed* (destined); *fuzzy* (unclear); *superficial* (on the surface; cosmetic); *species diversity* (the wide range and differentiation of species).

GRAMMAR **PRESENTATION:** Adverbs: Viewpoint, Focus, Negative, Location, Sequence (pages 366–369)

See the General Suggestions for Grammar Presentation on page 3.

NOTE 1: To clarify the concept of viewpoint adverbs, explain that sentences with viewpoint adverbs derived from adjectives can be restated using *I am* + adjective + *that* . . . or *It is* + adjective + *that* . . . For example:

Sadly, Mary was unable to do anything. = It is sad / I am sad that she was unable to do anything.
Luckily, Jerry wasn't hurt in the accident. = It is lucky that Jerry wasn't hurt in the accident.

In a sentence like the following, however, the adverb is not a viewpoint adverb:

The child behaved badly. ≠ It is bad that the child misbehaved.

NOTE 2: To present focus adverbs, take a sentence with the word *only* or *just* and show how the meaning changes when *only* or *just* is moved.

Just John came to the dinner. (John was the only one who came.)
John just came to the dinner. / John came just to the dinner. (He came only to the dinner—not to anything else.)

Helen just doesn't like me. (She doesn't like me. It's that simple.)
Helen doesn't just like me. = (It's far more than "like." She loves me.)

NOTE 3: Using the adverb *even* correctly is often a difficult concept to master. Explain that *even* is used to talk about things that are not expected. For example:

Mary seems to like everyone. She likes her teachers. She likes her boss at the fast food restaurant where she works. She likes her younger brothers and sisters. She even likes the new principal at school.
(This is unexpected. No one else likes the new principal. We would expect Mary to have a similar view.)
Steve is the opposite. He seems angry at everyone. He doesn't like his teacher. He doesn't like his parents. He doesn't like the new principal. He doesn't even care for his girlfriend.
(This is unexpected. Although Steve doesn't seem to like many people, we would expect him at least to care for his girlfriend.)

NOTE 4: Your students may be familiar with the concept of negative adverbs that force the inversion of the subject and the auxiliary when the adverb comes first in the sentence. This occurs in sentences such as *Neither do I* and *Neither does Ali*, so you may want to begin with simple sentences like these. Students must simply learn which adverbs behave in this fashion. It may help to point out as an example that the words *seldom* and *occasionally* may have the same meaning in reference to quantity:

I seldom go to plays—only two or three times a year. (negative)
I occasionally go to plays—maybe two or three times a year. (positive)

However, *seldom*, like the other negative adverbs, is inherently negative, while *occasionally* is not. Give your students plenty of practice using inversion with the simple present and simple past tenses. The difficulty here is that, in affirmative sentences, *do*, *does*, and *did* are often not present.

NOTE 5: The inversion of subject and verb after *here* and *there* and sequence adverbs is probably new to your students. Ask them to identify all uses of these in the opening reading. Then, to practice inversion with *here* and *there*, take some pictures to class showing motion toward a person and motion away from a person. Have the students construct simple sentences with *here / there* and nouns and then with *here / there* and pronouns. For example:

The train is going out of the station. → *There goes the train. There it goes.*
The bus is arriving. → *Here comes the bus. Here it comes.*

To practice inversion with sequence adverbs, give the students a starting sentence and have each student add to it. Instruct them to include sequence adverbs such as *then* and *along*. For example:

What had been a sunny day suddenly became just the opposite. Heavy, angry-looking clouds moved over the sun. Then came the rumble of thunder. Along with the thunder came a bolt of lightning. Then came a downpour of rain.

NOTE 6: Read the note in the Student Book with your class. Answer any questions.

FOCUSED PRACTICE (pages 370–373)

See the General Suggestions for Focused Practice on page 3.

1. Discover the Grammar, page 370
See the General Suggestions for Discover the Grammar on page 4.

2. Science and Technology, page 371
If your students need the practice, you can have them write all twenty-one sentences in their notebooks. Alternatively, you may want them to do the exercise orally.

DISCUSSION: Much has been said about the quality of genetically engineered tomatoes, which have been on the market in certain places for some time. Most people seem to feel the tomatoes are tasteless. Have any of your students eaten these tomatoes? Do they like them?

3. The Power of Technology, pages 371–372
After the students have completed this exercise, have them work in pairs and write two additional sentences for each negative adverb given.

4. Picture Time, page 372
At an advanced level, students should be able to produce sentences without much help. Accordingly, they are given only the adverb and the picture here. The goal is not to produce a perfect sentence so much as it is to use each adverb correctly.

5. Editing, page 373

See the General Suggestions for Editing on page 4.

You may want to point out the following vocabulary: *stomped* (moved heavily and often angrily); *roaming* (wandering without supervision).

CULTURE NOTE: April 15 is tax day in the United States, the last day a taxpayer may submit his or her tax return without penalty. Most Americans take this quite seriously, and there is considerable fear of and some animosity toward the I.R.S. (Internal Revenue Service).

DISCUSSION: You may want to discuss the concept of the open-campus policy with your students. Many American high schools allow students to leave the campus at lunchtime and at other times during the school day. Is this similar to the experience of your students? What policy do they think would be best?

COMMUNICATION PRACTICE (pages 374–375)

See the General Suggestions for Communication Practice on page 4.

6. Listening, page 374

You may want to point out that *go for it* means "pursue it."

DISCUSSION: What do your students think about the caller's statement about genetic engineering? Should it be used if it will result in healing or progress in fighting diseases?

7. Essay, page 375

The work prior to this point should prepare the students to write an essay on cloning. Stress the importance of providing plenty of supporting details for their positions.

8. Picture Discussion, page 375

Ask each pair to explain their reasons for approval and disapproval. This should provide lively discussion, especially the item about the man who wants a son only.

EXPANSION

Response to Sue's Letter: Have your students write letters in response to Sue's letter on page 373, taking on the role of her mother. Encourage them to use viewpoint adverbs, focus adverbs, and negative adverbs correctly.

UNIT 20 DISCOURSE CONNECTORS

GRAMMAR IN CONTEXT (pages 376–378)

See the General Suggestions for Grammar in Context on page 2.

ESTABLISH THE CONTEXT: The theme of the unit is memory. Discuss the cartoon. What do students think it means? Currently, some people seem to think that we are being bombarded with so much information (in this "Information Age") that there simply isn't space in our brain to store and access it all (that is, "our disks our full"). Do students think this is true?

Questions to Consider, page 376: Spend some time on these questions. You might even ask the students to write down their first memory and share it with the class. Ask for their methods of remembering things and write them on the board.

Reading, pages 376–378: Before the students read or listen to the reading, point out that many writers use discourse connectors to tie together their ideas. After they have heard or read the article once, ask them to read it again and mentally note words and phrases they think might be discourse connectors.

DISCUSSION: Ask your students if they think some people just naturally have a good memory, or whether memory is a skill that can be learned and improved upon. Have they ever had experience with any of the memory improvement materials on the market (Mega Memory, etc.)? If so, do they work? What is important about memory?

Understanding Meaning from Context, page 378
See the General Suggestions for Understanding Meaning from Context on page 2.

You may want to point out the following vocabulary: *frontal lobes* (rounded projections in the front part of the brain); *hippocampus* (a structure of the brain consisting mainly of gray matter and central to the memory process); *gloomy* (dark or unfortunate in outlook); *glucose* (a sugar found in most plant and animal matter); *vivid* (creating a strong and clear mental image).

GRAMMAR **PRESENTATION:** Discourse Connectors (pages 379–383)

See the General Suggestions for Grammar Presentation on page 3.

NOTE 1: After establishing the distinction between coordinating conjunctions and transitions, you may wish to ask students to identify the connectors in the opening reading and classify them as coordinating conjunctions or transitions.

NOTE 2: For practice with coordinating conjunctions, create several pairs of sentences and ask your students to join the sentences, using an appropriate coordinating conjunction. If students have difficulty with the conjunction *nor*, explain that it basically does the same thing as *and* but occurs in negative sentences. Make it clear that it functions in the same way as *neither* at the beginning of a sentence or clause. You will probably also want to point out that the conjunction *for* has roughly the same meaning as *because* or *since*, and that it is rare in conversation but common in writing, especially formal writing.

NOTES 3 AND 4: Read the notes in the Student Book with your class. Answer any questions.

NOTE 5: Students sometimes have difficulty distinguishing between *so, so . . . that*, and *so that*. To clarify these items, use the following example sentences:

I had been driving for hours and was starving, <u>so</u> I stopped at a restaurant to get something to eat.
I had been driving for hours and was <u>so</u> hungry <u>that</u> I had to stop at a restaurant to get something to eat.
I had been driving for hours and was starving. I stopped <u>so that</u> I could get something to eat.

To practice their use, ask students to work together to complete each one using *so, so . . . that*, and *so that*:

I couldn't remember people's names when I met them, . . .
I was broke, . . .
It was snowing hard, . . .
My best friend wasn't speaking to me, . . .

NOTE 6: Since transitions are often characteristic of more formal registers of language, your students may not have heard them often and will probably need practice with them. The following two methods are often effective in teaching transitions:

1. Create controlled cloze exercises by taking short newspaper or magazine passages and deleting all the transitions. Students fill in the blanks with transitions they consider appropriate.
2. Identify several transitions you consider important for your students to learn (for example, *however, therefore, moreover, otherwise, meanwhile, nevertheless, besides, in fact*). Create short sentences along with a transitional word for each that leads logically into a second sentence. For example:

   Having a good education is necessary. Moreover, . . .

Students work individually or in groups to write sentences using the transitions. For extra practice, write several complex sentences containing an independent clause and a dependent clause. Write each clause on a separate file card or piece of paper. Give each student a file card. The students go around the room to find the matching clauses to make sentences. For example:

although I never feel like doing exercises when I wake up in the morning +
they wake me up and contribute to my overall physical well-being =
Although I never feel like doing exercises when I wake up in the morning, they wake me up and contribute to my overall physical well-being.

NOTE 7: Read the note in the Student Book with your class. Answer any questions.

NOTE 8: It might be worth pointing out to your students that *beside* and *besides* are different in meaning. *Beside* is a preposition meaning "next to" (in a physical location). *Besides* is a transition meaning "in addition to."

NOTE 9: Stress that, while coordinating conjunctions and transitions often have similar meanings, they are punctuated differently. To give students practice in punctuating them correctly and in avoiding comma splices, go back to the unit opener. Identify several sentences with transitions or coordinating conjunctions. Ask students to rewrite them. For example:

It may sound silly, <u>but</u> it worked for me. =
It may sound silly. <u>However</u>, it worked for me. OR *It may sound silly; <u>however</u>, it worked for me.*

NOTES 10 AND 11: Read the notes in the Student Book with your class. Answer any questions.

FOCUSED PRACTICE (pages 384–387)

See the General Suggestions for Focused Practice on page 3.

1. Discover the Grammar, page 384
This exercise involves much searching and classifying, which should help your students make some cognitive connections.

2. A Memory Test, page 385
You may want to point out the following vocabulary: *aftermath* (a usually unpleasant result of something); *notoriously* (in a manner showing an unfavorable reputation); *hamper* (affect negatively); *make it* (to arrive). Play the tape with the students' books closed. Point out that it is harder to understand the text because the transitions have been deleted. Go through the memory exercise before you ask your students to fill in the blanks.

3. A String Around His Finger?, page 386
The goal here is to allow the advanced student to use his or her understanding of the grammar. The sentences produced do not have to be exact; the focus should merely be on the correct use of connectors and punctuation of sentences with coordinating transitions and conjunctions.

4. Editing, page 387
See the General Suggestions for Editing on page 4.

Make it clear to your students that they are not to change punctuation or word order. They are merely to find alternate connectors that work in the passage.

COMMUNICATION PRACTICE (pages 388–390)

See the General Suggestions for Communication Practice on page 4.

5. Listening, pages 388–389
See the General Suggestions for Listening on page 4.

DISCUSSION: After completing the listening task, ask your students the following questions: How important is it to remember other people's names? Have students give examples of times when someone has forgotten their name or they have forgotten someone else's. How did they feel? How does it feel to be called by your name when you are in a situation where you know few other people?

6. The Memory Game, page 389
This game should give your students the chance to be creative. Insist that each sentence produced contain a discourse connector.

7. Essay, page 389
The essay should be fairly easy for students to write. Potentially productive topics include remembering childhood experiences or embarrassing or dangerous experiences.

8. Picture Discussion, page 390
This should be an enjoyable discussion. You may wish to lengthen the time students are allowed to look at the picture to two minutes.

Forgotten Things: Ask your students if they have ever forgotten to do something important. Have them write essays about the experience. Encourage them to use discourse connectors correctly.

UNIT 21 — ADVERB PHRASES

GRAMMAR **IN CONTEXT** (pages 391–393)

See the General Suggestions for Grammar in Context on page 2.

ESTABLISH THE CONTEXT: The theme of the unit is compassion. The reading is about the couple from America who donated their son's organs to hospitals after their son had been shot by criminals and was unable to survive. Begin by asking students what they know about this situation. Someone will probably have heard of the incident. If not, summarize the situation for the class and then ask them how they think the parents' action demonstrates compassion.

Questions to Consider, page 391: Have your students give examples of compassionate acts they have heard of. Then play the tape or have students take turns reading.

Reading, page 391: See the General Suggestions for Reading on page 2.

Understanding Meaning from Context, page 393
See the General Suggestions for Understanding Meaning from Context on page 2.

Connect *floored* to pushing a gas pedal to the floor and *It gradually dawned on us* to the dawn of the day. Discuss the meaning of *irony* and the related word *ironic*. Ask students to give examples of irony. You may want to point out the following vocabulary: *the boot* (show a map of Italy and point out the boot area); *bandana* (a large cloth like a handkerchief worn around the neck, on the face, or around the head—traditionally worn by bandits); *shattering* (breaking into many pieces); *civility* (behaving in a civilized, proper fashion); *Calabrian* (from the Italian region named Calabria, which forms the "toe" of the boot); *a blow was struck for organ donation* (the cause of organ donation was advanced); *pledged* (promised).

Group Discussion, page 393
See the General Suggestions for Group and Pair Discussions on page 5.

Ask your students how they feel about organ donation. Are any students organ donors?

GRAMMAR **PRESENTATION:** Adverb Phrases (pages 394–397)

See the General Suggestions for Grammar Presentation on page 3.

NOTE 1: Read the note in the Student Book with your class. Answer any questions.

NOTE 2: Write short sentences containing adverb phrases on the board. Ask students to convert them into two sentences. For example:

Having eaten dinner, John lay down on the couch. (John ate dinner. Then he lay down on the couch.)

Given the chance, John would go to college. (Suppose that John is given the chance. John would go to college.)

NOTE 3: Ask the students to go back to the reading and identify adverb phrases with present and past participles.

One problem your students are likely to have with adverb phrases is knowing when to use the form with the present participle and when to use it with *having* + past participle. Tell the students to use the form with the present participle to describe two actions or states occurring in the same time frame. For example:

Sipping a soda, Denise wondered about the meaning of life. (Both actions, sipping and wondering, were occurring at the same time.)

Use the *having* + past participle form to show actions occurring in different time frames. For example: *Having sold his condominium, Michael had money to travel around the world.* (First Michael sold his condominium. Then he had money to travel around the world.)

Ask the students to write two sentences about two connected events from different time frames in their lives. They then combine them into one sentence with *having* + past participle.

NOTE 4: Students will be at least somewhat familiar with the infinitive of purpose from Unit 17: Infinitives. Remind them that infinitive of purpose constructions answer "why" or "for what purpose" questions. Have them practice this structure by completing prompts such as these:

To help myself remember names, I . . .
In order to get up on time, I . . .
To earn a decent salary, a person . . .
To find the right person to marry, one . . .
To protect themselves from disastrous circumstances, people . . .

NOTE 5: To teach your students to use adverb phrases, you can effectively use sentence-combining exercises. Bring in pictures or handouts with pairs of sentences. Have the class work in groups to produce sentences with adverb phrases in them. A game might be used, with prizes awarded to the group that can produce the greatest number of correctly combined sentences.

You also might write complex sentences with a main clause and an adverb phrase. Write each sentence part on a file card and give one card to each student. The students go around the room to find the matching parts to make sentences. For example:

having finished all the housework +
I was finally able to turn out the lights and go to bed
Having finished all the housework, I was finally able to turn out the lights and go to bed.

FOCUSED PRACTICE (pages 398–401)

See the General Suggestions for Focused Practice on page 4.

1. Discover The Grammar, page 398
Briefly review adverb clauses (including subordinating conjunctions) with your students before they do Part E.

2. Sentence Combining, pages 398–399
If students understand how to combine sentences correctly, they are more likely to avoid dangling modifiers and generally improve the quality of their writing. After the students have done this exercise, ask each student to write two sentences that either can or cannot be combined. The students present their sentences to the class, and the class decides if they can be correctly combined.

3. Enterprise, pages 399–400
After the students have completed this exercise, have them discuss whether or not they think being enterprising is important. Should people try to improve their own situation, or should they wait for someone else to come to their aid?

4. Editing, page 401
See the General Suggestions for Editing on page 4.

You may want to point out the following vocabulary: *barraged* (attacked with or subjected to a continuing stream of words or actions); *tune out* (not pay attention); *numbed* (desensitized); *pocketed* (put in one's pocket—often wrongly); *scratch out a living* (to earn a living in difficult circumstances); *limp* (an irregular or jerky way of walking); *semblance* (something similar to; an approximation).

This exercise is designed to teach students to avoid the dangling modifier in adverb phrases. The key point students need to know is that the subject in the clause and the implied subject in the phrase must refer to the same thing. You can help your students to master this concept by creating incorrect sentences with dangling modifiers. Ask the students to correct them by adding a necessary subject and / or rearranging the sentence. For example, in the sentence

Running into the room, the accident was reported.

it sounds as if the accident was running into the room. It can be corrected by adding a subject that shows who ran into the room:

Running into the room, Mary reported the accident.

The six sentences with dangling modifiers, reasons why they are incorrect, and possible corrections follow:

1. *Subjected to many stimuli, only the crucial ones stick in my mind.* (The crucial ones are not subjected to many stimuli; my mind is.) POSSIBLE CORRECTION: *Subjected to many stimuli, my mind retains only the crucial ones.*

2. *By arguing that I don't have enough money anyway, the request is ignored.* (The request is not arguing; I am.) POSSIBLE CORRECTION: *By arguing to myself that I don't have enough money anyway, I ignore the request.*

3. *Having landed in Santa Simona, a taxi took me to my hotel . . . .* (A taxi did not land in Santa Simona; I did.) POSSIBLE CORRECTION: *Having landed in Santa Simona, I took a taxi to my hotel . . . .*

4. *Sitting on a dirty blanket . . . my eye was caught by her.* (My eye was not sitting on a dirty blanket.) POSSIBLE CORRECTION: *Sitting on a dirty blanket . . . she caught my eye.*

5. *While talking later with a nun . . . much worthwhile information was given to me.* (Information was not talking with a nun.) POSSIBLE CORRECTION: *While talking later with a nun . . . I was given much worthwhile information.*

6. *Selling her mangoes, a semblance of a living was earned . . . .* (A semblance of a living was not selling mangoes; she was.) POSSIBLE CORRECTION: *Selling her mangoes, Elena managed to earn a semblance of a living . . . .*

COMMUNICATION PRACTICE (pages 402–407)

See the General Suggestions for Communication Practice on page 4.

5. Listening, page 402
This newscast is hypothetical. You may want to point out the following vocabulary: *dissident* (someone who strongly disagrees with the positions of a government or religious order); *anonymity* (the condition of not having one's name identified; compare *anonymous*); *infusions* (amounts "poured" into something).

6. Information Gap: A Caring Elephant, pages 402–405 and 406–407
This is an authentic reading. You may want to point out the following vocabulary: *distressed* (upset, saddened); *makeshift* (temporary and perhaps of poor quality); *intravenously* (literally, "within a vein"—by injection); *protruding* (sticking out); *maternity leave* (for women about to give birth, time off from work, sometimes paid); *grief / grieve* (great sorrow / to be greatly sorry); *stillborn* (born dead); *lapped up* (drank up, as an animal would drink); *shed tears* (cry); *heaped* (piled); *quota* (regular prescribed amount); *drooping* (hanging loosely and without energy).

DISCUSSION: Spend a good amount of time on the discussion. Students will probably have many ideas on the subject. Encourage them to answer this question: What is the basis of compassion?

7. Essay, page 405
Students should have a fairly easy time writing the essay, which should simply be about a situation in which they were moved by someone's unselfish actions.

8. Picture Discussion, page 405
This activity can be linked with the discussion in Exercise 6. There are many such stories of animals who appear to have shown love of humans (for example, the Scottish story "Greyfriars Bobby," about a dog who came to his master's grave for years after his death).

EXPANSION

Compassion: Nature or Nurture?: Have your students write essays about the following topic: Do you think people are compassionate by nature? Or is compassion something that has to be learned? Encourage your students to support their ideas with reasons and examples and to use adverb phrases correctly.

REVIEW OR SELFTEST

See the General Suggestions for Review or SelfTest on page 6.

FROM GRAMMAR TO WRITING: SENTENCES AND FRAGMENTS

See the General Suggestions for From Grammar to Writing on page 6.

In this section, students review sentences and fragments and practice combining sentences using coordinating conjunctions and transitions. They share their writing with a partner and evaluate each other's work.

Introduction, page 413

Though fragments are considered incorrect, they are found in many pieces of writing. Good writers use them sparingly, selectively, and deliberately. To use fragments effectively, it is essential to understand the difference between sentences and fragments.

For students who have difficulty recognizing fragments, try the following exercise. Rewrite relatively short passages (a paragraph or two) from newspaper and magazine articles so that they include some fragments. Have the students read them aloud and correct them.

Have the students read the introductory text. Answer any questions. You may want to refer students to Appendices 18–20 on pages A–8 and A–9 for information about coordinating conjunctions, subordinating conjunctions, and transitions.

Exercise 1, pages 413–414

Have the students do the exercise in pairs. Go over the answers as a class, asking the students to give reasons for their choices.

Exercise 2, pages 414–415

Have the students complete the exercise in pairs, reading the paragraph aloud. Go over the answers as a class, asking different students to read portions of the paragraph orally. Ask them if the natural pauses in the oral reading correspond to the correct punctuation.

Exercise 3, page 415

Before dealing with the exercise, you may want to have the students practice punctuation of dependent clauses that establish a contrast. Prepare a few compound sentences containing *but* and write them on the board. Have the students rewrite them, changing one of the sentences to a dependent clause. For example:

I love my dog, <u>but</u> he's a lot of trouble. =
I love my dog, <u>although</u> he's a lot of trouble. OR *<u>Although</u> my dog is a lot of trouble, I love him.*

Point out that the contrastive dependent clause can come first or second, but there is a comma in both cases.

Have the students do the exercise individually. Then go over the answers as a class.

Exercise 4, page 416

Before dealing with the exercise, prepare a few compound sentences. Elicit suggestions for rewriting them as sentences with subordinating conjunctions and then with transitions. For example:

Train travel is slow, <u>but</u> it's enjoyable.
<u>Although</u> it is slow, train travel is enjoyable. (with a subordinating conjunction)
Train travel is slow; <u>however</u>, it's enjoyable. (with a transition)

Have the students work on this exercise at home and then check their work in pairs in class. Go over the answers as a class.

Exercise 5: Apply It to Your Writing, page 416

Have the students complete their paragraphs outside of class. Insist that they include at least one coordinating conjunction, one subordinating conjunction, and one transition. Take the time to have the students edit each other's work in class.

PART IX NOUN CLAUSES

NOUN CLAUSES: SUBJECTS AND OBJECTS

GRAMMAR **IN CONTEXT** (pages 420–421)

See the General Suggestions for Grammar in Context on page 2.

ESTABLISH THE CONTEXT: The theme of the unit is humor. A good way to begin the unit is to ask students to tell about something they think is funny—a joke, a funny story, or a humorous happening. Ask the class whether they agree that the examples are funny and why.

Questions to Consider, page 420: See the General Suggestions for Questions to Consider on page 2.

Reading, pages 420–421: Play the cassette/CD. Ask the students to reconstruct the joke.

Understanding Meaning from Context, page 422
You may want to point out the following vocabulary: *ladylove* (girlfriend, fiancée); *with an attitude* (having an impatient, critical, or sarcastic attitude); *stuffy* (not well enough ventilated); *Say what?* (What was that you said?); *pilings* (cylindrical supporting structures); *pontoons* (floating structures that support a bridge); *environmental impact statement* (a detailed description of how a proposed project will affect the environment, often required by law).

Comprehension, page 422: Follow the General Suggestions for Group and Pair Discussions on page 5.

GRAMMAR **PRESENTATION:** Noun Clauses: Subjects and Objects, page 423

See the General Suggestions for Grammar Presentation on page 3.

NOTE 1: To give your students practice using noun clauses conversationally, you might construct conversations of this type:

A: *What do you think of the joke about the genie?*
B: *I think (that) it's funny.*
A: *OK. Tell me what's funny about it.*
B: *What I like about it is . . .*

Similar conversations can be constructed with prompts such as:

What I don't understand is . . .

NOTE 2: Make sure that your students understand the difference between the two meanings of *however*.

NOTE 3: Since many native speakers don't observe the distinction (at least in conversation) between *who / whom*, *whoever / whomever*, they are likely to be forgiving of language learners who don't use them correctly. Nonetheless, it is worthwhile teaching your students the distinction so that they are prepared to use it in writing.

NOTE 4: Read the note in the Student Book with your class. Answer any questions.

NOTE 5: Probably the most difficult type of noun clause to master is the embedded question—specifically, the change from question word order to statement word order. Remind your students that embedded questions are not direct questions. Spend time having your students ask and answer questions like these:

A: *What time is it?*   B: *I'm not sure what time it is.*
A: *What's my sister's name?*   B: *I have no idea what your sister's name is.*
A: *What does* kosher *mean?*   B: *I don't know what* kosher *means.*

NOTE 6: Read the note in the Student Book with your class. Answer any questions.

Note 7: You may want to spend some time reviewing direct and indirect speech, using questions like these:

A: *Alicia, how long have you been studying English?*
B: *I have been studying English for five years.*
C: *Toshiro asked Alicia how long she had been studying English. Alicia said she had been studying English for five years.*

Note 8: Read the note in the Student Book with your class. Answer any questions.

FOCUSED PRACTICE (pages 426–430)

See the General Suggestions for Focused Practice on page 3.

1. Discover the Grammar, page 426
After your students have identified and classified the noun clauses in the opener, you may wish to ask them to indicate the subject, verb, and object within each clause.

2. Parts of Noun Clauses, page 426
You may want to have your students do this exercise in pairs.

3. A Thumbnail Sketch of Humor, pages 427–428
The principal goal of this exercise is to practice embedded questions. Have the students go through Part A before they read the article. Then ask them to answer the questions by searching the reading. You may want to point out the following vocabulary: *thumbnail sketch* (a very brief summary, brief enough to "fit on a thumbnail"); *bare* (without socks; naked); *incongruous* (lacking harmony; not fitting together).

Discussion: Ask the students to give original examples of each of the types of humor given in the reading.

4. Bumper Stickers, page 429
For additional bumper sticker humor, visit the website www.rider.edu/users/grushow/humor/bumper.html.

Other examples from this website that you may wish to use in class are:

*I came, I saw, I did a little shopping. (*This recalls Julius Caesar's "I came, I saw, I conquered.")
My karma ran over your dogma.
Save California; when you leave take someone with you.
This is not an abandoned vehicle.
It's been lovely, but I have to scream now. (This pokes fun at the often empty saying "It's been lovely.")
If you're happy and you know it, see a shrink. (*shrink* = psychiatrist)
The worst day fishing is better than the best day working.

You may also want to ask your students for examples of bumper stickers they themselves have seen.

5. Editing, page 430
See the General Suggestions for Editing on page 4.

You may want to point out the following vocabulary: *vulgar* (indecent; lacking taste or refinement); *punch line* (the humorous, "clinching" statement which completes a joke).

Discussion: Ask your students if they agree with the advice in this exercise. You may wish to ask selected students to tell a joke to the class or to their partners.

COMMUNICATION PRACTICE (pages 431–433)

See the General Suggestions for Communication Practice on page 4.

6. Listening, page 431
When students have completed the Listening task, have them discuss whether they agree with Greg's reservations about jokes. Have they had similar experiences?

7. Group Discussion: What's Funny About That?, pages 431–432
This is an authentic reading. You may want to point out the following vocabulary: *dour* (stern, harsh, appearing gloomy or humorless); *demeanor* (behavior, appearance); *culled* (selected);

quips (clever, witty remarks); *faux paws* (a takeoff on the expression *faux pas*, meaning "false step," and referring to the paws of animals); *bereaved* (feeling great sorrow at the loss of a loved one); *dog pound* (a place where stray animals, including dogs, are taken by city officials and kept); *live bugs* (Point out that the adjective *live* rhymes with "dive," meaning *living*, the opposite of *dead*.).

DISCUSSION: Ask the students to share any humorous airline experiences they have had.

8. Essay, page 433
Encourage your students to write about something they found really funny. They should have an enjoyable time writing their essays.

9. Picture Discussion, page 433
This cartoon is typical of Gary Larson's *Far Side* drawings. Encourage your students to first describe what is happening literally. Then encourage them to explain what the artist had in mind. On which of the principles discussed in "A Thumbnail Sketch of Humor" on page 428 does the humor in the cartoon seem to depend? Is the cartoon satirical? Do the dogs represent humans in some way?

EXPANSION

What's So Funny?: Have your students find cartoons that they find funny. Have them write descriptions of the cartoons and explain the humor. Encourage them to use noun clauses correctly.

 UNIT 23 NOUN CLAUSES AND PHRASES: COMPLEMENTS

GRAMMAR **IN CONTEXT** (pages 434–436)

See the General Suggestions for Grammar in Context on page 2.

ESTABLISH THE CONTEXT: The theme of the unit is happiness. You might begin by simply asking students what they understand by happiness. How many people do they know who could be termed happy? Is happiness really an important goal?

Questions to Consider, page 434: Discuss the questions. What do your students think happiness really is? Is it different from joy?

Reading, pages 434–436: See the General Suggestions for Reading on page 2.

Understanding Meaning from Context, page 436
See the General Suggestions for Understanding Meaning from Context on page 2.

You may want to point out the following vocabulary: *elusive* (hard to find or identify); *fade* (go away, become less strong); *equilibrium* (balance); *Huntington's disease* (a rare disease of the central nervous system); *adverse* (difficult).

DISCUSSION: Ask students to summarize the main points. Do they agree with them? For example, do they agree with this statement at the end of paragraph 5:

It's not things or people or relationships in themselves that make us happy; it's the process of experiencing and adapting to them that brings us joy and satisfaction.

GRAMMAR **PRESENTATION**: Complements (pages 437–439)

See the General Suggestions for Grammar Presentation on page 3.

NOTE 1: On the board, write two or three sentences containing noun clauses functioning as complements. For example:

It's important <u>that children get a good education</u>.
There's a common belief <u>that it's essential for us to be happy in life</u>.

Explain that the word *it* in sentences of the first type is merely a "dummy" subject similar to *there* in *there is / there are* types of sentences. It has no lexical meaning. Then have them work in groups to complete these sentences:

It is essential (obvious, fortunate, a fact, obvious, desirable, etc.) that . . .

NOTE 2: Read the note in the Student Book with your class. Answer any questions.

NOTE 3: Probably the most difficult point to master in this unit is the use of the subjunctive (base) form after adjectives of urgency, necessity, and advice. Stress the fact that the base form is used after these adjectives. Have the students practice the structure by completing these sentences:

To be happy, it's important (essential, etc.) that a person have . . .

To practice the use of *be* after adjectives of urgency, necessity, and advice, ask students to complete these sentences:

To be a good parent (leader, etc.), it's important that a person be . . .

Also have them practice making negative sentences:

To be a good parent, it's important that a person not . . .

You may also want to practice the subjunctive structure in past tense sentences. Point out that the base form, not the past form, is used. Have students complete these sentences:

When I was younger, I felt that it was important that I . . .
When I was a child, my parents felt it was necessary that I . . .

NOTE 4: Read the note in the Student Book with your class. Answer any questions.

NOTE 5: After your students have become familiar with subjunctive forms, introduce noun phrases to them. Ask them to convert the sentences they wrote earlier to phrases with *for . . . to*. For example:

To be happy, it's essential <u>for</u> a person <u>to</u> . . .

Stress that in noun phrases, the infinitive is used.

FOCUSED PRACTICE (pages 440–442)

See the General Suggestions for Focused Practice on page 4.

1. Discover the Grammar, page 440
See the General Suggestions for Discover the Grammar on page 4.

2. A Family, pages 440–441
Perfect sentences are not expected. The goal of the exercise is to familiarize students with producing sentences containing noun clauses as complements. Advanced-level students should be able to do this.

DISCUSSION: Ask the students what they think of this family's situation. It appears from the picture that they don't have an overly-extravagant lifestyle. What role do material possessions play in happiness?

3. What Makes You Happy?, page 441
Allow the students time to do this exercise, including part C, thoroughly. The goal is to allow students to express themselves in using the noun phrase and noun clause patterns.

4. Editing, page 442
See the General Suggestions for Editing on page 4.

You may want to point out the following vocabulary: *reputed* (supposed, said); *"Mickey Mouse"* (so easy that even Mickey Mouse could do it); *breeze through* (complete easily); *pets* (favorites).

COMMUNICATION PRACTICE (pages 443–445)

See the General Suggestions for Communication Practice on page 4.

5. Listening, page 443
You may want to point out the following vocabulary: *décor* (the way in which the restaurant is furnished and decorated). After the students have completed the listening task, it might be worthwhile to discuss what they heard. Is this situation typical of the way marriages are planned in the students' culture? If not, how are things different?

6. Moods, pages 443–444

This is an authentic reading. You may want to point out the following vocabulary: *Y-chromosomed counterparts* (men, from the chromosome associated with male characteristics); *juggle* (do several things at one time, as a juggler keeps several objects in the air without dropping them); *emotional antennae* (range of emotions; compare this with insects' *antennae*); *foul* (terrible); *stressors* (things that cause stress).

7. Essay, page 445

Encourage students to provide plenty of supporting details in their essays to show why they are happy, unhappy, or somewhere in the middle.

8. Picture Discussion, page 445

Try to elicit the fact that the ad is based on emotional appeal.

EXPANSION

What Makes Us Happy?: Have your students interview five to ten people about what makes them happy and then write summaries of the results. Encourage them to use adjective and noun complements correctly.

REVIEW OR SELFTEST

See the General Suggestions for Review or SelfTest on page 6.

FROM GRAMMAR TO WRITING: WRITING DIRECT AND INDIRECT SPEECH

See the General Suggestions for From Grammar to Writing on page 6.

In this section, students learn the principles of writing direct and indirect speech and apply by writing both a conversation and a report of that conversation. They share their writing with a partner and evaluate each other's work.

Introduction, pages 451–452

Have the students read the introductory text. Answer any questions.

To teach the conventions of writing direct and indirect speech, divide the class into groups and have each group write a short conversation containing statements, questions, and exclamations. The groups then exchange papers and rewrite each other's conversations as indirect speech. Remind the students that, in indirect speech, verbs are usually shifted one tense into the past.

Exercise 1, page 452

Have the students complete the exercise in pairs. Go over the answers as a class.

Exercise 2, page 453

Have the students complete the exercise in pairs. Go over the answers as a class.

Exercise 3, page 453

Before dealing with the exercise, make sure the students understand each of the reporting verbs in the box. If you think they need extra practice, find an article in a magazine or newspaper that contains these and other reporting verbs. Have the students identify all of the reporting verbs used. Then have them complete the exercise in pairs. Go over the answers as a class.

Exercise 4, page 454

Have the students complete the exercise individually, either at home or in class. Go over the answers as a class.

Exercise 5: Apply It to Your Writing, page 454

Take the time to do this exercise thoroughly, insisting that students interview someone. They may want to tape record their interviews. If they have difficulty finding someone who speaks English, you might allow them to interview you, another teacher, or even each other (as long as the conversation is entirely in English).

Some of your students may have seen quotations within quotations. You can show them that, in American usage, a quotation inside a larger quotation is punctuated with single quotes. (However, in British usage, it is punctuated with double quotes.) The quote within a quote is normally preceded by a comma. For example:

Frank asked Mr. Quackenbush, his history teacher, "Did President Harry Truman live by his statement, 'The buck stops here'?"

PART X UNREAL CONDITIONS

 UNIT 24 UNREAL CONDITIONALS AND OTHER WAYS TO EXPRESS UNREALITY

GRAMMAR **IN CONTEXT** (pages 458–459)

See the General Suggestions for Grammar in Context on page 2.

ESTABLISH THE CONTEXT: The theme of the unit is intuition. Ask students what "intuition" means. Then ask whether women are usually considered to be more intuitive than men and whether or not they believe this is true. Is following one's intuition merely whimsical?

Questions to Consider, page 458: After discussing the questions, ask students what they would be doing if they hadn't signed up for this class, where they might be, and so on. This will prepare them to focus on the unreal conditionals in the story.

Reading, pages 458–459: See the General Suggestions for Reading on page 2.

CULTURE NOTE: The yard or garage sale, at which individuals try to sell possessions they no longer want at reduced prices, is a fixture of life in North America.

DISCUSSION: Some people have commented that this story is too far-fetched, could never happen, etc. However, it is based on a documented happening in which a mysterious benefactor left a married couple a considerable amount of money after they had shown kindness to him. Ask students what they think. Have they heard of any happenings of this type?

Understanding Meaning from Context, page 459
You may want to point out the following vocabulary: *beastly* (extremely); *serial killer* (murderer who kills a series of people); *chest of drawers* (a dresser without a mirror, a piece of furniture for storing clothes); *token* (an indication or symbol of something); *fluttered* (waved or flew slowly and erratically).

GRAMMAR **PRESENTATION:** Unreal Conditionals and Other Ways to Express Unreality (pages 460–462)

See the General Suggestions for Grammar Presentation on page 3.

Go over each sentence in the grammar charts, asking students to paraphrase the meanings. For example:

If you hadn't come along when you did and taken me to the pharmacy, I might have died. (You did help me. I didn't die.)

NOTE 1: Review real conditionals with present meaning. Show students the example from the reading:
If I don't take my medicine regularly, I go into shock.

Point out that this describes a habitual or regularly occurring action. Have your students produce similar sentences. For example:

Water freezes if the temperature drops below 32° F / 0° C.
Students tend to learn things well if they are motivated.
I'm tired all day if I don't eat a good breakfast.

Review real conditionals with future meaning, reminding students that the simple present tense is used in the *if*-clause. Show them an example from the reading and have them construct similar sentences. For example:

If I don't get my homework done, I won't be able to go to the concert.

To practice present unreal conditionals, give the students a series of prompts. Working together in groups, they make sentences like these:

If I were president of the country, I'd / I wouldn't . . .
If I had ten thousand extra dollars, I'd . . .
If I didn't have to work / go to school tomorrow, I'd . . .
If I could talk to one famous person in history, I'd choose to talk to . . .

To practice the past unreal conditional, ask students to write about a significant past event that happened to them or someone close to them. The students then read their sentences aloud. Take one or two of the examples and ask them to speculate as to what would or might have happened if events had proceeded differently. For example:

My parents met at a party. My mother's best friend invited her to go to the party. My mother didn't want to go, but her friend insisted. She met my father at the party.

(*If my mother's friend <u>hadn't insisted</u>, my mother <u>wouldn't have gone</u> to the party. She probably <u>wouldn't have met</u> my father.*)

Once your students are conversant with this structure, have them construct sentences using prompts like these:

If I had grown up in a different town . . .
If I had moved to a different city ten years ago . . .
If I hadn't (gotten married / taken piano lessons, etc.) . . .

Practice the present result of a past conditional situation, showing your students how past and present conditionals can be mixed. For example:

<u>If</u> my parents <u>hadn't moved</u> to this town, <u>I wouldn't be attending</u> this school.
<u>If</u> computers <u>hadn't been invented</u>, the world <u>would be</u> very different today.

Remind your students that conditional sentences beginning with an *if*-clause must have a comma after the *if*-clause.

NOTE 2: The structure that your students may struggle with the most in this unit is the use of *wish*, particularly present and future wishes. Remind them that the central meaning of *wish* is a desire that a situation be different from what it is. That is, a wish involves a contrary-to-fact situation. Ask your students to write down three general situations (not actions) that they want to be different. Then have them make a wish-statement about each. For example:

My husband / wife works about 60 hours a week, and I don't get to see him / her very much. I wish he / she had a different job.
I don't earn enough money. I wish I earned / could earn more money.

Next, ask them to write a sentence with *wish* + *would* + base form expressing a single action that would change each situation wished about. For example:

I <u>wish</u> my husband / wife <u>would look for</u> a better job with fewer hours.

For more practice with this use of *wish*, ask the class to write a list of things they would like to happen. These can be both single actions and habitual actions. For example:

I <u>wish</u> my children <u>would visit</u> me more often.

For more practice with this, bring in newspaper or magazine pictures in which someone in the picture is experiencing some kind of discomfort or distress. For example, a picture of a homeless person on the street might elicit the sentence:

He probably wishes someone would give him some money.

NOTE 3: *If only* is similar to *wish*. You can use the same or similar procedures as in Note 2. Ask students to write sentences about things they wish had gone differently in the past.

NOTE 4: To practice unreal conditionals after *as if* and *as though*, you can select a series of pictures showing strange situations. Have students work in pairs or groups to create sentences. For example: *She looked as if she'd seen a ghost.*

FOCUSED PRACTICE (pages 463–468)

See the General Suggestions for Focused Practice on page 3.

1. Discover the Grammar, pages 463–464

Have your students discuss their endings for Part B. Some people feel that, regardless of Quentin Wilkerson's motivation in giving them $50,000, it would be unethical for Thain and Aurora to cash the check because it would suggest that they were accepting payment for kindness. What do your students think? What would they do in a similar situation?

2. Hopes and Wishes, pages 464–465

Ask students to write as many variations of the basic sentence for each picture as they can.

3. Tragedy, pages 465–466

Most readers understand Frost's poem quite well with a little guidance. Ask your students to look for examples of personification (assigning human qualities to something inanimate) in the poem. They may mention the saw and the fact that the saw "snarled," "leaped out at the boy's hand," etc. You may want to point out the following vocabulary: *snarled* (made a noise like an angry predatory animal); *drew across* (touched); *rueful* (regretful); *keep the life from spilling* (to stop the blood from flowing); *ether* (an anesthetic used to induce unconsciousness).

This poem will be relatively easy for your students to understand if they hear it aloud. Read it to your class as dramatically as possible, or have certain students read it.

DISCUSSION: Ask the class to summarize what happened. Then discuss the poem. Note that the title is an allusion to a speech from Shakespeare's *Macbeth*, in which King Macbeth is mourning the death of his wife. Ask students what they think of the meaning of the last two lines. Did the ones not dead immediately forget about the boy? Or is this more of a "life goes on" type of statement?

4. What Would Have Happened If . . . ?, page 467

You may want to point out the following vocabulary: *might as well* (should take advantage of the situation); *twisted his arm* (persuaded him); *scanned* (briefly looked at); *inkling* (an intuitive feeling); *grumbled* (complained).

Students should be able to construct at least six past conditional sentences from the story.

5. Editing, page 468

See the General Suggestions for Editing on page 4.

You may want to point out the following vocabulary: *acts as if the world owes her a living* (acts as if the world is responsible for giving her the things she feels she deserves); *inner voice* (conscience).

COMMUNICATION PRACTICE (pages 469–471)

See the General Suggestions for Communication Practice on page 4.

6. Listening, page 469

You may want to point out the following vocabulary: *for good* (permanently); *to put yourself down* (to criticize yourself).

CULTURE NOTE: Explain that matchmaking services, which attempt to find romantic or friendship partners for clients, are common in North America. Have any of your students ever participated in this sort of thing? Is it likely to work?

7. The Conditional Game, pages 469–470

Give students time to play this game. Insist on correct usage of conditional sentences for points to be scored.

8. Essay, page 470

Explain that "gut" feelings are intuitive feelings. Most students will have past experiences they can use as the basis for this essay. If students don't want to write about intuition, an alternative topic is how their life might have proceeded differently if a certain event had or had not happened in the past.

9. Picture Discussion, page 471

Have students write the conversation the family might be having. Encourage them to compare the picture situation with similar events that have happened in their lives, when things went wrong.

EXPANSION

Thank You Letters: Have your students review the story on pages 458–459. Ask them to imagine that they are Thain or Aurora, and have just received the letter and check for fifty thousand dollars from Quentin Wilkinson. Have them write thank you letters to Mr. Wilkinson. Encourage them to use unreal conditionals correctly.

 UNIT 25 THE SUBJUNCTIVE; INVERTED AND IMPLIED CONDITIONALS

GRAMMAR **IN CONTEXT** (pages 472–473)

See the General Suggestions for Grammar in Context on page 2.

ESTABLISH THE CONTEXT: The theme of the unit is assertiveness vs. aggressiveness. You might begin the unit by asking students to recall the advice column on page 27 in Unit 2. Do they think that people can be helped by advice columnists? Ask the students what they think assertiveness and aggressiveness are. Is one better than the other? Why or why not?

CULTURE NOTE: In the last twenty to thirty years in North America, there has been considerable interest in self-help programs, books, and groups, especially in relation to assertiveness. There is an abundance of services and books designed to help individuals become more assertive.

Questions to Consider, page 472: See the General Suggestions for Questions to Consider on page 2.

Reading, pages 472–473: See the General Suggestions for Reading on page 2.

DISCUSSION: Ask your class whether they agree or disagree with the columnist's advice. What advice would they have given? Have they been in similar situations, or do they know someone who has? How was the situation handled?

Understanding Meaning From Context, page 473
See the General Suggestions for Understanding Meaning from Context on page 2.

You may want to point out the following vocabulary: *defaulted* (was unable to make necessary payments on a loan); *self-esteem* (self-concept; opinion of oneself); *notarized* (legally signed and witnessed); *small claims court* (a court in which people bring legal action against other people in order to recover small amounts of money).

GRAMMAR **PRESENTATION:** The Subjunctive; Inverted and Implied Conditionals (pages 474–475)

See the General Suggestions for Grammar Presentation on page 3.

Go carefully through each sentence in the grammar charts. Have students paraphrase each sentence. For example:

I'd say it's time you got some assertiveness training. (You need to get some assertiveness training.)
In fact, had I known what was going to happen, I never would have said yes. (If I had known this was going to happen, I never would have said yes.)

NOTE 1: The subjunctive has been partly lost in English, but it is still very much alive in verb phrases containing verbs or adjectives of urgency, necessity, or advice. The key point here is that these verbs requiring the subjunctive are followed by the base form, both in present and past. Remind students that they studied adjectives of urgency, necessity, and advice in Unit 23. Ask them to make subjunctive sentences with phrases like *it is important (essential) that . . . .* Then have them work in pairs or groups to make subjunctive sentences with the four principal verbs taking the subjunctive: *demand, suggest, insist,* and *recommend.* For example:

My teachers always <u>demanded</u> we be quiet in class.
A friend of mine <u>suggested</u> I take this class.
My parents always <u>insisted</u> that I eat everything on my plate.
My teacher <u>recommended</u> I read this book.

For more practice, have the students practice making subjunctive sentences with other verbs from Appendix 21 on page A-10 that can take either pattern. For example:

He <u>asked that I lend</u> him some money. / He <u>asked me to lend</u> him some money.

NOTE 2: To teach inverted conditionals, have students work in groups to create their own *if*-clauses with *If I had . . . , If she should come . . . , If I were, . . . ,* etc. Each group presents their sentences to the other groups, who practice inverting them (*Should she come . . . ,* etc.).

NOTE 3: To teach implied conditionals (*if so, if not, otherwise, with, without, what if*), create a series of prompts and have students work in pairs or groups to complete them. For example:

I'd better balance my checkbook. Otherwise, <u>I'm likely to bounce several checks</u>.

When students have completed the sentences with implied conditionals, have them practice "filling out" the conditionals with clauses. For example:

If I don't balance my checkbook, <u>I'm likely to bounce several checks</u>.

NOTE 4: Explain that the expressions *it's time* and *would rather* are followed by subjunctive forms, usually the simple past but occasionally the simple present. Sentences like *It's time we left* are quite common.

Ask students to make recommendations, using *it's time* and *would rather*. For example:

<u>*It's time*</u> *I decided what my career is going to be.*
<u>*I'd rather*</u> *we didn't have any homework tonight.*

FOCUSED PRACTICE (pages 476–480)

See the General Suggestions for Focused Practice on page 3.

1. Discover the Grammar, page 476
See the General Suggestions for Discover the Grammar on page 4.

2. Growing Up, page 477
You may want to point out that *dropped off* means "taken to a certain destination and left."

DISCUSSION: Is this a typical parent-child conversation? At what point should parents allow their children to "fly with their own wings"?

3. Job Hunting, page 477
You may want to point out that *fallen into a rut* means "become trapped in a situation that is repetitive."

DISCUSSION: Have your students had similar experiences in which they acted without worrying much and succeeded in their goals?

4. Aggressive or Assertive? page 478
Allow for a variety of responses here. The goal is not for everyone to create the same sentence but rather for everyone to be able to use subjunctive verb forms.

5. Editing, page 480
See the General Suggestions for Editing on page 4.

You may want to point out the following vocabulary: *tide me over* (last until a certain time); *where I stand* (what I think).

COMMUNICATION PRACTICE (pages 481–483)

See the General Suggestions for Communication Practice on page 4.

6. Listening 1, page 481
You may want to point out the following vocabulary: *look into* (research, find out about); *swore* (promised); *manipulated* (have your behavior controlled by someone else); *boiling* (extremely angry).

7. Listening 2, pages 481–482
You may want to point out the following vocabulary: *set foot in* (enter); *big time* (in a major way); *mad* (angry).

DISCUSSION: What do your students think of the radio show host's advice? Do they agree or disagree? How can one deal with manipulative parents?

8. Discussion, page 482
Allow the students plenty of time to carefully consider the quiz questions and discuss them with each other.

9. Essay, page 483
The students should be well-prepared to write the essay after having dealt with the quiz in Exercise 8.

10. Picture Discussion, page 483
Ask your students what they think a classroom should be like. How should teachers treat their students?

EXPANSION

Dear April: Have your students take on the role of Helen and respond to April's letter on page 480. Encourage them to use the subjunctive and inverted and implied conditionals correctly.

REVIEW OR SELFTEST

See the General Suggestions for Review or SelfTest on page 6.

FROM GRAMMAR TO WRITING: AVOIDING RUN-ON SENTENCES AND COMMA SPLICES

See the General Suggestions for From Grammar to Writing on page 6.

In this section, students review and expand the sentence-recognition skills they studied earlier by learning to recognize and avoid comma splices and run-on sentences. They share their writing with a partner and evaluate each other's work.

Introduction, page 489
The following analogy helps illustrate the difference between the run-on sentence and the comma splice. The run-on sentence is like a situation in which a driver approaches a stop sign or red light and doesn't even slow down before speeding through the intersection. A comma splice is like a situation in which a driver approaches a stop sign or red light, slows and perhaps shifts into second or third gear, and goes through the intersection without stopping but with some caution. From the viewpoint of a nearby police officer, both are illegal actions, though the "run-on sentence" is more serious.

Have the students read the introductory text. Answer any questions.

Exercise 1, pages 490–491

To prepare students for the exercise, find a paragraph and delete all the punctuation. Write the paragraph on the board and ask the students to read it to themselves. Ask them to identify each place where one sentence ends and the next begins. Then have them complete the exercise in pairs. Go over the answers as a class.

Exercise 2, pages 491–492

Find a paragraph and delete some of the periods, replacing them with commas. Have the students read the information about comma splices on page 490. Then write the paragraph on the board, asking the students to point out each comma splice. Have them complete the exercise in pairs and then go over the answers as a class.

Exercise 3, page 492

Have the students complete the exercise in pairs. Then go over the answers as a class.

Exercise 4, page 493

Have the students complete the exercise individually, either at home or in class. Then go over the answers as a class. Point out alternate ways of correctly punctuating the paragraph (i.e., by using a period or a semicolon).

Exercise 5: Apply It to Your Writing, page 493

Make sure that the students do not include any punctuation in the first draft of the paragraph. After they exchange papers, have them make punctuation suggestions in pencil so that they can make changes when discussing their papers.

A FINAL NOTE

Be sure to make it clear that the word *then* is not a coordinating conjunction. It behaves like the transitions *however* and *therefore* and must be preceded by a semicolon or period.

TAPESCRIPT

UNIT 1 EXERCISE 9, PAGE 14. LISTENING.

MOM: Tim? Come on! We're going to be late if you don't get up right now.

TIM: Why? Where are we going?

MOM: To the historical museum. Remember?

TIM: Do we have to? Amy and I want to go to the West Edmonton Mall.

AMY: That's right, Mom. Museums are boring.

DAD: But this is a really interesting museum. There'll be all kinds of things to learn.

TIM: Why do we have to learn things when we're on vacation?

AMY: Dad, can't you and Mom drop us off at the mall? Then you can go to the museum.

MOM: It's all arranged, kids. We're meeting the tour bus at 9:30. In fact, if we don't get down to the lobby, we're going to miss it.

TIM: Oh, no! Not a tour.

DAD: Yes. Sometimes a tour is the best way to see things.

AMY: I hate tours. If we have to go to the historical museum, can't we at least go by ourselves?

MOM: Come on, kids. We're going to be late.

AMY: Can we go to the mall later?

DAD: Sure. Tell you what. As soon as we get back from the tour, we'll go to the mall.

TIM: Sure, Dad.

UNIT 2 EXERCISE 8, PAGE 29. LISTENING.

In other news, the first-ever wedding of a couple jumping from a plane in parachutes took place yesterday in the skies over Saskatoon, Saskatchewan, Canada. Samantha Yang and Darrell Hammer hired Minister Robert Martinez to jump with them out of a twin-engine Cessna and marry them in the air before they landed. Yang and Hammer met four years ago at a meeting of the Saskatoon Sky-Divers, of which they have been members for many years. To date, each of them has made over thirty jumps. Interviewed as to why they wanted to get married in such an unusual way, Yang said, "We're just adventurous souls, I guess. We like new and different things. We didn't want a conventional wedding." Hammer agreed, adding, "We were going to get married on a bungee jump, but when we got to thinking about it, we decided that might be just a little too dangerous. Plus, we couldn't find a minister who would bungee-jump with us."

Reverend Martinez had never made a parachute jump before yesterday. Asked if he had ever performed such an unusual wedding ceremony before, Martinez responded, "No, I think this one takes the cake. I used to be a pastor in Arizona. I would get some fairly unusual requests. I mean, for example, once I married two people on horseback. But nothing quite like this."

Would he do another parachute-jump wedding—or even another parachute jump? "I don't think so," Martinez said. "No, I think this is one for the scrapbook. At this point, I can just say, 'Been there, done that.'"

That's the news on the half hour. Stay tuned for our next broadcast at the top of the hour.

EXERCISE 5, PAGE 44. LISTENING.

Good afternoon. This is science and technology news from WQQR.

Our subject today is robots. Have you ever considered buying one of the new personal robots for your household? Personal robots have been available for several years but have been very expensive until now. The firm Ready Robotics has announced that its new affordable personal robot, nicknamed Robert, will go into mass production this month. Researchers have been developing Robert the Robot for the past five years. The company predicts that they will have sold a million units by the end of this year. Robert will be able to speak twelve languages and to perform virtually all household tasks. Its batteries will need recharging once every three months.

And speaking of robots, Frances Parker of Winnipeg, Manitoba, was awakened at 3 A.M. last night by a strange noise in the kitchen. When she investigated, she discovered that the intruder was a robot that had gotten away from its owner because of a programming malfunction. Parker said that the robot was friendly and was simply trying to locate its owner. It had apparently decided that it lived in Parker's house and that its immediate responsibility was to clean up Parker's kitchen. When Parker found the robot in the kitchen, it was washing the dishes that Parker had left in her sink. The robot had already cleaned the refrigerator and mopped the floor.

And that's science and technology news for today. Tune in tomorrow at this time for another edition.

EXERCISE 6, PAGE 71. LISTENING.

EMILY: Hello?

JASON: Hi, Em. It's your big brother.

EMILY: Jason! Hey, I just got your letter yesterday. Thanks. But you know, you should have at least sent Mom and Dad a postcard.

JASON: I know. I'll write them next time. But, anyway, here's the reason I called.

EMILY: You mean you didn't call just to talk to me?

JASON: Well, sure I did. But I've got a problem, too. I lost my passport.

EMILY: Oh, no! Well, why don't you just go to the embassy, or something. Where are you, anyway?

JASON: We're still in Nairobi.

EMILY: Nairobi? I thought you were going to Cairo.

JASON: We were supposed to, but our flight was canceled and then we couldn't get another one for several days. There are a lot of people traveling right now. We finally managed to get a ticket to Cairo for seven o'clock this morning. Well, we had to leave really early to get to the airport. All my identification was in my small backpack, and . . . I guess I left it at the hotel. Anyway, I don't have it. I called the hotel, but no one knows anything about it.

EMILY: You ought to go to the embassy and apply for a new one.

JASON: I did. I'm at the embassy now. But I don't have any of my IDs, and I can't even remember my passport number. I know I should have written it down and kept it in a special place, but I forgot. But you have to have some form of identification to get a new passport.

EMILY: Doesn't the embassy have ways to find your records? I mean, they have computers, don't they?

JASON: Well, sure, but so far they can't find any proof that I even exist.

EMILY: Wow! Well, what should *I* do?

JASON: Go over to my apartment and look in my desk. There's a folder with a copy of my passport application form and other IDs. Then just fax it to the embassy.

EMILY: OK. What's the fax number?

JASON: It's 1-5-5-5-1-7 . . .

PROFESSOR: OK, folks. Today we're going to talk about a question related to hearing. I want to begin by telling you about an experience I had the first time I heard my voice on tape. It was in a speech class when I was in college. The professor recorded our voices and then played them back. When I heard mine, I said, "That couldn't have been me. I don't sound like that. There's got to be some mistake." Now, I'd venture to say that all of you must have had this experience at one time or another. Am I right? Let me see a show of hands. . . . Uh-huh, just as I thought. Now, the question is why. Why do we hear our voices differently than others do? Based on what we've been studying, you should be able to figure this out. Allison, what do you think?

ALLISON: I think it must be because we're hearing the sound in a different way.

PROFESSOR: Very good! You've got the right idea. Now, anybody want to expand on that? Bart?

BART: It could be because the sound is traveling through different substances.

PROFESSOR: Right. Go on. Can you explain?

BART: Well, let's see. When somebody speaks, the sound of that person's voice comes to us through the air. We hear our own voice through our own heads.

PROFESSOR: Good, good. Uh, Kathy, can you add something?

KATHY: I agree with Bart when he says we hear our own voice through our own head. But don't we also hear it through the air? It might be a combination of the two things.

PROFESSOR: Yes. You're both right. You see, when we hear our own voice, we hear partly through our ears—externally. But we also hear through the bone in our head and through the fluid in our inner ear—internally. Most of the sound that we hear internally comes through liquid. . . . Now, here's one more question. Which sound is the "real" sound? The way other people hear our voices, or the way we hear them? Uh, Darren?

DARREN: I think the sound others hear has to be the real sound.

PROFESSOR: Anybody else?

KATHY: I'd say the opposite. The sound we hear must be the real sound.

PROFESSOR: Actually, Kathy is right. Internal hearing is of higher fidelity than external hearing.

SENTENCES

1. That couldn't have been me.
2. There's got to be some mistake.
3. Now, I'd venture to say that all of you must have had this experience at one time or another.
4. Based on what we've been studying, you should be able to figure this out.
5. I think it must be because we're hearing the sound in a different way.
6. It could be because the sound is traveling through different substances.
7. It might be a combination of the two things.
8. I think the sound others hear has to be the real sound.
9. The sound we hear must be the real sound.
10. Internal hearing is of higher fidelity than external hearing.

Hello, everyone, and welcome to Global Gourmet. I'm Flo Nyberg, and today we're going to be making a wonderful dish called "pelmeni." Pelmeni is a traditional Russian food that requires some time and work to prepare, but it is well worth the effort.

Pelmeni are little balls of a delicious meat mixture in dough. Here are the ingredients you'll need: 1½ pounds of hamburger (or other ground meat such as chicken or pork), 1½ chopped onions, 2 egg yolks, 3 tablespoons of water, 1 teaspoon of salt, and ½ teaspoon of pepper. To make the dough, you'll need 2 cups of flour, 1 teaspoon of salt, 3 egg yolks, and ½ cup of water.

All right. Got your ingredients? Do you have them all assembled and ready? I hope so. Here we go, then. First you need to make the dough. Sift the flour and salt together. Then mix it with the egg yolks and some of the water. Stir this mixture with a fork. Add the rest of the water. Knead the mixture until it's smooth and not lumpy. Let the dough stand for one hour. Then roll it out with a rolling pin as thinly as possible.

The next step is to prepare the meat mixture. Simply mix the hamburger (or other meat), the chopped onions, the egg yolks, the salt, the pepper, and the water together.

The next step: Use a round cookie cutter to make circles from the dough. Each circle should be approximately two inches in diameter. Place a small amount of the meat mixture in the middle of each circle. Fold the edges of the circle over and pinch the edges together. Voila! You've got lots and lots of little pelmeni balls. Drop a large number of these into boiling water and let them cook. They'll be finished cooking when they rise to the surface. Spoon them out and serve them with sour cream and yellow mustard.

In Russia, hundreds of pelmeni balls are often made at one time—perhaps for banquets or perhaps to be frozen until needed. One person can easily eat 15 or 20 of them. Good luck and bon appetit.

I'm Flo Nyberg. I'll be back tomorrow with another recipe on Global Gourmet.

UNIT 6 EXERCISE 7, PAGE 115. LISTENING.

1. An individual particle of a cereal grown in warm and wet areas is called a grain of rice.
2. A collection of bovine mammals is called a herd of cattle.
3. A continuing flow of electrons is termed a current of electricity.
4. A small piece of a very fine, sometimes powdery material is termed a speck of dust.
5. A particular staging of an athletic competition played on an outdoor field and using a round ball is called a game of soccer.
6. A subcategory of that science which deals with the study of planets, stars, and galaxies is called a branch of astronomy.
7. A statement of recommended behavior is a piece of advice.
8. An individual particle of a material produced by the disintegration of stone and rocks is called a grain of sand.
9. A single discharge of electrical current between clouds or between clouds and the earth is a bolt of lightning.
10. A single movable structure on which one sits or sleeps is called a piece of furniture.
11. An item worn to cover the body is called an article of clothing.
12. An instance of loud sound usually accompanying lightning is a clap of thunder.

UNIT 7 EXERCISE 5, PAGE 130. LISTENING.

WIFE: Anything interesting in the paper?

HUSBAND: Not much. There's a story about the standoff between the environmentalists and that Indian tribe that wants to kill whales.

WIFE: Oh, yeah. What does it say?

HUSBAND: Oh, the usual nonsense. It's on the side of the environmentalists.

WIFE: Why do you think it's nonsense?

HUSBAND: Because it's too pro-environmentalist. It doesn't look at the Indians' point of view.

WIFE:	You mean you support the Indians?
HUSBAND:	Well, yes, basically.
WIFE:	Why? Do you think they should be allowed to kill whales?
HUSBAND:	Well . . . yes, I think I do. I mean, after all, whale hunting was traditionally their livelihood. They just want to get that back.
WIFE:	Well, I don't support them. I believe in saving the whales.
HUSBAND:	Why?
WIFE:	Well, once I saw a whaling ship bring in a whale and cut it up. It was a horrible experience. Whales should be left alone. Hunting them is cruel.
HUSBAND:	Hmm. But do you feel that way about all animals? What about cattle? We had roast beef for dinner last night. Isn't it cruel to slaughter cattle for meat?
WIFE:	That's different. Cattle are domestic animals. They're raised for food. Whales are different. They're intelligent creatures. And some of them are endangered. If we allow whale hunting, they could become extinct.
HUSBAND:	Yeah. You've got a point. But I still think we have to consider the Indians' point of view. They've hunted whales for centuries.

UNIT 8 — EXERCISE 5, PAGES 146–147. LISTENING.

DR. TANAKA:	OK, Josh, let's get started. Our first meeting is only going to be a thirty-minute session. We don't want to make this a brain-breaker. Now, first I want you to tell me exactly how you feel when your teacher asks you to read.
JOSHUA:	I feel like a total, complete idiot. And I feel like I have an ugly, high-pitched, squeaky voice.
DR. TANAKA:	Your voice sounds fine, Josh. You're just going through an adolescent growth spurt, so your voice is changing. It happens to a lot of twelve-year-old boys. All right. Now, the key to getting you over this fear-of-oral-reading problem is to distract you from thinking about how well you're doing. Let's think of a short, easy-to-remember phrase that you can keep in the back of your mind. When you're reading and you start to feel nervous or frustrated, you say it and distract yourself.
JOSHUA:	How about "Roses are red, violets are blue"?
DR. TANAKA:	That'll do fine. All right, let's put it to the test. I want you to read this passage. If you start feeling anxious, just start saying the phrase.
JOSHUA:	"It was an icy, dark, stormy evening. It promised to be one of those legendary three-dog nights." . . . What's a three-dog night?
DR. TANAKA:	It's a night that's so cold that you need three large, warm, furry dogs to sleep with to keep you warm. Anyway, you read that beautifully. Did you feel nervous?
JOSHUA:	Just for a second, and I started saying the line from the poem. After that it was fine. I think I'm going to like this.

UNIT 9 — EXERCISE 5, PAGES 164–165. LISTENING.

GRANT:	United Central Bank. This is Nancy Grant speaking. May I help you?
ANDREWS:	Hello, Ms. Grant? This is Jack Andrews.
GRANT:	Oh, yes, hello Mr. Andrews. What can I do for you?
ANDREWS:	I wanted to ask if I could have a little more time on this month's payment.
GRANT:	OK. Let me just look at your file. Hmm . . . well, we've received no payments for three months, and your file shows that few of your payments have been made on time since you took out the loan. I'm sorry, but I can't recommend any more extensions.

ANDREWS: I know, Ms. Grant, but I just started a new job. I'll be earning much more money than I did in my last position, but I won't be getting paid for a month.

GRANT: Well, Mr. Andrews, we try to be helpful here, but we do have certain policies that we have to uphold. There's little I can do at this point. In fact, I'm going to have to turn your account over to a collection agency if you don't pay at least a little on your outstanding balance.

ANDREWS: Could I have just a few more days to try to come up with some money? I'm sure I can arrange something if I can just have a bit more time.

GRANT: How much more time would you need?

ANDREWS: How about ten days?

GRANT: All right, Mr. Andrews. If you can make a payment within ten days, we'll reopen your account. I can't do much for you otherwise.

ANDREWS: Thank you, Ms. Grant.

UNIT 10 — EXERCISE 5, PAGE 193. LISTENING 1.

JENNIFER: Hi, Bob. How's your new job?

BOB: Well, the pay is good, which is why I took the job in the first place. Other than that, it's pretty grim.

JENNIFER: Why?

BOB: Well, my boss is a slave-driver, for one thing. He's got me doing a lot of paperwork, which really makes me angry. I didn't take this job to be a paper pusher. The other thing is that I have a co-worker who's making things difficult for me. She's one of those passive-aggressive types who can never say directly what's bothering them. They assigned me to be her partner without even consulting me, which is really irritating.

JENNIFER: Two months ago you told me you wanted this job more than anything. Now you're dissatisfied, which really surprises me. What happened?

BOB: Well, I guess I didn't investigate the company well enough, which makes me wonder whether I was too impulsive in the first place.

UNIT 10 — EXERCISE 7, PAGES 193–194. LISTENING 2.

1. The supervisor of our dorm floor, who lives right down the hall from me, is pretty lenient.
2. I really like my roommates who are from Canada. They're great to hang around with.
3. My English class, which is really tough, is going to require a lot of writing.
4. My history class that's held in the afternoon looks like it's going to be the easiest.
5. The girls who live on the second floor eat with us at the cafeteria.
6. My advisor, who is from Minneapolis, has really given me a lot of help.

UNIT 11 — EXERCISE 6, PAGE 205. LISTENING.

Good evening. I'm Penelope Truman with this week's Movie Mania. Run, don't walk, to the film festival being held this holiday weekend on the university campus. A series of all-time classics, some recent and some of which haven't been shown on the big screen in more than a decade, will be screened in the film school auditorium. For the ten-dollar admission price, you can see eight movies. Here are my special picks.

First: *Fargo*, the creation of director Joel Coen and his brother Ethan, is a black comedy, based on a true-life murder case, about a car salesman who tries to solve his debt problem by having his wife kidnapped. Frances McDormand won a best actress Oscar for her amazing performance as a police investigator.

Second: *Forrest Gump*, a heartwarming comedy-drama, is about a slow-witted young man trying to figure out how to navigate in life. The movie catapulted Tom Hanks to superstar status. This film, deserving of its Academy Award for Best Picture, still makes me cry.

Third: We don't see too many musicals anymore, which is too bad. Even if you're not a fan of musicals, though, this one deserves your attention. *Evita*, starring Madonna as Eva Peron, the famous first lady of Argentina who died so young, and Antonio Banderas as Che Guevara, will surprise you. Madonna does a good job of acting and singing, but for my money it's Banderas who steals the show. Who would have thought he could sing so well?

Fourth: *Back to the Future*, the movie responsible for launching Michael J. Fox in his screen career, is about a teenager who has to travel back in time to arrange for his own parents to meet so that he won't cease to exist! *Back to the Future* is especially fun because it gives us a semi-objective comparison of our own era and an earlier one.

Finally: For all of you old-timers out there, a kiss may be just a kiss, but *Casablanca*, showcasing the talents of Humphrey Bogart and Ingrid Bergman, is more than just a movie. This picture is a must-see for all regarding themselves as serious movie junkies. This movie, filmed in black and white, may not be a pretty picture, but it's certainly a profound one.

So, there they are. My spies tell me that tickets are likely to sell like hotcakes, in which case you'd better call right away if you want to attend. I'm Penelope Truman for Movie Mania, and I'll see you at the movies!

REVIEWER'S SENTENCES

1. Run, don't walk, to the film festival being held this holiday weekend on the university campus.
2. A series of all-time classics, some recent and some of which haven't been shown on the big screen in more than a decade, will be screened in the film school auditorium.
3. *Fargo*, the creation of director Joel Coen and his brother Ethan, is a black comedy, based on a true-life murder case, about a car salesman who tries to solve his debt problem by having his wife kidnapped.
4. *Fargo*, the creation of director Joel Coen and his brother Ethan, is a black comedy, based on a true-life murder case, about a car salesman who tries to solve his debt problem by having his wife kidnapped.
5. *Forrest Gump*, a heartwarming comedy-drama, is about a slow-witted young man trying to figure out how to navigate in life. The movie catapulted Tom Hanks to superstar status. This film, deserving of its Academy Award for Best Picture, still makes me cry.
6. This film, deserving of its Academy Award for Best Picture, still makes me cry.
7. Even if you're not a fan of musicals, though, this one deserves your attention.
8. *Evita*, starring Madonna as Eva Peron, the famous first lady of Argentina who died so young, and Antonio Banderas as Che Guevara, will surprise you.
9. *Back to the Future*, the movie responsible for launching Michael J. Fox in his screen career, is about a teenager who has to travel back in time to arrange for his own parents to meet so that he won't cease to exist!
10. This movie, filmed in black and white, may not be a pretty picture, but it's certainly a profound one.
11. *Casablanca*, showcasing the talents of Humphrey Bogart and Ingrid Bergman, is more than just a movie. This picture is a must-see for all regarding themselves as serious movie junkies.

UNIT 12 — EXERCISE 5, PAGE 230. LISTENING.

SADLER: OK, Mr. Akimura—just a few questions. The koala's keeper was found by the janitor?

AKIMURA: Yes. I had him examined by our resident physician. Apparently he'd been drugged. He's all right now.

SADLER:	He hadn't been hit?
AKIMURA:	No, there are no marks of any kind on his body.
SADLER:	Have any other animals been stolen?
AKIMURA:	Well . . . yes, as a matter of fact. Two sea turtles were taken two weeks ago.
SADLER:	Why weren't we notified immediately?
AKIMURA:	Well, you've heard that the zoo is currently being expanded, haven't you? The expansion depends on a 50% yes vote in the election. The bond issue isn't likely to get approved by the voters if they hear that animals are missing.
SADLER:	What time was the keeper found?
AKIMURA:	About 8 P.M. The laboratory and food preparation area gets cleaned every evening after the animals have been fed. The janitor was just starting his work when he noticed the keeper's body behind a table.
SADLER:	Do you have any idea why these animals were taken? And by whom?
AKIMURA:	Well, they're very valuable. They could be sold on the black market for a handsome profit. We can only imagine that some underworld group is behind this.
SADLER:	What about the janitor?
AKIMURA:	What do you mean?
SADLER:	Well, is he reliable? Has his background been checked?
AKIMURA:	Well, no, not really. He gave us good references when he was interviewed.
SADLER:	All right. I'll get his references checked out when I go back to the office. We'll be in touch, Mr. Akimura.

UNIT 13   EXERCISE 4, PAGE 243. LISTENING 1.

We interrupt our regularly scheduled program to bring you this news bulletin. A massive series of earthquakes has struck the nation, causing extreme damage to most major cities. The earthquakes are said to have registered a nine on the Richter Scale, although this information is considered preliminary. The minister of science has stated that the epicenter of the quakes was located in the Atlantic Ocean some forty miles west of the Pillars of Hercules. According to unconfirmed reports, vast sections of the coastline are reported to be underwater as a consequence of a gigantic tidal wave which hit the coastal areas in the aftermath of the earthquakes. The exact number of casualties of the tidal wave is not known, although it is estimated that more than 200,000 people have drowned. Serious flooding is believed to have occurred in cities farther inland. The president, who had been vacationing at his mountain retreat, has returned to the capital. Looting is alleged to be taking place in most major cities, and it is assumed that the president will be speaking to the nation shortly in an effort to reestablish law and order. As he was boarding a plane for the flight to the capital, the president said, "A grave tragedy has struck our nation. It is to be hoped that the citizens of Atlantis will conduct themselves in a calm, gentle, and law-abiding manner in our time of need." In the meantime, Atlanteans are advised to gather provisions and head for the highest ground that they can find. Stay tuned for further bulletins.

UNIT 13   EXERCISE 5, PAGES 243–244. LISTENING 2.

QUIZMASTER:	All right, contestants, are you ready to begin? Here we go. For $500: A revolutionary leader from Venezuela, he was called the Liberator and is considered the father of South American democracy.
CONTESTANT 1:	Simón Bolívar?
QUIZMASTER:	That's correct. Next question, for another $500: He is thought to have been the author of "The Iliad" and "The Odyssey," both from Greek literature. However, it is not known for certain whether he was one specific person or a composite of many people.

CONTESTANT 3: Aristotle?

QUIZMASTER: I'm sorry. That is incorrect.

CONTESTANT 2: Homer.

QUIZMASTER: Yes, that is correct. For $800: He was a philosopher who lived in Greece from approximately 427 B.C. to 347 B.C. His *Dialogues* are studied today all over the world. He was born in Greece in 427 B.C. Some people say that the myth of Atlantis was created by him.

CONTESTANT 2: Plato?

QUIZMASTER: Absolutely correct. For another $800: Born in India, he is known as the father of Buddhism, a religion that is practiced by many people in Asia.

CONTESTANT 1: Gandhi?

QUIZMASTER: No, I'm sorry. That is not correct.

CONTESTANT 2: Siddhartha Gautama?

QUIZMASTER: Yes, correct. Now for the last question. Contestant 2 is in the lead. For $1000: One of the daughters of the ruling royal family in Russia, she was thought to have been murdered in the 1917 revolution which brought the Bolsheviks to power. In the years since then, however, it has been persistently rumored that this one daughter somehow survived the assassination attempt and eventually made her way to America.

CONTESTANT 2: Anastasia Romanova?

QUIZMASTER: Absolutely right! Congratulations, Contestant 2. You are the winner.

UNIT 14 — EXERCISE 6, PAGE 270. LISTENING.

MARY: Good evening. I'm Mary Mobley with tonight's edition of *Do the Right Thing*. The toll-free number is 1-800-555-9999. Caller number one, Sally from Toronto, you're on the air.

SALLY: Hi, Mary. First let me tell you how much I enjoy your show. I don't care much for a lot of the stuff on radio, but I DO listen to you.

MARY: Thanks, Sally. What's on your mind tonight?

SALLY: Well, I've been dating a man named Bob for a long time. We're engaged to be married, but I just don't feel I can go through with it.

MARY: Why not? Don't you love him?

SALLY: I DID love him at first—or at least I thought I did—and I DO think a lot of him as a person. But the wedding is in three weeks. I've been thinking of just running away and never coming back.

MARY: Why haven't you done something before this?

SALLY: I DID try to tell him a couple of weeks ago, but he just dismissed it as typical pre-wedding jitters.

MARY: Well, Sally, to me you don't sound at all sure of your feelings.

SALLY: No, I AM sure. I'm just worried about hurting him.

MARY: You don't have to hurt Bob, but you DO have to level with him and tell him the truth. I wish you good luck. . . . Hello, Jerry from Tulsa.

JERRY: Evening, Mary. Thank you for taking my call. I wanted to ask you about a problem with my children.

MARY: OK, go ahead. What's the problem?

JERRY: They call me only when they want something, and all they really seem to care about is getting their inheritance. I'm not a rich man, but I AM pretty well off, and I HAVE got some money put away for them. The trouble is that they never come to see me. We DO live in different parts of the country, so I guess that part is understandable. They've both written me recently, asking if they could have their inheritance early. My son wants to buy a house. He doesn't have the cash for a down payment, but he **DOES** earn enough to make the monthly payments. And my daughter and her husband want to buy a boat.

MARY: How old are they?

JERRY: They're both in their late twenties.

MARY: OK. What's your problem, then?

JERRY: I agreed to send the money. Can I withdraw my offer? I mean, would it be ethical? Or right?

MARY: Well, your children **DO** sound a bit selfish. If you feel it'd be wrong to give them this money now, I'd suggest you just tell them that you've changed your mind. That **MAY** start them thinking a bit and might even make them a little more concerned about you in the long run. Good luck. . . . Now, caller number 3, Helen from Kingston, New York, talk to me . . .

UNIT 15 EXERCISE 5, PAGE 286. LISTENING.

BEV: Hello?

DAD: Hi, Bev. This is Dad.

BEV: Dad! Where are you? The surprise party is supposed to start in fifteen minutes! Everybody's already shown up. We're just waiting for you and Ray and Mom.

DAD: Great. You don't think your mother has figured out what's going on, do you?

BEV: No, I'm sure she hasn't. She thinks we're all going to a concert this afternoon. She says she's really looking forward to it.

DAD: Good. Anyway, here's the problem, Bev. Ray and I are at the department store trying to find a gift for your mom, and we can't come up with anything. Do you think we could get away with not giving her a present today? If we took a little more time, we could find something really nice.

BEV: Dad! Of course not! Everybody who's here has brought something. You and Ray will be the only ones.

DAD: Well, what do you suggest?

BEV: What about a camera?

DAD: She's got three cameras. In fact, she just got rid of one of her old cameras last week.

BEV: How about some article of clothing?

DAD: Great idea. A dress, maybe?

BEV: Dad! You can't just buy her a dress. She'd never buy a dress without trying on several first.

DAD: Well, Bev, we're running out of time, here. Can't you think of something?

BEV: Hmm . . . . How about a couple of nice scarves?

DAD: Good! What material? What color?

BEV: Well . . . let's see. Why don't you look for a couple of silk scarves in some subdued, conservative color?

DAD: Good idea. Will do. We'll get there as soon as we can.

BEV: OK, Dad. But hurry up.

UNIT 16 EXERCISE 6, PAGE 313. LISTENING.

JANE: Hello?

BRIAN: Hello. May I speak with Jane Travanti?

JANE: This is Jane.

BRIAN: Jane, my name is Brian Hansen. Dr. Ralph Stevens gave me your number. I understand that you belong to an orienteering group. I'm interested in joining a group like that, and . . . he suggested calling you to find out some details. Would you mind giving me some information about your club and maybe about becoming a member?

JANE: Sure, I'd be glad to. Are you new in town?

BRIAN: Yeah, I've been here about five months and haven't really met anyone. Doctor Stevens thinks I need to stop working so hard and try to enjoy myself more. He's probably right. Ever since I started working at my job here, it's been pretty much of a go-go rush-rush situation. It seems like there just isn't any time for having fun. It's . . . a rat race.

JANE: Have you ever done any orienteering before?

BRIAN: No, I haven't. Do you need to be experienced?

JANE: Not necessarily. You can learn. We've got several different levels of participants. You do need to be in good physical condition.

BRIAN: Well, I haven't been doing much exercising lately, but Dr. Stevens says I'm basically in good physical shape. . . . So can you give me some details? How often do you go orienteering, and where do you go, and stuff like that?

JANE: Sure! We try to go at least twice a month, normally on Saturdays. Usually we go to the Sherwood Forest area. Sometimes we manage to go only once a month, but most months it's at least twice. In the summer we get around by running, but right now we navigate by cross-country skiing. Do you know how to ski?

BRIAN: I tried cross-country skiing a couple of years ago, but I haven't done it since then. I did pretty well at it, though. I still have my skis.

JANE: Great. Let's see, what else? Uhmm, oh the group is pretty diverse. There are some married people and their kids, some singles, all ages. But we're an actual club. We have dues of $40 a year. That's to pay for organizing the activities.

BRIAN: Sounds great to me. When's your next activity?

JANE: We're meeting on Saturday morning, the 15th, at 6 A.M. in front of Darcy's Coffee Shop in Stapleton. We'll be carpooling. Do you know where Darcy's is?

BRIAN: I think so.

JANE: OK, good. Don't forget to bring your skis. And remember to bring along a lunch—hopefully with a lot of high-protein stuff in it.

BRIAN: Super. I'll see you Saturday morning at 6 A.M. Thanks a lot.

JANE: Sure. I'll look forward to meeting you in person. Bye.

UNIT 17 EXERCISE 6, PAGE 332. LISTENING.

KENNY: Mom, you said you'd type my term paper. I just finished writing it. It's due tomorrow. Will you be able to?

MOM: Kenny, not again! It's 5:45. Your father and I are supposed to go to a party at the Carrolls', and you expect me to type it now? I won't have time to. We have to leave in an hour.

KENNY: But Mom, it's due tomorrow. I'll get an "F" if I don't turn it in, and I won't be able to unless you do it tonight. I don't want to get kicked out of school. You have to, Mom. Please, just this once?

MOM: Kenny, you're not going to get kicked out of school. Don't be silly.

KENNY: Well, but I might fail history. And if I fail history, I might have to repeat the whole year, and . . .

MOM: Kenny, what did I tell you the last time this happened?

KENNY: You told me I had to start getting my work done at a reasonable time. You told me you weren't going to type any more last-minute assignments. But Mom, I had to take Rover for his walk. In fact, I've had to every day for the last two weeks. And he started barking at someone and ran off down the street, and it took a long time to catch him. That's why I haven't had time to finish the paper.

MOM: Kenny, that's no excuse.

KENNY: But Mom, if you'll just do it this one time, I'll get my work done in plenty of time in the future. I promise to.

MOM: Kenny, I'm sorry, but I meant what I said. I told you I wasn't going to bail you out at the last minute, and I'm not going to this time. You'll have to type it yourself.

KENNY: But Mom, I only type ten words a minute.

MOM: Well, you'd better get a snack and be ready to stay up all night. You may need to.

KENNY: Aw, Mom . . .

MOM: No, Kenny, my mind is made up.

UNIT 18 — EXERCISE 5, PAGE 360. LISTENING.

MARY: Thanks for tuning in to *Sports Talk,* all you listeners out there. I'm Mary Mobley, and today we're talking with Lillian Swanson, champion swimmer, whose Team Jamaica just won the world championship. Lillian will be participating in the upcoming Olympics as part of the Jamaican national team. Lillian, thanks so much for being here with us.

LILLIAN: Thank you for having me, Mary.

MARY: There are a million questions I could ask, Lillian, but I'll start with this one: From all appearances, you've had a charmed athletic career. Everything has gone your way. To what do you attribute your success?

LILLIAN: Well, Mary, whenever I've been asked that question—which has been a lot of times—I've always answered in the same way: It was because my parents loved and supported me.

MARY: OK. Tell us more. How did it all happen?

LILLIAN: Well, it started when I was a girl in Jamaica. I learned to swim when I was four. I swam in the Caribbean, and swimming wasn't a big deal. It's the most natural thing in the world in Jamaica. However, it's a lot more difficult to swim in the Caribbean than it is to swim in a pool. That's what made me a good swimmer, I think—the difficulty, I mean.

MARY: Who taught you to swim?

LILLIAN: My parents. My family and I spent a lot of time at the beach because we didn't have a lot of toys or video games or things like that.

MARY: What did you mean when you said that your parents supported you?

LILLIAN: Well, when I was twelve, I decided I wanted to become a champion swimmer and maybe even make it to the Olympics someday. My parents said they'd pay for lessons and training if I stuck to it and practiced daily. So I did. They helped me become a disciplined person.

MARY: Twelve is pretty young to make a decision like that. Didn't you ever get tired of practicing all the time?

LILLIAN: Sure I did, many times. I didn't have as much time to just have fun and be a kid as my school friends did.

MARY: Any regrets?

LILLIAN: None at all. Swimming is such a passion for me that I can't imagine myself doing anything else. But I owe it all to my parents. Once I started, they wouldn't let me quit.

MARY: Well, Lillian, thanks very much for talking with us. And good luck in the Olympics.

LILLIAN: My pleasure.

UNIT 19 — EXERCISE 6, PAGE 374. LISTENING.

RUSSELL: Our next caller is from Hong Kong, China. Here's Mu Han. Mu, what's your view?

MU HAN: Hello, Russell. Before I give my viewpoint, I just want to say how much I enjoy your show. I get a chance to listen only once a week or so, but I really like it.

RUSSELL: Thanks. That's nice to hear. So how do you feel about what these first two callers said? Do you agree with either of them?

MU HAN: Well, I'm sort of in between. Basically, I guess I'm closer to the lady from England. I disagree with what the man said about using technology just because it exists. But he does have one or two good ideas.

RUSSELL: OK. Give me some specifics.

MU HAN: Well, I agree with what the lady says about not cloning humans. I'm not actually in favor of cloning any animals.

RUSSELL: Not even lower animals?

MU HAN: Not even them. But I think genetic engineering has something to be said for it.

RUSSELL: Yeah? OK. Explain.

MU HAN: Take what the man said about dread diseases. AIDS, for example. It's a death sentence. What if scientists find a genetic engineering solution to the problem? If we can offer AIDS victims a chance for a normal life, I think we ought to go for it.

RUSSELL: All right. Thanks for your comments. Call me back sometime. . . . We'll be back after this commercial message.

UNIT 20 EXERCISE 2, PAGE 385. A MEMORY TEST.

_____ we focus on the aftermath of the recent California earthquake. Investigators have determined that it will cost approximately six billion dollars to rebuild damaged highways. According to the governor, two actions have to be taken: _____, the federal government will have to approve disaster funds to pay for reconstruction; _____, insurance investigators will need to determine how much their companies will have to pay in the rebuilding effort. With luck, the governor says, some key highways could be rebuilt within six months. He cautioned, _____, that the six-month figure is only an estimate. The process depends on timely allocation of funds, and certain insurance companies have in the past been slow to approve such funds. The rebuilding effort could, _____, drag on for at least a year. _____, bad weather could hamper the speedy completion of the project. _____, it is taking some people as long as four hours to commute to work, and others haven't been able to get to work at all. Interviewed by our news team, one commuter who works in an office downtown said, "This has been ridiculous. It took me six hours to drive to work last Friday. I knew I'd have to find some other way of getting there; _____, I'd never make it. Well, yesterday I took the train and got there in 50 minutes. _____ you know, the trip was really pleasant. I had the chance to read the morning paper. _____, I'm going to switch permanently to the train."

UNIT 20 EXERCISE 5, PAGES 388–389. LISTENING.

LEADER: All right, folks, we're ready to start Part 2 of the workshop. Let's just review the points we made before. First, it's important to instill people's names in your short-term memory. When you're meeting clients, it's crucial to be able to remember and use their names. Clients respond well to that, and it's good for business. Therefore, it's absolutely essential that you say the people's names when you meet them. Second, you need to notice one particular thing about each person and link that thing with the person's name. For example, suppose that person has strong, prominent eyebrows. And suppose the person's name is Ed. You can link the "e" in eyebrows with the "e" in Ed, and then you have an easier . . .

LEADER: Yes, may I help you?

VISITOR: Yes. My name is Cameron Kendall.

LEADER: Excuse me, Ms. Kendall, but we're in the middle of a workshop here. I'd . . .

VISITOR: I will not keep you long. I want everyone to put your hands up. Hands up!

SARAH: She's got a gun.

VISITOR: Hands up! Quick! Everyone! . . . Thank you. You have all been most cooperative. You may put your hands down now. Thank you. Aloha.

BOB: What in the world was that all about?

MICHELLE: Come on, you guys. She wasn't for real.

SARAH: What? Are you kidding?

MICHELLE: Didn't you notice? That was a toy gun she had. Besides that, Marsha, you didn't really act like it was an interruption. So this must have all been staged.

LEADER: Yes, Michelle. You're right. It was all staged. But I'll bet she had you going for a minute. Right, Bob?

BOB: I'll have to admit it.

LEADER: All right. The question is what you got out of the experience. Let's see what you remember. How was she dressed?

LINDA: She had on a long dress, something like a gown, that went all the way down to her feet?

LEADER: OK. What color was the dress? . . . No one remembers? All right. What about her shoes? What color were they?

MIKE: Brown?

LEADER: Sorry. As a matter of fact, they were black. What was her name?

SARAH: Uh . . . I think her first name was . . . uh . . . Cameron?

LEADER: That's right. Good. Now why do you think you were able to remember that name?

SARAH: Well, it's an unusual name for a woman—or for anyone as a first name.

LEADER: What was her last name?

MIKE: I think it was Kendall. I don't think I would have remembered it, except for the fact that you repeated it when you said, "Excuse me, Ms. Kendall."

LEADER: Right. Very good. Now what was the last word she said?

BOB: Aloha.

LEADER: Excellent. Why were you able to remember it?

BOB: Well, it's not the usual way we say good-bye. Everyone knows the word, of course. But people don't say it much.

LEADER: Right. OK. Now let's just sum up the point here. You were able to remember some of the particulars about our visitor but not all of them. It's true that you were distracted. That was deliberate. But . . . most importantly, if you're going to improve your memory and use your memory well, you're going to have to learn to focus your attention consistently. You were able to remember the flashy things, and that's a good start. But it's the ordinary things you have to work on. You have to pay attention to those things, too.

UNIT 21 EXERCISE 5, PAGE 402. LISTENING.

Good afternoon. This is the news from the World Broadcasting Network. The cease fire has been broken in Franconia. When asked whether he would attend the upcoming peace conference in Geneva, dissident leader Amalde declined to commit himself, saying that the success of the conference depends on the good-faith actions of Mr. Tintor, the country's president. Mr. Amalde went on to say that Mr. Tintor could demonstrate good faith by agreeing to free and unconditional talks. Interviewed about Mr. Amalde's comments, an aide to President Tintor, speaking on the condition of anonymity, said that he did not expect the peace conference to take place as planned. One of the key issues to be discussed is the return of the 40,000 refugees displaced by the war.

Meanwhile, researchers from the Global Health Foundation announced plans to test a new vaccine for AIDS. Acknowledging that the current vaccine is ineffective, the researchers claim that their new vaccine is a marked improvement over the old one and believe that it holds great promise.

Scientists at WASA, the World Aeronautics and Space Association, announced plans to launch a new space telescope with four times the magnification power of the existing space instrument. Having conducted successful repairs and identified flaws on Magna Maria, WASA's existing instrument, the agency is confident that the new telescope will be well worth its billion-dollar price tag.

Finally, a new nation comes into existence at midnight tonight. To be known as Illyria, the new nation has been carved out of the eastern portion of Spartania. According to its new president, Illyria will need massive infusions of foreign aid in order to be a viable state. That's the news from the World Broadcasting Network. Stay tuned for further developments.

UNIT 22 EXERCISE 6, PAGE 431. LISTENING.

JEAN: Hi, Greg.

GREG: Hi, yourself. How's it going?

JEAN: Great. Hey, want to hear a joke?

GREG: A joke? Why do you think I'd want to hear a joke?

JEAN: Don't you like jokes?

GREG: Not usually.

JEAN: Why not?

GREG: Well . . . what bothers me about jokes is that they're too . . . stimulus-response.

JEAN: I don't know what you mean.

GREG: Somebody tells a joke, and you're expected to laugh, whether you think it's funny or not.

JEAN: You're too sensitive. Don't laugh if you don't think it's funny.

GREG: But everybody thinks you're no fun if you don't laugh. And then you feel stupid.

JEAN: What?

GREG: Well, a lot of times I don't get what the point of the joke is. I feel stupid when that happens.

JEAN: I know what: I'll tell you a funny story—not exactly a joke—and let's see if you understand.

GREG: Oh, all right. Go ahead.

JEAN: OK, here we go. According to a report on the radio, there was a middle school in Oregon that was faced with a unique problem. A lot of girls were beginning to use lipstick, and they would put it on in the girls' bathroom. There was nothing wrong with that, but after they'd put it on, they'd press their lips against the mirror just to make sure the lipstick was on right, and that would leave dozens of little lip prints all over the mirror. So finally the principal of the school decided something had to be done about the problem.

GREG: So what did he do?

JEAN: It wasn't a he; it was a she. Anyway, here's what she did: She told all the girls to report to the bathroom, and she met them there with the school custodian. She explained to the girls that all the lip prints were causing a major problem for the custodian because he had to clean the mirrors every day. To show the girls how difficult it was to clean the mirrors, she asked the custodian to clean one of them. He took out a squeegee with a long handle, dipped it into the toilet, and then cleaned the mirror with it. Ever since then there haven't been any lip prints on the mirror.

GREG: Gross! Pretty funny, though.

JEAN: Are you sure you're not just saying that so that I don't feel stupid?

GREG: Nope. It wasn't exactly a joke, but it was funny.

MIKE: Isn't this a great place, Carol?

CAROL: Yes, it is. I really like the décor.

MIKE: How's your steak?

CAROL: Oh, it's really good. What about your fish?

MIKE: Wonderful. Carol, you know there's a really important reason why I asked you out tonight.

CAROL: There is?

MIKE: Well, sure. You know, I just can't begin to tell you how great I think our relationship is. I don't know if I've ever been this happy.

CAROL: Yes, we have a nice . . . relationship.

MIKE: Yes, we sure do. Anyway, I expect you know what I'm going to say.

CAROL: I do?

MIKE: Well yeah. Carol, you'll make me the happiest man in the world if you'll marry me. Now I'm not sure if this is really what you want in a ring. I know I don't have very good taste. But anyway, take a look.

CAROL: Mike, I . . . don't know what to say.

MIKE: Just say yes. You know, I was out driving the other day, and I saw this house that would be perfect for us, a really cute little house, and . . .

CAROL: Mike . . .

MIKE: What?

CAROL: Mike . . . I don't think I'm ready for marriage.

MIKE: What?

CAROL: I . . . I just don't think I'm ready. This is all happening too fast.

MIKE: But Carol, when two people love each other like we do . . .

CAROL: Mike, I think a lot of you, and I really value our friendship, but . . .

MIKE: But . . . what?

CAROL: Mike, we have a wonderful friendship. Why don't we just keep it that way?

MIKE: Friendship? Carol, I've got lots of friends. I don't need any more friends. I want someone to spend my life. . . .

PHYLLIS: Hey Rosa, what do you think of Warm Hearts?

ROSA: It's good. I wouldn't have met the interesting people I've met if I hadn't joined. How about you?

PHYLLIS: Well, Warm Hearts is fine. I'm the one who's to blame. I wish I'd followed my gut feeling.

ROSA: Why? What happened?

PHYLLIS: Well, after I joined, the agency arranged for me to meet two men, Wayne and Les. I talked to both of them on the phone. Les was fun to talk to, and I liked him better than Wayne, but you know what they say about how you should choose someone of the same educational level? Wayne has a degree and Les doesn't, so I went out with Wayne. I wish I'd gone out with Les instead. If I'd paid attention to my intuition, I might be in a good relationship right now. Anyway, with Wayne it was OK for the first few dates, but after that it was a disaster. Wayne acted as if he were in charge of me. He was insanely jealous. I broke off the relationship, but he kept calling me. I had to get an unlisted phone number. I hope he's gone for good.

ROSA: What about Les? Is he still in the picture?

PHYLLIS: I don't know. If I weren't such a coward, I'd call him.

ROSA: Come on, Phyllis. I really wish you wouldn't put yourself down so much. You can be stronger than that. Give it a try. Call him up again.

PHYLLIS: You really think so? Well, all right. I just hope he hasn't found someone else.

UNIT 25 — EXERCISE 6, PAGE 481. LISTENING 1.

A few minutes ago, your friend Mary called and asked that you baby-sit her children for the fifth time in the last three weeks. Had you known she was going to call, you wouldn't have answered the phone. The last time this happened, it was ten o'clock at night and you finally had to call and insist that she come and pick up her kids. You politely suggested that Mary look into day care, but she said she wouldn't be able to afford it until she got a job. After that you swore you wouldn't be manipulated again, but when Mary called up and said, "Just this once," you gave in and said yes. Now you're boiling inside, because you feel Mary treats you as if you were her slave. Does this sound like you? If so, we can help. We're Lionhearts, and we specialize in assertiveness training. With a little bit of practice, you can learn how to say what you think and not feel guilty about it. Call 555-9195 now for an appointment. Money back if you're not completely satisfied.

UNIT 25 — EXERCISE 7, PAGES 481–482. LISTENING 2.

FORREST: Good evening. I'm Forrest Taylor. Welcome to *Wimp No More*, the program that helps you to stop being a doormat. In a moment, we'll start taking your calls; we ask only that you turn down your radio when you're on the air and that you keep your language clean. Caller Number 1, Mildred from Saskatoon, talk to me.

MILDRED: Hi, Forrest. I've got a problem with my mother-in-law. A year ago she moved in across the street from us, and since then she's taken control of our life. She demands that Buddy, my husband, take her shopping every day and that he have dinner with her every Sunday—just the two of them. When she comes over to our house, she makes it seem as if she owned the place and I were some sort of intruder in it. I'd rather she didn't set foot in the house at all, but I have Buddy's feelings to consider.

FORREST: Have you talked to Buddy about this?

MILDRED: Yes, but he says it's really important that we not excite her too much because of her high blood pressure. She could have a heart attack.

FORREST: The old illness excuse, eh? Well, it's time you took some action here, because you're obviously being manipulated big time. If I were you, I'd sit down with Buddy and tell him this can't go on. I'd insist that he find her a new place to live, maybe a retirement center where she could be with people her own age.

MILDRED: What if he were to get mad and choose her over me? I'm afraid he might do that.

FORREST: Well, Mildred, that's what it all boils down to, isn't it? I suggest that you give Buddy a chance to show who he's married to. Lay it on the line to him. If he chooses his mother, he's not worth fretting over. Good luck. Caller Number 2, Jason from Anaheim, what's on your mind?

DIAGNOSTIC AND FINAL TESTS AND ANSWER KEY

These exams, which are linked to the twelve parts of the Student Book, test the material presented in the Grammar Charts, Grammar Notes, and Focused Practice exercises.

The results of each **Diagnostic Test** enable you to tailor your class to the needs of individual students. The format of both the Diagnostic and Final Tests is the same, and all but the final two or three sections of each test are labeled by unit title. This labeling allows you to pinpoint each student's strengths and weaknesses. The final sections of each test are called Synthesis; these exercises cover the grammar points of the entire part. Included in the Synthesis section are questions in the format of the Structure and Written Expression sections of the TOEFL.

Students who do well on the part's Diagnostic Test should feel good about their high scores, but they should also realize that knowledge of a language requires communication in open-ended situations. If these students are weak in comprehension or communication skills, they should concentrate on the Listening and Comprehension Practice exercises in the book.

Students who do poorly on the Diagnostic Test will want to divide their time between the Focused Practice and Communication Practice exercises.

Students of diverse skills and abilities can be divided into groups that concentrate on the kinds of exercises they need the most. The teacher can work with the different groups and help each student to overcome his or her weaknesses.

The **Final Test** for each part gives students the chance to make certain that they understand the grammar points presented in the part. The tests are straightforward, and since the format of the Final Test is the same unit-by-unit format as the Diagnostic Test, the Final Test offers students who have studied the chance to succeed and gain a sense of accomplishment and confidence in their ability to learn and understand grammar.

NOTE: **The Tests, which are perforated so that they can be removed and copied, follow the Answer Key.**

DIAGNOSTIC AND FINAL TESTS
ANSWER KEY

Note: In this Answer Key, where the contracted form is given, the full form may also be correct, and where the full form is given, the contracted form may also be correct.

PART I

Diagnostic Test

I. (Unit 1: Present and Future Time)
Total: 13 points—1 point per item
2. 'll be studying
3. have
4. need
5. 'm writing
6. 'll have been
7. think
8. 'll throw
9. 've wanted / 've been wanting
10. haven't had
11. 's
12. find
13. 'll call
14. get

II. (Unit 1: Present and Future Time)
Total: 11 points—1 point per item
2. 'm making
3. Do . . . want
4. haven't had
5. is . . . getting / is . . . going to get
6. comes
7. 's feeling
8. cries
9. needs
10. is bringing / is going to bring
11. 're going to dance / 'll be dancing
12. 'll have / 're going to have

III. (Unit 2: Past Time)
Total: 13 points—1 point per item
2. ended
3. got
4. did . . . do
5. thought
6. was
7. would fail / was going to fail / had failed
8. did / 'd done
9. studied
10. 've studied
11. paid off
12. were . . . doing
13. called
14. was thinking about

IV. (Unit 2: Past Time)
Total: 10 points—1 point per item
2. used to live
3. would go
4. used to have
5. would go
6. would meet
7. would go
8. would go
9. used to be
10. used to have
11. would come

V. (Unit 2: Past Time)
Total: 4 points—1 point per item
2. I was sure that I'd learn to speak Swahili fluently,
3. I expected that I would make a lot of new friends,
4. I didn't think I'd have time to visit South Africa,
5. I wasn't going to spend a lot of money,

VI. (Unit 3: Past, Present, and Future)
Total: 15 points—1 point per item

2. I hadn't seen
3. I ran into
4. Did she seem
5. She's being
6. I think
7. she's
8. thought
9. she was
10. gotten
11. were seeing
12. broke up
13. I'm having
14. I'll
15. She'll be
16. You'll have

VII. (Unit 3: Past, Present, and Future)
Total: 12 points—1 point per item

(I ~~felt~~ ^I've been feeling very homesick lately,) but ~~I've~~ ^I made an important decision last night: The time has ~~been coming~~ ^come to stop moping around! I'm here in the United States, and ~~I'm needing~~ ^I need to take advantage of this wonderful opportunity. I've always ~~been making~~ ^made friends easily, and I've met some terrific people since I ~~get~~ ^got here. From now on, I will make more of an effort to enjoy life. In fact, a really nice guy named Alan ~~was inviting~~ ^invited me for dinner tomorrow night. Unfortunately, I told him I ~~won't~~ ^wouldn't be able to go, but I think ~~I~~ ^I'll call him later and tell him I'm ~~being~~ free tomorrow night after all.

~~I'm having~~ ^I have to start taking better care of myself, too. The food in the cafeteria ~~is tasting~~ ^tastes really awful, so I should stop eating there. I'm going to start having breakfast and lunch at the nice health-food cafe across the street from the dorm. When ~~I'll~~ ^I start eating more healthfully, I'm sure I'll feel better.

VIII. (Units 1–3: Synthesis)
Total: 12 points—1 point per item

2. C	6. D	10. B
3. D	7. B	11. B
4. C	8. B	12. C
5. A	9. C	13. A

IX. (Units 1–3: Synthesis)
Total: 10 points—1 point per item

2. D	6. D	9. B
3. A	7. B	10. D
4. B	8. B	11. C
5. D		

PART I

Final Test

I. (Unit 1: Present and Future Time)
Total: 13 points—1 point per item

2. rings and rings
3. have
4. 'll have left
5. 'll enjoying / 'm going to be enjoying
6. 're thinking
7. cost
8. 've wanted / 've been wanting
9. sounds
10. leaves
11. 'll be walking
12. 'll have taken
13. 'll tell
14. see

II. (Unit 1: Present and Future Time)
Total: 11 points—1 point per item

2. are going / have been going
3. has been working
4. 're going / 're going to go
5. comes / 'll come
6. won't believe / aren't going to believe / 're not going to believe
7. 'm going / 'm going to go
8. 've . . . wanted
9. gets
10. is . . . going / is . . . going to go
11. stops / 's going to stop
12. will . . . be / are . . . going to be

III. (Unit 2: Past Time)
Total: 13 points—1 point per item

2. said
3. were going to call / would call
4. heard
5. has been happening / has happened
6. was considering / 'd been considering
7. gave
8. was
9. 'd worked / 'd been working / worked
10. did . . . react
11. got
12. 'd . . . seen
13. Have . . . found / Did . . . find
14. didn't take

IV. (Unit 2: Past Time)
Total: 10 points—1 point per item

2. used to teach
3. would spend / used to spend
4. would teach
5. would take
6. would have / used to have
7. used to teach
8. would spend / used to spend
9. used to have
10. used to enjoy
11. would count

V. (Unit 2: Past Time)
Total: 4 points—1 point per item

2. I didn't think my courses were going to be too difficult,
3. I didn't think I'd have to get a job,
4. I had the feeling my roommate and I were going to become best friends,
5. I was sure I'd have a great time,

VI. (Unit 3: Past, Present, and Future)
Total: 15 points—1 point per item

2. Have you been waiting
3. you told
4. you'd
5. I've been
6. you hear
7. forgive
8. I'm starving
9. looks
10. Do you smell
11. didn't you want
12. I worked
13. I was trying
14. had left
15. I'm
16. got

VII. (Unit 3: Past, Present, and Future)
Total: 12 points—1 point per item

(~~I've had~~ *I had* dinner with Stacy the night before last.) I ~~haven't~~ *hadn't* seen her in a really long time before that evening, and I ~~forget~~ *had forgotten* how much I like her. In fact, ~~I'm thinking~~ *I've been thinking* about her night and day since ~~I've seen~~ *I saw* her. I got to the restaurant late, and I was afraid ~~she'll~~ *she'd* be angry, but she ~~was being~~ *was* really nice about it. ~~I'm~~ *I* always ~~feeling~~ *feel* very comfortable with Stacy. We talked all through dinner. After dinner, we went for a long walk down by the river. ~~I'm thinking~~ *I think* it was one of the best evenings ~~I was ever having~~ *I've ever had*. ~~I'll~~ *I'm going to call* her tomorrow to invite her to a movie on Saturday night. Maybe ~~she's saying~~ *she'll say* yes. Maybe ~~she's liking~~ *she likes* me, too.

VIII. (Units 1–3: Synthesis)
Total: 12 points—1 point per item

2. C
3. C
4. B
5. C
6. C
7. D
8. A
9. C
10. B
11. A
12. B
13. A

IX. (Units 1–3: Synthesis)
Total: 10 points—1 point per item

2. C
3. D
4. C
5. A
6. D
7. A
8. C
9. B
10. D
11. D

PART II

Diagnostic Test

I. (Unit 4: Modals: Necessity)
Total: 18 points—1 point per item

2. had to
3. didn't have to
4. don't have to
5. should / ought to / must
6. shouldn't
7. has to / must
8. shouldn't have
9. should / ought to / must
10. shouldn't
11. mustn't
12. doesn't have to
13. must
14. had better
15. Shall
16. should / ought to / had better
17. should / ought to / had better
18. can
19. can / should

II. (Unit 4: Modals: Necessity)
Total: 6 points—1 point per item

2. a
3. b
4. b
5. a
6. b
7. b

III. (Unit 5: Modals: Certainty)
Total: 12 points—1 point per item

2. might have gone
3. must not have heard
4. may take
5. could have caused
6. can't have arrived
7. couldn't have committed
8. Shouldn't I feel / Shouldn't I be feeling
9. Couldn't they have chosen
10. must have been grading
11. Could he be taking
12. might have gone
13. must be talking

IV. (Unit 5: Modals: Certainty)
Total: 12 points—1 point per item

2. b
3. a
4. c
5. c
6. a
7. c
8. a
9. c
10. a
11. c
12. b
13. a

V. (Units 4–5: Synthesis)
Total: 12 points—1 point per item

2. ought to
3. don't have to
4. aren't supposed to
5. must have
6. Shall
7. can't have
8. must not have
9. had better not
10. shouldn't have stayed
11. must not
12. Aren't
13. don't have to

VI. (Units 4–5: Synthesis)
Total: 15 points—1 point per item

(I̶'̶d̶ ̶b̶e̶t̶t̶e̶r̶) [*I should*] be sleeping because I have ₍to₎ get up early tomorrow, but I'm too confused to sleep. Tonight Mom and Dad told me that they're worried about me. They think I ought ₍to₎ see a counselor. They think I c̶a̶n̶ [*might / could*] be depressed, and talking to someone might m̶a̶k̶e̶s̶ [*make*] me feel better about myself and my life. They said that a counselor c̶a̶n̶ [*will*] be able to help me understand why I'm feeling so negative about everything these days.

I must t̶o̶ admit that I have been really sad lately, and I haven't been doing anything that I'm supposed to d̶o̶i̶n̶g̶ [*do*]. Mom says I m̶u̶s̶t̶ ̶n̶o̶t̶ [*don't have to*] go to the counselor if I don't want to, but I think it might t̶o̶ be the smart thing to do. I read a book a few months ago about a girl who wasn't able to c̶o̶m̶m̶u̶n̶i̶c̶a̶t̶e̶d̶ [*communicate*] with anyone; she s̶h̶o̶u̶l̶d̶n̶'̶t̶ [*couldn't*] find anything that interested her. She must ₍have₎ felt the same way I do. She finally decided she had g̶o̶t̶ to do something about the situation, so she went to see the guidance counselor at her high school. The counselor must h̶e̶l̶p̶ [*have helped*] her a lot because a few months later, she auditioned for a school play and got the leading role. Now, ten years later, she's a very successful Hollywood actress and a very happy person. Talking to a counselor might ^{not}be such a bad idea!

VII. (Units 4–5: Synthesis)
Total: 12 points—1 point per item

2. B	6. C	10. C
3. B	7. C	11. A
4. A	8. D	12. C
5. D	9. D	13. D

VIII. (Units 4–5: Synthesis)
Total: 13 points—1 point per item

2. C	7. D	11. C
3. C	8. B	12. A
4. C	9. D	13. C
5. D	10. A	14. D
6. C		

PART II

Final Test

I. (Unit 4: Modals: Necessity)
Total: 18 points—1 point per item

2. can't
3. should / ought to
4. can't / mustn't
5. can
6. couldn't
7. shouldn't have
8. should / had better / must / ought to
9. should / ought to / had better
10. should / ought to / had better
11. don't have to
12. should
13. should / ought to
14. should have
15. have to
16. had to
17. didn't have to
18. should / ought to / had better
19. Shall

II. (Unit 4: Modals: Necessity)
Total: 6 points—1 point per item

2. a	4. b	6. a
3. a	5. a	7. b

III. (Unit 5: Modals: Certainty)
Total: 12 points—1 point per item

2. might be
3. might not have heard
4. must not like
5. must have had
6. can't be
7. might be practicing
8. must have gotten
9. might be studying
10. should be
11. Could he have forgotten
12. Could they be playing
13. can't have finished

IV. (Unit 5: Modals: Certainty)
Total: 12 points—1 point per item

2. a	6. b	10. c
3. b	7. a	11. a
4. b	8. b	12. c
5. c	9. a	13. b

V. (Units 4–5: Synthesis)
Total: 12 points—1 point per item

2. Are we supposed to
3. must not be
4. might be
5. could have caught
6. didn't have to
7. ought
8. is
9. might have dropped
10. Are you allowed to
11. able to
12. had better
13. ought to

VI. (Units 4–5: Synthesis)
Total: 15 points—1 point per item

(Today, John and I asked Brenda what we ought ^{to}do about our wedding.) Then I made the mistake of asking my mother. As you might have ~~guess~~ ^{guessed}, whatever Brenda says we don't ~~had~~ ^{have} to do, my mother says ~~we~~ ^{we're} supposed to do. For example, my mother thinks we must ~~to~~ invite all her friends who live far away. Most of them have never even met me, so they can't ~~have wanted~~ ^{want} to fly all the way here just for my wedding. And when I told Mom we might ~~have been having~~ ^{be having} an outdoor wedding, she said, "You must ^{be}crazy! You ~~had~~ ^{have} to have your wedding in the same place Dad and I got married!" John thinks I ~~have~~ ^{had} better listen to my mother since she and Dad

are paying for much of the wedding, but
I think I ~~should~~ *shouldn't have* asked her for advice. Many
of her ideas are old-fashioned and may not
~~have been~~ *be* appropriate for weddings today.
I'm beginning to think that ~~I'll~~ *I'd* better hire a
wedding consultant. A consultant
can't ~~have been~~ *be* too expensive and ~~to~~ must
know what to do. And we ~~had~~ ought to hire
one soon!

VII. **(Units 4–5: Synthesis)**
Total: 12 points—1 point per item

2. D	6. C	10. A
3. A	7. B	11. C
4. B	8. D	12. C
5. A	9. D	13. B

VIII. **(Units 4–5: Synthesis)**
Total: 13 points—1 point per item

2. D	7. B	11. A
3. C	8. C	12. C
4. B	9. D	13. B
5. D	10. D	14. D
6. A		

PART III

Diagnostic Test

I. **(Unit 6: Count and Non-Count Nouns)**
Total: 9 points—1 point per item

2. Pollution	7. milk
3. a work	8. Film
4. an iron	9. talk
5. coffees	10. a matter
6. a red wine	

II. **(Unit 6: Count and Non-Count Nouns)**
Total: 5 points—1 point per item

2. speck of	4. bolt of	6. piece of
3. drop of	5. branch of	

III. **(Unit 6: Count and Non-Count Nouns)**
Total: 5 points—1 point per item

2. is	4. were	6. is
3. is	5. were	

IV. **(Unit 7: Definite and Indefinite Articles)**
Total: 9 points—1 point per item

2. a	5. the	8. the
3. the	6. the	9. The
4. Ø	7. Ø	10. The

V. **(Unit 7: Definite and Indefinite Articles)**
Total: 9 points—1 point per item

2. the wheel	7. electricity
3. beets	8. the whale
4. The dinosaurs	9. the telephone
5. Iron	10. the clarinet
6. An orangutan	

VI. **(Unit 7: Definite and Indefinite Articles)**
Total: 15 points—1 point per item

(⋀*The* Statue of Liberty is located in New York
Harbor.) It was ⋀*a* gift of ~~the~~ friendship
from ⋀*the* people of France to ⋀*the* American people. It is one of the most famous symbols
of ~~the~~ freedom in ⋀*the* world. ~~The visitors~~
to ⋀*the* Statue of Liberty National Monument
can climb to ⋀*the* crown of ⋀*the* statue. There is
also ⋀*an* elevator. ~~An~~ *The* elevator goes to ⋀*the* top
of ⋀*the* pedestal, but not to ⋀*the* crown.

VII. **(Unit 8: Modification of Nouns)**
Total: 9 points—1 point per item

2. new pink satin
3. cute Canadian fox terrier puppy
4. first three eligible
5. his own country
6. all six of the Romanian orphans
7. interesting American
8. narrow Chinese silk
9. interesting and worthwhile training
10. five unprofitable South African diamond

VIII. **(Unit 8: Modification of Nouns)**
Total: 5 points—1 point per item

2. ten-year-old	5. In-class
3. citizen-initiated	6. twelve-year-old
4. forty-pound	daughter

IX. (Unit 9: Quantifiers)
Total: 9 points—1 point per item

2. fewer	6. Either	9. a great
3. Much	7. a few	many
4. little	8. less	10. All
5. number		

X. (Units 6–9: Synthesis)
Total: 12 points—1 point per item

2. A	6. D	10. B
3. D	7. A	11. A
4. B	8. D	12. A
5. B	9. A	13. C

XI. (Units 6–9: Synthesis)
Total: 13 points—1 point per item

2. A	7. C	11. B
3. B	8. B	12. D
4. D	9. D	13. C
5. C	10. C	14. B
6. A		

PART III

Final Test

I. (Unit 6: Count and Non-Count Nouns)
Total: 9 points—1 point per item

2. a white	5. a chance	9. a televi-
wine	6. Matter	sion
3. water	7. a powder	10. sodas
4. Cinema	8. a work	

II. (Unit 6: Count and Non-Count Nouns)
Total: 5 points—1 point per item

2. branch of	4. current of	6. flash of
3. piece of	5. grain of	

III. (Unit 6: Count and Non-Count Nouns)
Total: 5 points—1 point per item

2. have	4. are	6. are
3. are	5. has	

IV. (Unit 7: Definite and Indefinite Articles)
Total: 9 points—1 point per item

2. The	5. The	8. the
3. the	6. the	9. the
4. the	7. a	10. the

V. (Unit 7: Definite and Indefinite Articles)
Total: 9 points—1 point per item

2. A cetacean	7. the radio tele-
3. hydroelectric	scope
power	8. cooked carrots
4. the dolphins	9. The passenger
5. the phonograph	pigeon
6. the piano	10. Radium

VI. (Unit 7: Definite and Indefinite Articles)
Total: 15 points—1 point per item

(The Golden Gate Bridge in ~~the~~ San Francisco) had ^the^ longest span in ^the^ world at ^the^ time of its construction in 1937. It was named after the Golden Gate Strait, which is ^the^ entrance to ~~the~~ San Francisco Bay from ^the^ Pacific Ocean. ~~The~~ ^An^ army captain gave ~~the~~ strait its name because it reminded him of ^a^ harbor in Istanbul. ~~A~~ ^The^ bridge is actually not gold but orange. ~~A~~ ^The^ people in charge chose ~~the~~ color orange because it blends well with ^the^ environment. However, ^the^ United States Navy wanted to paint ^the^ bridge black and yellow so that passing ships could see it more easily.

VII. (Unit 8: Modification of Nouns)
Total: 9 points—1 point per item

2. their own soft drink
3. all six of the available properties
4. first three
5. old yellow gingham
6. lovable Scottish border collie puppy
7. contemporary Canadian
8. elegant French silk
9. difficult and frustrating review
10. four least profitable Chilean copper

VIII. (Unit 8: Modification of Nouns)
Total: 5 points—1 point per item

2. Open-book	5. eighty-year-old
3. twenty-year-old	mother
4. eight-hour	6. voter-initiated

IX. (Unit 9: Quantifiers)
Total: 9 points—1 point per item

2. little	6. much	9. A great
3. number	7. fewer	many of
4. Either	8. less	10. All
5. a few		

X. (Units 6–9: Synthesis)
Total: 12 points—1 point per item

2. D	6. B	10. B
3. B	7. D	11. A
4. A	8. C	12. A
5. B	9. A	13. A

XI. (Units 6–9: Synthesis)
Total: 13 points—1 point per item

2. A	7. D	11. C
3. B	8. C	12. A
4. D	9. D	13. B
5. D	10. D	14. D
6. A		

PART IV

Diagnostic Test

I. (Unit 10: Adjective Clauses: Review and Expansion)
Total: 9 points—1 point per item

2. which is now one of the ten largest cities in the United States
3. whom you met at the business luncheon last month
4. that I find most charming
5. whose dog escaped and chased our cats
6. which are located off northern British Columbia
7. you introduced me to at the party
8. when everything seems to change
9. where the treasure had been buried
10. which is what is so endearing about her

II. (Unit 10: Adjective Clauses: Review and Expansion)
Total: 5 points—1 point per item

2. which	4. whose	6. in which
3. to whom	5. that	case

III. (Unit 10: Adjective Clauses: Review and Expansion)
Total: 10 points—2 points per item

2. Mexico City, which is the largest city in the Western Hemisphere, has a population of at least twenty million.
3. Nancy Armenta, whom you met at the Prettos' party, is the new assistant to the president.
4. The scholarship will be awarded to the student who gets the faculty recommendation.
5. The man whose dogs have been barking all night has agreed to take better control of his animals.
6. The boy whom/that/who/ø we saw on the train is standing over there.

IV. (Unit 10: Adjective Clauses: Review and Expansion)
Total: 5 points—1 point per item

2. The daughter who lives in California is an oceanographer.
3. The daughter who lives in Costa Rica is a linguist.
4. Joe Morgan, whose father has been nominated for the Senate, is planning on going into politics himself.
5. Cuneiform writing, which was developed by the Sumerians, is the oldest known writing system.
6. The company for which Priscilla works is Tucson Tutorials.

V. (Unit 10: Adjective Clauses: Review and Expansion)
Total: 5 points—1 point per item

2. The woman you met
3. The company Jane has been working for
4. the house Jack built
5. *Pronoun cannot be removed.*
6. *Pronoun cannot be removed.*

VI. (Unit 10: Adjective Clauses: Review and Expansion)
Total: 4 points—1 point per item

2. a	3. a	4. a	5. b

VII. (Unit 11: Adjective Clauses with Qualifiers: Adjective Phrases)
Total: 9 points—1 point per item

2. responsible for this prank
3. interested in obtaining concert tickets
4. including Washington, St. Louis, and Cincinnati

5. in that sports car
6. starring Vanessa Redgrave and David Hemmings
7. located in the southeastern part of the Yukon
8. directed by Steven Spielberg
9. the second-largest city in Mexico
10. Lasting from 1338 to 1453

VIII. (Unit 11: Adjective Clauses with Quantifiers: Adjective Phrases)
Total: 8 points—2 points per item

2. *E.T.* and *Jurassic Park*, both of which were directed by Steven Spielberg, have been huge financial successes.
3. The company has proposed two options, neither of which seems viable.
4. The president has been defeated on many pieces of legislation, several of which have been fundamentally sound.
5. Many issues will be debated in the next legislative session, among which are universal health care and welfare reform.

IX. (Unit 11: Adjective Clauses with Quantifiers; Adjective Phrases)
Total: 10 points—2 points per item

2. New Orleans, known for its French Quarter, is an exciting city to visit.
3. The Mediterranean and Red seas, now connected by the Suez Canal, have figured prominently in Middle Eastern history.
4. The drama department will put on several classical plays this year, including *King Lear, Oedipus Rex,* and *Frogs.*
5. We are staying in a cabin on Lake Saratoga.
6. *Casablanca*, starring Humphrey Bogart and Ingrid Bergman, won the Academy Award for Best Picture in 1942.

X. (Units 10–11: Synthesis)
Total: 15 points—1 point per item

2. who had	7. which	12. that
3. both of	8. produced	13. who
4. who	9. including	14. for which
5. who	10. which	15. in which
6. which	11. for which	16. who

XI. (Units 10–11: Synthesis)
Total: 11 points—1 point per item

2. A	6. B	10. A
3. D	7. C	11. A
4. D	8. D	12. D
5. C	9. A	

XII. (Units 10–11: Synthesis)
Total: 9 points—1 point per item

2. A	5. A	8. A
3. C	6. B	9. C
4. B	7. A	10. C

PART IV

Final Test

I. (Unit 10: Adjective Clauses: Review and Expansion)
Total: 9 points—1 point per item

2. which is the largest metropolitan area in Canada
3. whom the governor just appointed his press secretary
4. that I find most beautiful
5. whose pet raccoons have been raiding our garbage cans
6. which are two islands located in the West Indies
7. we met on the train to Stockholm
8. when our company is financially strapped for funds
9. where the original village stood
10. which is what is so irritating about him

II. (Unit 10: Adjective Clauses: Review and Expansion)
Total: 5 points—1 point per item

2. which	4. whose	6. in which
3. to whom	5. who	case

III. (Unit 10: Adjective Clauses: Review and Expansion)

Total: 10 points—2 points per item

2. São Paulo, which is the largest city in Brazil, is also the largest city in South America.
3. Peter Glisson, whom/who we ran into at the picnic, is the new assistant to the dean.
4. The scholarship will likely be given to the candidate who gets the committee's recommendation.
5. The woman whose cats have been stealing fish from our pond has agreed to keep her pets indoors.
6. The little girl whom/that/who/ø we saw at the park is eating a lollipop.

IV. (Unit 10: Adjective Clauses: Review and Expansion)

Total: 5 points—1 point per item

2. The son who lives on Prince Edward Island writes novels for a living.
3. The son who lives in Bermuda does genetic research.
4. Theresa Tafoya, whose grandmother was also a well-known artist, has a painting on exhibit in the Museum of Contemporary Art.
5. *Don Quixote,* which was written by Miguel de Cervantes, is considered one of the world's greatest novels.
6. The company to which Henry applied has gone out of business.

V. (Unit 10: Adjective Clauses: Review and Expansion)

Total: 5 points—1 point per item

2. we were introduced to
3. we've been living in
4. *Pronoun cannot be removed.*
5. *Pronoun cannot be removed.*
6. *Pronoun cannot be removed.*

VI. (Unit 10: Adjective Clauses: Review and Expansion)

Total: 4 points—1 point per item

2. a   3. a   4. a   5. a

VII. (Unit 11: Adjective Clauses with Quantifiers; Adjective Phrases)

Total: 9 points—1 point per item

2. guilty of tax evasion
3. interested in joining the soccer team
4. including California, Washington, and Alaska
5. in the first row
6. starring Gregory Peck as Captain Ahab
7. located on Great Slave Lake
8. directed by Federico Fellini
9. the industrial center of Mexico
10. Beginning in 1929

VIII. (Unit 11: Adjective Clauses with Quantifiers; Adjective Phrases)

Total: 8 points—2 points per item

2. *Grease, The Sound of Music,* and *My Fair Lady,* all of which are musicals, have been quite financially successful.
3. My broker says I have two business options, neither of which is particularly attractive.
4. The president has vetoed many bills passed by Congress, some of which had the overwhelming support of the electorate.
5. The Constitution guarantees to the people certain unalienable rights, among which are life, liberty, and the pursuit of happiness.

IX. (Unit 11: Adjective Clauses with Quantifiers; Adjective Phrases)

Total: 10 points—2 point per item

2. Venice, known for its many canals, is a charming and beautiful city to visit.
3. Colombia and Panama, connected by a narrow isthmus, were at one time one nation.
4. The repertory company will perform several contemporary plays this year, including *An Inspector Calls, Equus,* and *One Flew over the Cuckoo's Nest.*
5. We are renting the house on Main Street.
6. *The Silence of the Lambs,* starring Anthony Hopkins and Jodie Foster, won the Academy Award for Best Picture in 1991.

X. (Units 10–11: Synthesis)
Total: 15 points—1 point per item

2. which	7. where	12. including
3. belonging	8. which	13. which
4. whose	9. which	14. for which
5. who	10. of which	15. who
6. influential	11. when	16. leading

XI. (Units 10–11: Synthesis)
Total: 11 points—1 point per item

2. C	6. A	10. D
3. C	7. D	11. C
4. A	8. A	12. C
5. A	9. C	

XII. (Units 10–11: Synthesis)
Total: 9 points—1 point per item

2. A	5. A	8. A
3. B	6. D	9. A
4. A	7. A	10. C

PART V

Diagnostic Test

I. (Unit 12: The Passive: Review and Expansion)
Total: 7 points—1 point per item

2. were directed
3. will not be completed
4. am easily awakened
5. was composed
6. are required
7. was invented
8. is going to be presented

II. (Unit 12: The Passive: Review and Expansion)
Total: 5 points—1 point per item

2. are going to get beaten	4. got included
	5. get sidetracked
3. gets distracted	6. will get done

III. (Unit 12: The Passive: Review and Expansion)
Total: 5 points—1 point per item

2. was being repaired	4. are getting fed
	5. are being treated
3. been getting overcharged	6. be getting trained

IV. (Unit 12: The Passive: Review and Expansion)
Total: 5 points—1 point per item

2. 's been done
3. had been tampered with
4. has gotten done / has been getting done
5. have been advised
6. have been deposited

V. (Unit 12: The Passive: Review and Expansion)
Total: 5 points—1 point per item

2. should not be left alone
3. must have been reported
4. has to be attended to
5. should have been taken
6. was supposed to be watered

VI. (Unit 13: Reporting Ideas and Facts with Passives)
Total: 5 points—1 point per item

2. are believed	5. is alleged
3. are said	6. is regarded
4. are considered	

VII. (Unit 13: Reporting Ideas and Facts with Passives)
Total: 5 points—1 point per item

2. is found	4. is bordered
3. was / is more commonly known	5. is not related
	6. are connected

VIII. (Unit 13: Reporting Ideas and Facts with Passives)
Total: 10 points—2 point per item

3. Her plane wasn't allowed to land in New York until 10:00 P.M.
4. Mrs. Adams had to take a taxi to her hotel.
5. Mrs. Adams arrived at her hotel very late.
6. Because of her late arrival, her hotel room had been given away.
7. Mrs. Adams spent a very uncomfortable night on a couch in the hotel lobby.

IX

(Units 12–13: Synthesis)
Total: 15 points—1 point per item

(Crop circles, small areas of crops in elaborately swirled patterns, are a modern-day mystery. They have been ~~spotting~~ spotted all over the world.) One ~~was~~ reported in England in the 1960s. More were ~~documenting~~ documented in England and the Australian outback in the 1970s. Crop circles also appeared on a farm in Switzerland. On this farm, the grass stalks within the circles ~~had~~ been bent flat, but they had not ~~being~~ been broken. The grass continued to grow in a swirled pattern. Meanwhile, a farmer in Canada noticed several dome-shaped aircraft in the air above his field. When the aircraft left, they had left several crop circles in the field. More circles appeared during the next few nights.

In the 1980s, people began to research crop circles. It was ~~proposing~~ proposed by one meteorologist that they might have ~~been~~ caused by an unusual weather phenomenon. Since strange lights or spacecraft resembling UFOs had often been ~~seeing~~ seen around the same time these circles were ~~form~~ formed, some people believed that these formations could have been ~~using~~ used as landing strips for alien spacecraft.

In the 1990s, two men claimed to have created all the formations by using a plank of wood and a piece of rope. However, they later admitted that they had lied. It ~~was~~ then suggested that these men had been ~~plant~~ planted by the government to cover up evidence of UFOs. The idea that crop circles had ~~been~~ created by UFOs was becoming more widely ~~believing~~ believed, since the formations had begun to occur in even more elaborate patterns. The size of the formations had also increased. One, ~~find~~ found in England in 1996, was 4100 feet across!

In the twentieth century, these Crop Circles remain a mystery. What do you think they're ~~cause~~ caused by?

X

(Units 12–13: Synthesis)
Total: 15 points—1 point per item

2. are caused by
3. have been proposed
4. is not known
5. is believed
6. have been suggested
7. known
8. are regarded
9. created
10. have been disproven / have been disproved
11. located
12. has been alleged
13. were created / have been created
14. are considered
15. have been offered
16. is being investigated / will be investigated

(Units 12–13: Synthesis)
Total: 14 points—1 point per item

2. C	7. B	12. C
3. B	8. A	13. B
4. B	9. C	14. C
5. D	10. A	15. A
6. B	11. A	

(Units 12–13: Synthesis)
Total: 9 points—1 point per item

2. A	5. B	8. A
3. D	6. C	9. C
4. C	7. D	10. C

PART V

Final Test

I. (Unit 12: The Passive: Review and Expansion)
Total: 7 points—1 point per item

2. are arrested
3. are mined
4. were written
5. will not be finished
6. is going to be discussed
7. am frequently bothered
8. was composed

II. (Unit 12: The Passive: Review and Expansion)
Total: 5 points—1 point per item

2. gets intimidated
3. got hit
4. is going to get defeated
5. will get assigned
6. got incorporated

III. (Unit 12: The Passive: Review and Expansion)
Total: 5 points—1 point per item

2. is being built
3. was being resurfaced
4. been getting undercharged
5. be getting counseled
6. is being monitored

IV. (Unit 12: The Passive: Review and Expansion)
Total: 5 points—1 point per item

2. had been put out
3. has been tampered with
4. 's been done
5. have been finished
6. has gotten done

V. (Unit 12: The Passive: Review and Expansion)
Total: 5 points—1 point per item

2. should not be allowed
3. was supposed to be reinvested
4. must have been taken
5. have to be watered
6. should have been advised

VI. (Unit 13: Reporting Ideas and Facts with Passives)
Total: 5 points—1 point per item

2. is alleged
3. is regarded
4. are thought
5. is believed
6. are said

VII. (Unit 13: Reporting Ideas and Facts with Passives)
Total: 5 points—1 point per item

2. are separated
3. is located
4. are found
5. is / was more commonly known
6. is bordered

VIII. (Unit 13: Reporting Ideas and Facts with Passives)
Total: 10 points—2 points per item

3. The ship wasn't allowed to leave Kingston harbor for a week.
4. To pass the time, Henry, Martha, and the other passengers played card games.
5. The passengers also spent many hours reading books from the ship's library.
6. Fortunately, Henry and Martha made many new friends
7. Because of the inconvenience, the passengers were given free tickets for another cruise.

IX. (Units 12–13: Synthesis)
Total: 15 points—1 point per item

(Easter Island $\overset{is}{\wedge}$located over 2,000 miles west of the Chilean mainland.) The island is probably best ~~knowing~~ $\overset{known}{}$ for its mysterious huge stone statues that are ~~scattering~~ $\overset{scattered}{}$ along the coastline. ~~Calling~~ $\overset{Called}{}$ *Te Pito O Te Henua*, or "Navel of The World" by the early settlers, the isolated island$\overset{was}{\wedge}$renamed Easter Island by Admiral Roggeveen, who landed there on Easter Day in 1722. Today, the land, people, and language$\overset{are}{\wedge}$referred to locally as *Rapanui*.

Where did the statues come from? How were they ~~move~~ $\overset{moved}{}$? It was ~~suggesting~~ $\overset{suggested}{}$ by explorer and archaeologist Thor Heyerdahl that the people who built the statues$\overset{were}{\wedge}$related to the natives of Peru, since there are marked similarities between Rapanui and Incan stonework. It$\overset{was}{\wedge}$proposed by author Erich von Däniken that the statues could have$\overset{been}{\wedge}$left by extraterrestrials, since they are too large and heavy for people to move. Others thought that the island could have once been part of a lost continent. Today, it is widely ~~believing~~ *believed* that the island was ~~discover~~ *discovered* by Polynesians around 400 A.D.

As the population on the island grew, the forests ∧ *were* destroyed for agriculture, and natural resources became scarce. Later, civil war erupted and most of the statues on the coast ~~tore~~ *were torn* down by the islanders. The population decreased even further after contact with Western peoples. Many of the inhabitants were ~~enslave~~ *enslaved* or contracted fatal diseases.

Today, Easter Island is part of Chile, but the Polynesian influence still remains. It is now a fascinating living museum in a beautiful, natural setting.

X. (Units 12–13: Synthesis)
Total: 15 points—1 point per item

2. were . . . moved
3. is . . . located
4. was annexed
5. is believed / was believed
6. known
7. was discovered
8. found
9. Are . . . related
10. unearthed
11. was theorized
12. had been made / were made
13. was proposed / has been proposed
14. are called
15. were inspired / had been inspired
16. was created

XI. (Units 12–13: Synthesis)
Total: 14 points—1 point per item

2. B	7. D	12. A
3. C	8. D	13. D
4. D	9. C	14. C
5. A	10. C	15. B
6. C	11. A	

XII. (Units 12–13: Synthesis)
Total: 9 points—1 point per item

2. D	5. D	8. A
3. B	6. B	9. C
4. A	7. A	10. C

PART VI

Diagnostic Test

I. (Unit 14: Auxiliaries)
Total: 10 points—1 point per item

2. doesn't	6. didn't	9. didn't
3. weren't	7. isn't	10. don't
4. weren't	8. was	11. has
5. weren't		

II. (Unit 14: Auxiliaries)
Total: 12 points—2 points per item

2. A. hasn't she	5. A. won't he
B. she has	B. he won't
3. A. can't he	6. A. didn't they
B. he can't	B. they did
4. A. do you	7. A. should they
B. I do	B. they shouldn't

III. (Unit 14: Auxiliaries)
Total: 9 points—1 point per item

2. So do I	5. so does	8. not either
3. Neither do I	6. do too	9. does too
	7. neither is	10. is too
4. so do		

IV. (Unit 14: Auxiliaries)
Total: 6 points—1 point per item

2. am	5. did go
3. do speak	6. will check
4. has traveled	7. had acted

V. (Unit 15: Phrasal Verbs)
Total: 14 points—1 point per item

2. c	7. c	12. a
3. c	8. b	13. b
4. b	9. a	14. b
5. a	10. a	15. c
6. b	11. b	

VI. (Unit 15: Phrasal Verbs)
Total: 10 points—1 point per item

2. show up	8. putting off
3. cut down on	9. figure out
4. showing off	10. running out of
5. get rid of	11. 'm concerned
6. do without	about
7. found out	

VII. (Unit 15: Phrasal Verbs)
Total: 5 points—1 point per item

2. try it on	5. set them aside
3. cut her off	6. think it over
4. give them up	

VIII. (Unit 15: Phrasal Verbs)
Total: 9 points—1 point per item

How to Perform Well on an Exam

- Get _{to} know your teachers early in the semester. You may want to ask them questions later.)

- Don't put ~~up~~ ^{off} studying until the last minute. Set ~~it~~ aside an hour each night to study for a few weeks before the exam. Brush up ^{on} any materials you don't understand well.

- Show ~~off~~ ^{up} at the examination room a few minutes early.

- Wait ~~him or her~~ for the teacher to give you directions before you begin.

- Think ~~up~~ ^{about} each question before you answer it. If you can't figure ~~it~~ out the answer to a question, don't waste too much time thinking ~~it about~~ ^{about it}. Otherwise, you might run out ~~for~~ ^{of} time.

IX. (Units 14–15: Synthesis)
Total: 15 points—1 point per item

2. C	7. B	12. D
3. B	8. C	13. C
4. B	9. A	14. A
5. B	10. A	15. C
6. C	11. D	16. C

X. (Units 14–15: Synthesis)
Total: 10 points—1 point per item

2. D	6. D	9. D
3. C	7. A	10. D
4. C	8. D	11. A
5. A		

PART VI

Final Test

I. (Unit 14: Auxiliaries)
Total: 10 points—1 point per item

2. isn't	6. hadn't /	9. won't
3. aren't	didn't	10. isn't
4. don't	7. doesn't	11. has
5. haven't	8. don't	

II. (Unit 14: Auxiliaries)
Total: 12 points—2 points per item

2. A. can't he	5. A. won't you
B. he can	B. I won't
3. A. aren't they	6. A. weren't you
B. they aren't	B. I was
4. A. does she	7. A. should he
B. she does	B. he shouldn't

III. (Unit 14: Auxiliaries)
Total: 9 points—1 point per item

2. So did I	7. So do
3. Neither have I	8. Neither can I
4. So do I	9. do too
5. does too	10. can't either
6. don't either	

IV. (Unit 14: Auxiliaries)
Total: 6 points—1 point per item

2. am
3. does know
4. has produced
5. did make
6. will send
7. had worked

V. (Unit 15: Phrasal Verbs)
Total: 10 points—1 point per item

2. a
3. b
4. a
5. a
6. c
7. a
8. a
9. c
10. b
11. a
12. a
13. a
14. a
15. a

VI. (Unit 15: Phrasal Verbs)
Total: 10 points—1 point per item

2. come up with
3. set aside
4. was familiar with
5. found out
6. insisted on
7. run . . . by
8. turned down
9. ran out of
10. wait for
11. show . . . off

VII. (Unit 15: Phrasal Verbs)
Total: 5 points—1 point per item

2. put it off
3. showing it off
4. figured them out
5. open them up
6. break them up

VIII. (Unit 15: Phrasal Verbs)
Total: 9 points—1 point per item

(How to Get Your Girlfriend or
Boyfriend to Break Up ^with You)

* Never be concerned ^about his or her feelings.
* Never give ~~up~~ ^in to him or her when making plans. Always insist ~~for~~ ^on doing whatever you want to do. Alternatively, make plans without running ~~it~~ ^them by him or her.
* Always show up ^for dates at least half an hour late.
* Always show off ~~of~~ when you are in public together. Whenever he or she starts to say something, cut ~~off him or her~~ ^him or her off.
* Forget ~~his or her birthday about~~ ^about his or her birthday.
* Start a rumor that you are going out ^with someone else.

IX. (Units 14–15: Synthesis)
Total: 15 points—1 point per item

2. B
3. C
4. C
5. D
6. C
7. C
8. D
9. B
10. C
11. C
12. C
13. C
14. A
15. C
16. D

X. (Units 14–15: Synthesis)
Total: 10 points—1 point per item

2. D
3. A
4. D
5. D
6. D
7. D
8. C
9. D
10. C
11. B

PART VII

Diagnostic Test

I. (Unit 16: Gerunds)
Total: 5 points—1 point per item

2. watching
3. Quitting
4. skiing
5. having
6. exercising

II. (Unit 16: Gerunds)
Total: 5 points—1 point per item

2. our sitting down and discussing
3. John's having
4. my getting
5. teacher's insisting
6. parents' having

III. (Unit 16: Gerunds)
Total: 5 points—1 point per item

2. having earned
3. having perceived
4. having gone
5. having had
6. having written

IV. (Unit 16: Gerunds)
Total: 5 points—1 point per item

2. Getting accepted
3. being chosen
4. getting infected
5. getting struck
6. Being invited

V. (Unit 17: Infinitives)
Total: 5 points—1 point per item

2. not to talk
3. To enjoy
4. to help
5. To know
6. to be

VI. (Unit 17: Infinitives)
Total: 5 points—1 point per item

2. to have submitted
3. to have mastered
4. to have written
5. to have escaped
6. to have fiddled

VII. (Unit 17: Infinitives)
Total: 5 points—1 point per item

2. to get elected
3. To be given
4. to get hired
5. to be treated
6. to be rewritten

VIII. (Unit 17: Infinitives)
Total: 10 points—1 point per item

2. He certainly ought to go on a diet.
3. I didn't have time to mop the floors.
4. They're planning to buy a new house in October.
5. I'd love to go camping this weekend.
6. He has to register for the selective service.

IX. (Units 16–17: Synthesis)
Total: 7 points—1 point per item

2. going
3. becoming
4. to review
5. not to dress
6. to be
7. getting
8. having gotten

X. (Units 16–17: Synthesis)
Total: 19 points—1 point per item

2. to spend
3. kayaking
4. going
5. kayaking
6. to learn
7. to be
8. to use
9. to have
10. to maneuver
11. paddling
12. getting
13. kayaking / to kayak
14. to try
15. to bring
16. wearing
17. to get
18. bringing
19. to take
20. to leave

XI. (Units 16–17: Synthesis)
Total: 14 points—1 point per item

2. B
3. A
4. C
5. C
6. C
7. A
8. C
9. D
10. A
11. C
12. A
13. C
14. B
15. D

XII. (Units 16–17: Synthesis)
Total: 15 points—1 point per item

2. B
3. A
4. B
5. B
6. D
7. B
8. B
9. B
10. C
11. B
12. B
13. B
14. D
15. C
16. B

PART VII

Final Test

I. (Unit 16: Gerunds)
Total: 5 points—1 point per item

2. eating
3. fixing
4. smoking
5. Quitting
6. Tipping

II. (Unit 16: Gerunds)
Total: 5 points—1 point per item

2. my needing
3. Mrs. Martin's having
4. parents' having
5. their trying
6. Doris's having

III. (Unit 16: Gerunds)
Total: 5 points—1 point per item

2. having led
3. having warned
4. having signed
5. having recognized
6. having gotten

IV. (Unit 16: Gerunds)
Total: 5 points—1 point per item

2. getting cheated
3. Being selected
4. getting hit
5. being given
6. Getting nominated

V. (Unit 17: Infinitives)
Total: 5 points—1 point per item

2. To appreciate
3. to make
4. to learn
5. not to turn in
6. To live

VI. (Unit 17: Infinitives)
Total: 5 points—1 point per item

2. to have developed
3. to have hit
4. to have said
5. to have been
6. to have signed

VII. (Unit 17: Infinitives)
Total: 5 points—1 point per item

2. to be taken
3. to be reroofed
4. to be considered
5. to get invited
6. To be given

VIII. (Unit 17: Infinitives)
Total: 10 points—1 point per item

2. I'd like to come to the card party on Saturday
3. She has to pay child support.
4. I don't want to go to the movies tonight.
5. He ought to start working out.
6. I didn't have time to mow the lawn.

IX. (Units 16–17: Synthesis)
Total: 7 points—1 point per item

2. working
3. to go
4. to get
5. not to smoke
6. to be
7. getting
8. having received

X. (Units 16–17: Synthesis)
Total: 19 points—1 point per item

2. to find out
3. having
4. to eat
5. going
6. to take
7. sampling
8. eating
9. to diet
10. trying
11. paying
12. ordering
13. to serve
14. to go
15. to spend
16. to go
17. to change
18. to be
19. to take
20. to drive

XI. (Units 16–17: Synthesis)
Total: 14 points—1 point per item

2. A
3. A
4. C
5. B
6. D
7. B
8. D
9. D
10. B
11. C
12. B
13. A
14. A
15. C

XII. (Units 16–17: Synthesis)
Total: 15 points—1 point per item

2. B
3. A
4. B
5. B
6. C
7. A
8. C
9. C
10. C
11. D
12. A
13. A
14. D
15. C
15. A

PART VIII

Diagnostic Test

I. (Unit 18: Adverb Clauses)
Total: 5 points—1 point per item

2. <u>Wherever there is poverty,</u> there is the potential for strife. (place)
3. Elena is such a good cook <u>that she could get a job in a world-class restaurant.</u> (result)
4. <u>Even though you made a few mistakes in calculation,</u> you passed the exam with a score of 88 percent. (contrast)
5. I learned more in my high school Spanish class <u>than I did in any college course.</u> (comparison)
6. You'll pass the course <u>if you pass the final exam.</u> (condition)

II. (Unit 18: Adverb Clauses)
Total: 10 points—2 points per item

2. Joyce has been successful in her small business because she works hard and keeps excellent records.
3. You'll be able to reduce your mortgage payment if you make a large down payment.
4. Whenever I ignore my inner voice, I go wrong.
5. Unless you make a payment this week, we'll have to send your account to a collection agency.
6. Frank did so well on the advanced placement biology test that he earned college credit.

III. (Unit 19: Adverbs: Viewpoint, Focus, Negative, Location, and Sequence)
Total: 16 points—2 points per item

2. here (location)
3. On no account (negative)
4. certainly (viewpoint)
5. even (focus)
6. Unfortunately (viewpoint)
7. almost (focus)
8. only (focus)
9. Rarely (negative)

IV. (Unit 19: Adverbs: Viewpoint, Focus, Negative, Location, and Sequence)

Total: 15 points—1 point per item

2. Apparently
3. is not at all
4. Actually
5. The dictionary clearly
6. does cloning occur
7. even occur
8. came the technology
9. only thing that's new
10. is
11. perhaps it will
12. Maybe it will
13. even
14. will it
15. almost certinly won't
16. surely

V. (Unit 20: Discourse Connectors)

Total: 4 points—1 point per item

2. nor   3. so   4. and   5. so

VI. (Unit 20: Discourse Connectors)

Total: 5 points—1 point per item

2. however   5. Second
3. Also   6. For example
4. Therefore

VII. (Unit 20: Discourse Connectors)

Total: 6 points—1 point per item

2. vegetables, nor   6. housework, and
3. March; however   7. assignments;
4. colors, though   therefore
5. house; otherwise

VIII. (Unit 21: Adverb Phrases)

Total: 5 points—1 point per item

2. To remember people's names
3. having already wiped out smallpox
4. by talking with my next-door neighbor
5. Given the choice between watching a video or going out to a theater
6. while visiting a nursing home last month

IX. (Unit 21: Adverb Phrases)

Total: 8 points—2 points per item

2. You can improve your English by listening to the radio
3. While vacationing alone in the mountains, Millie decided what she wanted as a career.
4. Having earned his bachelor's degree, Jonah was eager to enter the world of work.
5. Presented with attractive job prospects, most people will take the one that offers long-term stability.

X. (Units 18–21: Synthesis)

Total: 12 points—1 point per item

2. D	7. C	12. D
3. A	8. B	13. D
4. A	9. A	14. B
5. C	10. A	15. B
6. C	11. C	16. A

XI. (Units 18–21: Synthesis)

Total: 9 points—1 point per item

2. B	5. D	8. D
3. B	6. C	9. B
4. B	7. C	10. D

PART VIII

Final Test

I. (Unit 18: Adverb Clauses)

Total: 10 points—2 points per item

2. We can leave <u>as soon as the babysitter gets here</u>. (time)
3. <u>Whenever I feel afraid</u>, I sing a song at the top of my lungs. (time)
4. Esther is such a good swimmer <u>that she could be on the Olympic team</u>. (result)
5. <u>Although Shari's Spanish accent isn't perfect</u>, she's certainly fluent in the language. (contrast)
6. I learned more about gardening from my Uncle Joe <u>than I ever did in my master gardener class</u>. (comparison)

II. (Unit 18: Adverb Clauses)
Total: 10 points—2 points per item

2. Melanie is a successful student because she listens in class and takes excellent notes.
3. I'll be able to go on the picnic with you if I can get the afternoon off.
4. When I go to San Francisco, I ride the cable cars
5. The strike won't be settled anytime soon unless both sides make some concessions.
6. Kathy speaks so quietly that we can't hear her.

III. (Unit 19: Adverbs: Viewpoint, Focus, Negative, Location, and Sequence)
Total: 16 points—2 points per item

2. Apparently (viewpoint)
3. There (location)
4. only (focus)
5. Along (sequence)
6. only (focus)
7. certainly (viewpoint)
8. Little (negative)
9. Fortunately (viewpoint)

IV. (Unit 19: Adverbs: Viewpoint, Focus, Negative, Location, and Sequence)
Total: 15 points—1 point per item

2. totally
3. just had
4. is completely
5. to genetic programming at all
6. Basically
7. only an
8. even become
9. almost certainly
10. I just
11. Unfortunately, some
12. surely cash in
13. even
14. certainly not the society we
15. do most
16. only hope

V. (Unit 20: Discourse Connectors)
Total 4 points—1 point per item

2. and 3. so 4. but 5. so

VI. (Unit 20: Discourse Connectors)
Total: 5 points—1 point per item

2. however
3. Therefore
4. Also
5. Second
6. for instance

VII. (Unit 20: Discourse Connectors)
Total: 6 points—1 point per item

2. period; therefore
3. unopened, so
4. cat, but
5. school, nor
6. birthday; however
7. on time, though
8. mail; otherwise

VIII. (Unit 21: Adverb Phrases)
Total: 5 points—1 point per item

2. Gazing up at the sky on a warm August night,
3. having already seen it three times.
4. by following the instructions in my *Mr. Fixit Encyclopedia.*
5. Offered the choice between rafting on the Colorado and sunbathing in Hawaii,
6. while talking with my son's math teacher.

IX. (Unit 21: Adverb Phrases)
Total: 8 points—2 points per item

2. While digging for treasure in the back yard, Johnny unearthed a large bone.
3. Feeling the need to get in touch with nature, Lily enrolled in an Outward Bound course.
4. You can save money on groceries by purchasing many products in bulk.
5. Having been very successful at the state level, the governor decided to run for the presidency.

X. (Units 18–21: Synthesis)
Total: 12 points—1 point per item

2. C	6. B	10. B
3. A	7. B	11. A
4. A	8. C	12. C
5. C	9. A	13. C

XI. (Units 18–21: Synthesis)
Total: 9 points—1 point per item

2. B	5. B	8. C
3. D	6. B	9. A
4. B	7. B	10. D

Part IX

Diagnostic Test

I. **(Unit 22: Noun Clauses: Subjects and Objects)**
Total: 9 points—1 point per item

2. what we're going to do to solve the problem
3. Whatever you would like to do tonight
4. The fact that she returned your call
5. Whoever isn't ready to go right on to college
6. that Mary get this message today
7. whomever you like
8. However you want to handle this problem
9. that Jim needs to take some time off from work
10. if I take notes during our conversation

II. **(Unit 22: Noun Clauses: Subjects and Objects)**
Total: 7 points—1 point per item

2. whoever	5. what	8. the fact
3. However	6. whomever	that
4. It	7. whichever	

III. **(Unit 22: Noun Clauses: Subjects and Objects)**
Total: 10 points—2 points per item

2. where she will be attending college
3. that you don't like her
4. The fact that you have a good credit rating
5. However you want to arrange the financing
6. whatever we can

IV. **(Unit 22: Noun Clauses: Subjects and Objects)**
Total: 6 points—2 points per item

2. I'm not sure whether or not he's coming to the party / whether he's coming to the party or not.
3. Did you find out if the plane has landed yet?
4. Did you decide whether or not it's a good idea / whether it's a good idea or not?

V. **(Unit 22: Noun Clauses: Subjects and Objects)**
Total: 8 points—2 points per item

2. The fact that you passed the final exam
3. the fact that I wasn't ready for college
4. the fact that the house wasn't in perfect condition
5. the fact that people weren't protected from most diseases

VI. **(Unit 23: Noun Clauses and Phrases: Complements)**
Total: 8 points—2 points per item

2. It's clear that Bob doesn't understand your point of view.
3. It appears likely that the governor will not support our position.
4. It is wonderful that our son is marrying such a kind person.
5. It seems possible that my daughter will be the class valedictorian.

VII. **(Unit 23: Noun Clauses and Phrases: Complements)**
Total: 8 points—2 points per item

2. Is it advisable that Mary be present for the meeting?
3. It's important that we attend our daughter's wedding.
4. It's necessary that you make a payment on your loan.
5. It's crucial that the principal have all the facts about the incident.

VIII. **(Unit 23: Noun Clauses and Phrases: Complements)**
Total: 6 points—2 points per item

2. It was difficult for Glen to make friends as a child.
3. It will be mandatory for all passengers to wear seat belts once this law is passed.
4. It is unusual for Robin to be late.

IX. (Unit 23: Noun Clauses and Phrases: Complements)
Total: 15 points—3 points per item

2. (a) That people choose friends with similar interests is not uncommon.
3. (c) That we analyze each situation carefully before making a decision is essential.
4. (f) That people take advantage of opportunities while they're available is necessary.
5. (d) That we judge things by their real value rather than their apparent value is desirable.
6. (b) That people not assume things will happen until they happen is vital.

X. (Units 22–23: Synthesis)
Total 14 points—1 point per item

2. C	7. C	12. A
3. C	8. D	13. D
4. D	9. A	14. D
5. D	10. A	15. C
6. C	11. D	

XI. (Units 22–23: Synthesis)
Total 9 points—1 point per item

2. B	5. C	8. D
3. A	6. B	9. B
4. B	7. C	10. D

PART IX

Final Test

I. (Unit 22: Noun Clauses: Subjects and Objects)
Total: 9 points—1 point per item

2. what we're going to do to get them to pay us
3. Whatever you want to bring to the pot luck dinner
4. The fact that he came to your defense
5. Whoever wants to live healthily
6. that Phil get treatment for that burn immediately
7. whomever you want
8. However you want to arrange the sale
9. that the administration should give top priority to passing health-care legislation
10. if the mail has come yet

II. (Unit 22: Noun Clauses: Subjects and Objects)
Total: 7 points—1 point per item

2. However	5. whomever	7. the fact
3. It	6. whichever	that
4. what		8. What

III. (Unit 22: Noun Clauses: Subjects and Objects)
Total: 10 points—2 points per item

2. where he wants to work this summer
3. that you're a bad influence on her daughter
4. The fact that you have excellent faculty recommendations
5. However you want me to pay you
6. whatever it can

IV. (Unit 22: Noun Clauses: Subjects and Objects)
Total: 6 points—2 points per item

2. I'm not certain whether or not the Joneses plan to join us in this venture / whether the Joneses plan to join us in this venture or not.
3. Did Hal find out if he's been accepted at the university?
4. Have you decided whether or not you want to come along / whether you want to come along or not?

V. (Unit 22: Noun Clauses: Subjects and Objects)
Total: 8 points—2 point per item

2. The fact that you went out of your way to help
3. the fact that Sarah didn't like working here
4. the fact that there were only two channels
5. the fact that most things were new and unspoiled

VI. (Unit 23: Noun Clauses and Phrases: Complements)
Total: 8 points—2 points per item

2. It's clear that the job doesn't pay enough.
3. It appears likely that the senator is going to be reelected.
4. It is wonderful that my short story has been accepted for publication.
5. It seems possible that the Wrights are going to be our new neighbors.

VII. (Unit 23: Noun Clauses and Phrases: Complements)
Total: 8 points—2 points per item

2. It's important that you listen to your children
3. Is it necessary that I be in court to testify?
4. It's crucial that the investigators have all the information on the accident.
5. It is essential that Amanda seek professional help.

VIII. (Unit 23: Noun Clauses and Phrases: Complements)
Total: 6 points—2 points per item

2. It was difficult for Ludmilla to communicate when she first came to this country.
3. It will be mandatory for all employees to submit written requests for vacation days effective January 1.
4. It is not unusual for Tony to forget things.

IX. (Unit 23: Noun Clauses and Phrases: Complements)
Total: 15 points—3 points per item

2. (f) That many similar things happen at the same time is not uncommon.
3. (d) That we not exaggerate the importance of a problem is desirable.
4. (a) That people pursue their dreams in order to make them come true is necessary.
5. (e) That we be frugal in our use of material goods is important.
6. (b) That people think carefully about the consequences of their actions is vital.

X. (Units 22–23: Synthesis)
Total: 14 points—1 point per item

2. B	7. A	12. C
3. B	8. D	13. A
4. B	9. B	14. A
5. D	10. D	15. B
6. B	11. D	

XI. (Units 22–23: Synthesis)
Total: 9 points—1 point per item

2. C	5. C	8. A
3. C	6. C	9. A
4. C	7. C	10. B

PART X

Diagnostic Test

I. (Unit 24: Unreal Conditionals and Other Ways to Express Unreality)
Total: 9 points—1 point per item

2. R	5. U	8. U
3. R	6. R	9. R
4. R	7. U	10. U

II. (Unit 24: Unreal Conditionals and Other Ways to Express Unreality)
Total: 12 points—2 points per item

2. You probably would have gotten the job if you'd arrived on time to the interview.
3. If she hadn't been wearing her seat belt, she could have been badly injured.
4. Mort would be more credible if he didn't exaggerate so much.
5. We might never have gotten to know each other if we hadn't gone to that party.
6. If we didn't live in an apartment, we would get a dog.
7. If Ken were less shy, he would go to parties more often.

III. (Unit 24: Unreal Conditionals and Other Ways to Express Unreality)
Total: 12 points—2 point per item

2. Joe wishes (that) he'd gone to college.
3. I wish (that) we could get together more often.
4. Cynthia hopes (that) she'll be accepted to Columbia University.
5. Jack wishes (that) he hadn't broken off his relationship with Barbara.
6. Mike and Kelly hope (that) their son gets a good job.
7. I wish (that) I could afford a trip to Europe next summer.

IV. (Unit 25: The Subjunctive: Inverted and Implied Conditionals)

Total: 10 points—2 points per item

2. Were I to offer you a job, would you take it?
3. Should you return before Tuesday, give me a call.
4. I wouldn't have invested in that company had I known anything about its track record.
5. We'd need a strong indication that you could pay us back were we to lend you the money.
6. Please notify the registrar in writing should you want to drop a course.

V. (Unit 25: The Subjunctive: Inverted and Implied Conditionals)

Total: 4 points—1 point per item

2. With
3. Without
4. Otherwise
5. If so

VI. (Unit 25: The Subjunctive: Inverted and Implied Conditionals)

Total: 10 points—2 points per item

2. I move that the motion be accepted.
3. I insist that Marie be present at the meeting.
4. My broker is suggesting that I sell the property.
5. We recommend that you consider sending Wayne to a private school.
6. It is essential that you fill out this form completely.

VII. (Units 24–25: Synthesis)

Total: 7 points—1 point per item

2. told
3. were
4. had
5. hadn't
6. got
7. didn't talk
8. were

VIII. (Units 24–25: Synthesis)

Total: 11 points—1 point per item

2. tell
3. as though
4. finds
5. What if
6. Had
7. would
8. hope
9. speak
10. has done
11. were
12. What if

IX. (Units 24–25: Synthesis)

Total: 15 points—1 point per item

2. B	7. B	12. B
3. C	8. B	13. C
4. A	9. A	14. D
5. B	10. B	15. A
6. A	11. C	16. D

X. (Units 24–25: Synthesis)

Total: 10 points—1 point per item

2. A	6. A	9. B
3. D	7. C	10. B
4. C	8. B	11. A
5. A		

PART X

Final Test

I. (Unit 24: Unreal Conditionals and Other Ways to Express Unreality)

Total: 9 points—1 point per item

2. R	5. U	8. U
3. R	6. R	9. R
4. R	7. U	10. U

II. (Unit 24: Unreal Conditionals and Other Ways to Express Unreality)

Total: 12 points—2 points per item

2. Sally probably would have been accepted by the university if she'd applied on time.
3. If Josh hadn't been wearing his life preserver, he could have drowned.
4. Eve would be more popular if she didn't talk about herself so much.
5. They might never have gotten married if they hadn't bumped into each other on the bus.
6. If I weren't paying so much money on credit cards, I could afford a nicer apartment.
7. If Tom weren't so tired, he'd go out with us tonight.

III. (Unit 24: Unreal Conditionals and Other Ways to Express Unreality)
Total: 12 points—2 points per item

2. Chuck wishes (that) he hadn't spent all his money.
3. I wish (that) you lived closer to us.
4. Doug hopes (that) his loan will be approved.
5. Gary wishes (that) he hadn't sold the house on Maple Street.
6. Gerry and Hilda hope (that) Hugh makes the right decision.
7. Eric wishes (that) Mrs. Graham would come back and teach his class next year.

IV. (Unit 25: The Subjunctive: Inverted and Implied Conditionals)
Total: 10 points—2 points per item

2. Were I to tell you something confidential, could you keep it a secret?
3. Should the package arrive before I get back, please sign for it.
4. I'd never have asked Albert to do this had I known he would fall apart.
5. We would need a recommendation from your former boss were we to offer you a position.
6. Please contact our customer service department should you have any questions.

V. (Unit 25: The Subjunctive: Inverted and Implied Conditionals)
Total: 4 points—1 point per item

2. With
3. Without
4. Otherwise
5. If so

VI. (Unit 25: The Subjunctive: Inverted and Implied Conditionals)
Total: 10 points—2 points per item

2. I move that the motion be tabled.
3. The Illyrian government is demanding that the Redonian government withdraw its troops.
4. My doctor suggests that I exercise three times a week.
5. I recommend that you take some time off from work.
6. It is required that all employees submit to a medical examination

VII. (Units 24–25: Synthesis)
Total: 7 points—1 point per item

2. offered
3. were
4. had
5. had
6. were leaving
7. didn't go into
8. were

VIII. (Units 24–25: Synthesis)
Total: 11 points—1 point per item

2. Had
3. would have had
4. were
5. feel
6. can
7. told
8. called
9. feels
10. learn
11. What if
12. check

IX. (Units 24–25: Synthesis)
Total: 15 points—1 point per item

2. C
3. A
4. D
5. B
6. D
7. C
8. A
9. C
10. C
11. C
12. A
13. D
14. B
15. A
16. B

X. (Units 24–25: Synthesis)
Total: 10 points—1 point per item

2. A
3. A
4. C
5. A
6. A
7. C
8. B
9. B
10. B
11. D

TESTS

PART I TENSE AND TIME

DIAGNOSTIC TEST

(Note: In your answers, use contractions with pronoun subjects whenever possible.)

I. PRESENT AND FUTURE TIME

Complete the e-mail message with the correct forms of the verbs in parentheses.

Hi, Mona!

I __'ve been studying__ all afternoon, and I _____ until midnight because I
    1. (study)   **2. (study)**

_____ a huge exam at 8:00 tomorrow morning. I _____ a break, though,
  3. (have)   **4. (need)**

so I _____ you this note.
     5. (write)

     Can you believe that by the end of this month, I _____ here for an entire year?
                                                    6. (be)

I _____ I _____ a party next weekend to celebrate.
   7. (think)   **8. (throw)**

   I _____ to invite some people over, but I _____ any free time since
     9. (want)   **10. (not have)**

the start of the term.

     Well, it _____ time to say goodbye. If I _____ a spare moment,
                11. (be)   **12. (find)**

I _____ you tomorrow when I _____ home from my exam.
  13. (call)   **14. (get)**

Take care,

Jason

II. PRESENT AND FUTURE TIME

Jason has decided to have his party on Saturday night. He's calling friends to invite them. Complete Jason's conversation with the correct forms of the verbs in parentheses.

JASON: Hi, Ana. This is Jason. I _____**'m having**_____ a party on Saturday night. Can you come?
                                      1. (have)

ANA: Hi, Jay! Sure, I'd love to. What should I bring? I _____ some chocolate chip
                                               2. (make)

cookies. In fact, I'm about to put them in the oven now. _____ you

_____ me to bring some?
  3. (want)

JASON: Yes, that would be great. I _____ homemade cookies in ages.
                                              4. (not have)

ANA: And what time _____ everybody _____ to your house?
                                                            5. (get)

JASON: Around 8:00.

ANA: Is it OK if Gina _____ with me? I think she _____ homesick
                              6. (come)   7. (feel)

these days. I heard her crying the other day, and you know Gina: She never

_____ .
8. (cry)

JASON: Really? That's too bad. Yes! Bring her. A party is just what she _____ . Alan
                                                                                  9. (need)

_____ his CD collection, so we _____ . We _____ a
10. (bring)   11. (dance)   12. (have)

great time.

III. PAST TIME

Complete the phone conversation with the correct past forms of the indicated verbs.

A: Hello?

B: Hi, Barb. It's me, Luis.

A: Luis! How are you? Long time no see!

B: That's true. I ___'ve missed___ you. You sound happy. What's new with you?
                          1. (miss)

A: Well, the term _____ two weeks ago and I just _____ my grades.
                            2. (end)   3. (get)

B: How _____ you _____ ?
                              4. (do)

A: Much better than I _____ I would. I _____ sure I _____
                              5. (think)   6. (be)   7. (fail)

anthropology because I _____ really badly on the first exam. You know,
                              8. (do)

I _____ harder for that course than I _____ in my entire life.
      9. (study)   10. (study)

B: And it _____ ?
                11. (pay off)

A: For sure. I'm very proud of my grade. I got a B+!

B: So, what _____ you _____ when I _____ you?
                                  12. (do)   13. (call)

A: I _____ going to Mel's Diner for lunch. Do you want to go?
          14. (think about)

B: Great idea. I'll meet you there in fifteen minutes.

IV. PAST TIME

Complete the interview. Use would *or* used to *and the correct form of* be, come, go, have, live, *or* meet. *Use* would *when possible.*

REPORTER: Today we're talking to people on the street. Excuse me, ma'am. Do you have a minute?

INTERVIEWEE: Certainly.

REPORTER: Have you lived here long?

INTERVIEWEE: No, I haven't. I've been here for just over a year.

REPORTER: Where _____did_____ you _____use to live_____ ?

　　　　　　　　　　　　　　　　　　　　　1.

INTERVIEWEE: I _____ in Asbury Park, New Jersey.

　　　　　　　2.

REPORTER: Oh, I know Asbury Park. When I was a little girl, my family _____ there

　　　　　　　　　　　　　　　　　　　　　　　　　　　　　　　　　　　3.

every summer. We _____ a house near the beach. My father

　　　　　　　　　4.

_____ back and forth between Asbury Park and the city, spending the

　　　5.

weekends with us and going back to the city to work during the week. My mom and I

_____ him at the train station every Friday. Then, on Sunday night, he

　　6.

_____ back to the city. We _____ to the station and wave

　　7.　　　　　　　　　　　　　　　　　　　8.

good-bye. . . . Oh, I'm sorry. This interview was supposed to be about you.

INTERVIEWEE: That's OK. Your story is very interesting. I remember that Asbury Park

_____ a favorite vacation town for people living in the city. My grand-

　　9.

parents _____ a small grocery store. Folks from New York City

　　　　　　10.

_____ into the store and keep them busy all summer long.

　　11.

V. PAST TIME

A year ago, when Carl was preparing to spend a year in Africa, he wrote about his plans and expectations. It's a year later. Some of them came true, and some didn't. He's telling a friend about his experiences. Write the first part of Carl's sentences. Use the future-in-the-past constructions: was/were going to *or* would + *verb.*

Before the Trip

1. I'm positive that I'm going to climb to the top of Mount Kilimanjaro.
2. I'm sure that I'll learn to speak Swahili fluently.
3. I expect that I'll make a lot of new friends.
4. I don't think I'll have time to visit South Africa.
5. I'm not going to spend a lot of money.

After the Trip

1. ___I was positive that I was going to climb to the top of Mount Kilimanjaro,___ but I didn't.

2. _____ and I did.

3. _____ and I did.

4. _____ but I did.

5. _____ and I didn't.

VI.   PAST, PRESENT, AND FUTURE

Circle the most appropriate forms to complete the conversation.

ALAN: Did you see /(Have you seen) Gina lately?
1.

STACY: Well, I haven't seen / I hadn't seen her in ages, but I ran into / I was running into
2.   **3.**

her yesterday at the gym.

ALAN: Did she seem / Was she seeming okay to you? She was / She's being really distant these days.
4.   **5.**

STACY: I'm thinking / I think she's / she's being homesick.
6.   **7.**

ALAN: Yes, I guess she never has thought / thought that she's / she was going to miss Italy so
8.   **9.**

much. She just hasn't gotten / been getting used to living in the States.
10.

STACY: Also, she and Jim Carson saw / were seeing each other for a while, but they
11.

broke up / were breaking up up last week.
12.

ALAN: Oh, no. Poor Gina. Well, I'm having / I'll have dinner with some friends Friday night.
13.

Maybe I'm going to / I'll invite her to come along.
14.

STACY: She'll be / She's being glad to hear from you. You'll be having / You'll have fun together.
15.   **16.**

VII.   PAST, PRESENT, AND FUTURE

Read Gina Borrelli's diary entry. Find and correct the twelve errors in verb usage.

February 3

Dear Diary,

      've been feeling

I felt very homesick lately, but I've made an important decision last night: The time has been coming

to stop moping around! I'm here in the United States, and I'm needing to take advantage of this

wonderful opportunity. I've always been making friends easily, and I've met some terrific people since

I get here. From now on, I will make more of an effort to enjoy life. In fact, a really nice guy named

2. We stayed in _____ hotel. A B C D

(A) an interesting Victorian old
(B) a Victorian old interesting
(C) an old interesting Victorian
(D) an interesting old Victorian

3. My brother has a _____ car. A B C D

(A) ten year-old
(B) ten-year-old
(C) ten-years-old
(D) ten-year old

4. _____ my sisters live in Paris. A B C D

(A) Both of
(B) Either of
(C) Either
(D) Some

5. We asked the teacher to give us _____. A B C D

(A) example
(B) an example
(C) the example
(D) a example

6. This soup is missing something. Maybe we should add _____ salt. A B C D

(A) little
(B) a little
(C) few
(D) a few

7. Ouch! There's _____ sand in my eye. A B C D

(A) speck
(B) a speck
(C) speck of
(D) a speck of

8. Many people enjoy _____. A B C D

(A) ballroom-dancing
(B) a ballroom dancing
(C) ballroom dancing
(D) the ballroom dancing

9. _____ is now a global problem. A B C D

(A) Air pollution
(B) Air-pollution
(C) The air pollution
(D) An air pollution

10. I just bought _____ kimono. A B C D

(A) an old unusual Japanese silk
(B) an unusual old Japanese silk
(C) an old Japanese unusual silk
(D) an old silk unusual Japanese

11. Frank is selling tickets to the _____ ball. A B C D

(A) eleventh annual fireman's
(B) annual eleventh fireman's
(C) fireman's eleventh annual
(D) fireman's annual eleventh

12. _____ agree with the president's decision. A B C D

(A) Half of the voters
(B) Half of voters
(C) The half voters
(D) The half of the voters

13. The robber was wearing _____ trenchcoat. A B C D

(A) a tattered old black wool
(B) an old tattered black wool
(C) a black old tattered wool
(D) a black wool tattered old

XI. SYNTHESIS

Each sentence has four underlined words or phrases. The four underlined parts of the sentence are marked A, B, C, and D. Circle the letter of the ONE underlined part that is NOT CORRECT.

1. <u>A couple of people</u> told me <u>an interesting</u> <u>news</u> yesterday: Jeff is running   A Ⓑ C D
       A   B   C
   for <u>Parliament</u>!
       D

2. There is <u>a loaf bread</u>, <u>fried chicken</u>, and <u>some lemonade</u> on <u>the table</u>.   A B C D
          A   B   C   D

3. <u>The Joneses</u> say <u>that old big Cadillac</u> has been <u>a wonderful car</u> to drive   A B C D
      A   B   C
   in <u>the city</u>.
       D

4. <u>People</u> all around <u>the world</u> signed <u>a petition</u> to save <u>a whale</u>.   A B C D
      A   B   C   D

5. <u>Massive credit-card debt</u> is <u>a</u> <u>late-twentieth-century</u> <u>phenomena</u>.   A B C D
      A   B   C   D

6. <u>A telephone</u> is certainly <u>one of the most significant</u> <u>inventions</u> of <u>all time</u>.   A B C D
      A   B   C   D

7. I failed <u>the</u> <u>final exam</u> in <u>mathematics</u> because of those <u>silly four errors</u>.   A B C D
           A   B   C   D

8. <u>A great many people</u> are not <u>in favor of</u> <u>a cloning</u> for <u>religious reasons</u>.   A B C D
      A   B   C   D

9. <u>The construction</u> of <u>the Babbling Brook Expressway</u> is <u>a</u> <u>ten-years project</u>.   A B C D
      A   B   C   D

10. <u>A great number of</u> <u>people</u> in <u>the country</u> support <u>the gun control</u>.   A B C D
        A   B   C   D

11. After Rudy was in <u>a car accident</u>, he spent <u>four hours</u> in <u>emergency ward</u>   A B C D
                    A   B   C
    of <u>the city hospital</u>.
        D

12. <u>The fastest growing group</u> of <u>computer users</u> in <u>the state</u> are <u>senior citizens</u>.   A B C D
            A   B   C   D

13. <u>Subjects and verbs</u> of <u>the English sentences</u> must agree in <u>number</u> <u>all the time</u>.   A B C D
        A   B   C   D

14. <u>A great many</u> <u>of the students</u> couldn't finish <u>the reading assignment</u> because   A B C D
        A   B   C
    there were <u>many of unfamiliar words</u>.
           D

PART IV ADJECTIVE CLAUSES

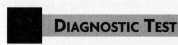

I. ADJECTIVE CLAUSES: REVIEW AND EXPANSION

Underline the adjective clause in each sentence.

1. That funny man <u>who lives on our street</u> is actually a clown in the circus.

2. Phoenix, which is now one of the ten largest cities in the United States, is the home of the Arizona Cardinals.

3. Mrs. Kenton, whom you met at the business luncheon last month, has been appointed vice president of the company.

4. The Canadian city that I find most charming is Toronto.

5. The woman whose dog escaped and chased our cats got a citation from the Animal Control Bureau.

6. The Queen Charlotte Islands, which are located off northern British Columbia, are beautiful and idyllic.

7. I was really impressed by the lady you introduced me to at the party.

8. Adolescence is a time when everything seems to change.

9. Captain Kidd discovered the place where the treasure had been buried.

10. Reiko is always considerate of others, which is what is so endearing about her.

II. ADJECTIVE CLAUSES: REVIEW AND EXPANSION

Complete each sentence with the correct relative pronoun.

1. The man _____who_____ is buying our house is originally from Newfoundland.
   (who / whom)

2. Eritrea, _____ became independent in 1993, is located on the Red Sea.
   (that / which)

3. The person _____ you seem to be referring is not being considered for the job.
   (to whom / to which)

4. The woman _____ son mowed our lawn last week is our block leader.
   (whom / whose)

5. The student _____ has earned the best grade-point average after four years will be named valedictorian.
   (who / which)

6. It may snow this afternoon, _____ you had better wear heavy clothing.
   (in that case / in which case)

III. ADJECTIVE CLAUSES: REVIEW AND EXPANSION

Combine each pair of sentences into one sentence with an independent clause and a dependent adjective clause. Make the second sentence the dependent clause.

1. This is the house. Jack built it.

   This is the house that Jack built.

   _____

2. Mexico City has a population of at least 20 million. It is the largest city in the Western Hemisphere.

   _____

   _____

3. Nancy Armenta is the new assistant to the president. You met her at the Prettos' party.

   _____

   _____

4. The scholarship will be awarded to the student. The student gets the faculty recommendation.

   _____

   _____

5. The man has agreed to take better control of his animals. His dogs have been barking all night.

   _____

   _____

6. The boy is standing over there. We saw him on the train.

   _____

   _____

IV. ADJECTIVE CLAUSES: REVIEW AND EXPANSION

Add commas where necessary.

1. Electronic television‚ which was invented in 1927 by Farnsworth‚ dominated twentieth-century life.
2. The Masons have two daughters. The daughter who lives in California is an oceanographer.
3. The daughter who lives in Costa Rica is a linguist.
4. Joe Morgan whose father has been nominated for the Senate is planning on going into politics himself.
5. Cuneiform writing which was developed by the Sumerians is the oldest known writing system.
6. The company for which Priscilla works is Tucson Tutorials.

V. ADJECTIVE CLAUSES: REVIEW AND EXPANSION

In each sentence, remove the relative pronoun if it is possible to do so.

1. The man who bought my Harley is a collector of motorcycles. *(Pronoun cannot be removed.)*
2. The woman whom you met at the dinner is going to be our new counselor.
3. The company that Jane has been working for is going out of business.
4. This is the house that Jack built.
5. The invention which most changed life in the late twentieth century is the computer.
6. The contestant who wins today's match gets to keep the cash.

VI. ADJECTIVE CLAUSES: REVIEW AND EXPANSION

Read each statement. Then circle the letter of the quotation that is true according to the statement.

1. The speaker has more than one brother.
   a. "My brother, who lives in Cincinnati, is a doctor."
   b. "My brother who lives in Cincinnati is a doctor."

2. Deb has only one math class.
   a. "Deb's math class, which is in the afternoon, is very difficult."
   b. "Deb's math class which is in the afternoon is very difficult."

3. Mike always wears the same pair of shoes to work.
   a. "The shoes, which Mike wears to work, are too tight."
   b. "The shoes which Mike wears to work are too tight."

4. All of the speaker's roommates are from Columbia.
   a. "My roommates, who are from Columbia, are very friendly."
   b. "My roommates who are from Columbia are very friendly."

5. There is only one dentist.
   a. "The dentist who specializes in cosmetic dentistry is on vacation."
   b. "The dentist, who specializes in cosmetic dentistry, is on vacation."

VII. ADJECTIVE CLAUSES WITH QUANTIFIERS; ADJECTIVE PHRASES

Underline the adjective phrase in each sentence.

1. The man <u>in that painting</u> is King Henry the Eighth.
2. All students responsible for this prank will be punished.
3. People interested in obtaining concert tickets may call 555-5555.

4. Certain cities, including Washington, St. Louis, and Cincinnati, have lost professional sports franchises.

5. The woman in that sports car is Jessica's great-aunt Minnie.

6. *Blowup,* starring Vanessa Redgrave and David Hemmings, is based on a short story by Julio Cortázar.

7. Whitehorse, located in the southeastern part of the Yukon, is the territory's capital.

8. A film directed by Steven Spielberg is likely to be a financial success.

9. Guadalajara, the second-largest city in Mexico, has a population of about 3 million.

10. Lasting from 1338 to 1453, the Hundred Years War is one of the longest in human history.

VIII. ADJECTIVE CLAUSES WITH QUANTIFIERS; ADJECTIVE PHRASES

Combine each pair of sentences into one sentence with a dependent adjective clause containing a quantifier. Make the second sentence the dependent clause.

1. Jim Babcock and Roger Alves are local writers. Both of them attended Simon Fraser University.

   <u>Jim Babcock and Roger Alves, both of whom attended Simon Fraser University, are</u>

   <u>local writers.</u>

2. *E.T.* and *Jurassic Park* have been huge financial successes. Both of them were directed by Steven Spielberg.

   _____

   _____

3. The company has proposed two options. Neither of them seems viable.

   _____

   _____

4. The president has been defeated on many pieces of legislation. Several of them have been fundamentally sound.

   _____

   _____

5. Many issues will be debated in the next legislative session. Among them are universal health care and welfare reform.

   _____

   _____

IX. ADJECTIVE CLAUSES WITH QUANTIFIERS; ADJECTIVE PHRASES

Combine each pair of sentences into one sentence with an independent clause and an adjectival modifying phrase. Make the second sentence the adjectival modifying phrase.

1. The cat ate the food. The food was on the counter.

   The cat ate the food on the counter.

2. New Orleans is an exciting city to visit. It is known for its French Quarter.

3. The Mediterranean and Red seas have figured prominently in Middle Eastern history. They are now connected by the Suez Canal.

4. The drama department will put on several classical plays this year. They include *King Lear, Oedipus Rex,* and *Frogs.*

5. We are staying in a cabin. The cabin is on Lake Saratoga.

6. *Casablanca* won the Academy Award for Best Picture in 1942. It starred Humphrey Bogart and Ingrid Bergman.

X. SYNTHESIS

Circle the most appropriate forms to complete the biography.

Peter Sellers, (who)/ which was born in London on September 8, 1925, was an actor

1.

had / who had many talents. His parents, both / both of whom performed onstage, probably

2.   **3.**

influenced his career choice. However, he also created his own opportunities for success. He got a

job working on radio by impersonating two BBC radio stars who / whom were popular at the time

4.

and recommending himself to a BBC producer. Later, he admitted his deception to the producer,

<u>who / which</u> was impressed with his talents. It wasn't long before Sellers got bigger and better roles.
5.

He starred in a new BBC radio show, *Crazy People*, <u>when / which</u> made its debut on May 28, 1951.
6.

The show was a collection of skits <u>where / which</u> allowed Sellers to demonstrate his talents and
7.

gain popularity.

Sellers's first feature film was *Penny Points to Paradise*, <u>produced / producing</u> in 1951. After
8.

performing in several British movies, <u>included / including</u> *London Entertains* and *The Ladykillers*,
9.

Sellers played several characters in the movie *The Mouse That Roared*, <u>that / which</u> was popular in
10.

America as well as Britain. In 1963, he played Inspector Clouseau in the film *The Pink Panther*, a

role <u>for which / in which</u> he became very famous in the four sequels <u>in that / that</u> followed. In 1964,
11.   12.

Sellers played several characters in *Dr. Strangelove*, Stanley Kubrick's tale about a mad general

<u>whose / who</u> launches a nuclear attack against Russia, <u>which / for which</u> he received his first Oscar
13.   14.

nomination. He got his second Oscar nomination for his role in the 1979 movie *Being There*,

<u>where / in which</u> he played Chance, a gardener <u>who / whom</u> is mistaken for a financial genius.
15.   16.

Sellers was still acting in movies when he died on July 24, 1980.

XI. SYNTHESIS

Circle the letter of the correct answer to complete each sentence.

1. Please give these books to the boy _____ is wearing a red T-shirt.   **A Ⓑ C D**

   (A) of whom   (C) whose

   (B) who   (D) which

2. *Whom* is a word _____ people use mainly in formal English.   **A B C D**

   (A) which   (C) for which

   (B) in which   (D) of which

3. *Perfectionists* are people _____ can't accept less than the best.   **A B C D**

   (A) who they   (C) they

   (B) whose   (D) who

4. Ben, _____ parents live in Brooklyn, now lives in Manhattan.   **A B C D**

   (A) which   (C) whom

   (B) who   (D) whose

5. The elevators may not be working, _____ you must use the stairs.   **A B C D**

   (A) in which   (C) in which case

   (B) that   (D) in that case

6. Have you ever lived in a country _____ you couldn't speak the language? A B C D

   (A) that   (C) which

   (B) where   (D) whose

7. Anyone _____ playing volleyball, please sign up here. A B C D

   (A) whose interested in   (C) interested in

   (B) with whom interested in   (D) who interested in

8. *Gigantic*, _____ Ronaldo DiCapio and Kit Winslow, is playing at a A B C D

   theater near you.

   (A) which starring   (C) in which starring

   (B) that starring   (D) starring

9. Each chapter in the textbook has a quiz, the answers _____ can be found A B C D

   at the back of the book.

   (A) for which   (C) where

   (B) which   (D) that which

10. Giselle has fond memories of the day _____ she met her husband. A B C D

   (A) when   (C) which

   (B) where   (D) whom

11. The people _____ the kidnapping have demanded a million dollars in A B C D

   small bills.

   (A) responsible for   (C) which responsible for

   (B) that responsible for   (D) who responsible for

12. Shania Twain is the singer _____ music I like best. A B C D

   (A) who   (C) who's

   (B) whom   (D) whose

XII. SYNTHESIS

Each sentence has four underlined parts or phrases. The four underlined parts of the sentence are marked A, B, C, and D. Circle the letter of the ONE underlined part that is NOT CORRECT.

1. The doctors <u>are examining</u> the dog <u>bit</u> the child for rabies, <u>which</u> is a A (B) C D
            A   **B**   **C**

   dangerous disease <u>requiring</u> immediate treatment.
                D

2. Alice Beardsley, <u>which</u> is the class valedictorian, <u>will attend</u> the Sorbonne, A B C D
           A   **B**

   <u>a famous university</u> <u>located</u> in Paris.
       C   **D**

3. The <u>lady wearing the red dress</u> <u>whom you met</u> <u>her at the party</u> <u>last weekend</u> A B C D
          A   **B**   **C**   **D**

   is Jerry's aunt.

4. The person to <u>whom</u> I was <u>talking to</u> <u>made me an offer</u> I <u>couldn't refuse</u>.
              A   B   C   D   **A B C D**

5. Taiwan, <u>that</u> is an island off the southeast coast of China, <u>used to</u> <u>be called</u>   **A B C D**
            A   B   C

Formosa, <u>meaning</u> "beautiful island" in Portuguese.
          D

6. Charlotte and Jacksonville, <u>both of</u> <u>whom</u> are cities <u>that</u> are in the southern   **A B C D**
                                   A   B   C

United States, <u>are</u> growing metropolitan areas.
              D

7. *The Deer Hunter,* <u>starred</u> Robert De Niro, Meryl Streep, and Christopher   **A B C D**
                       A

Walken, <u>is</u> a movie <u>about the war</u> <u>that occurred</u> in Vietnam.
       B   C   D

8. The realtor <u>with I've been working</u> <u>has found me a house</u> <u>that</u> I can afford,   **A B C D**
                         A   B   C

<u>which</u> is why I'd like to recommend her.
   D

9. The European Union, <u>consisting</u> of several member countries, <u>is</u> a West   **A B C D**
                             A   B

European organization <u>establishing</u> under the Treaty of Rome <u>to compete</u>
                     C   D

with other economic powers.

10. It's possible <u>that</u> it <u>will be</u> very cold today, <u>in that case</u> <u>you'd better wear</u>   **A B C D**
                    A   B   C   D

clothes that are warm.

PART IV ADJECTIVE CLAUSES

FINAL TEST

I. ADJECTIVE CLAUSES: REVIEW AND EXPANSION

Underline the adjective clause in each sentence.

1. That amusing woman <u>who won the singing contest</u> is Jeffrey's grandmother.

2. Toronto, which is the largest metropolitan area in Canada, is the home of the American League Blue Jays.

3. Lane Akimura, whom the governor just appointed his press secretary, is the former administrator of the city zoo.

4. The Mexican city that I find most beautiful is Guanajuato.

5. The man whose pet raccoons have been raiding our garbage cans has agreed to give his pets to the zoo.

6. Guadeloupe and Martinique, which are two islands located in the West Indies, are both part of the French Republic.

7. Jennifer was really amused by that fellow we met on the train to Stockholm.

8. This reversal comes at a time when our company is financially strapped for funds.

9. The archeologists discovered the place where the original village stood.

10. Curtis will never be serious, which is what is so irritating about him.

II. ADJECTIVE CLAUSES: REVIEW AND EXPANSION

Complete each sentence with the correct relative pronoun.

1. The family _____who_____ is moving in next door is originally from New Brunswick.
   (who / whom)

2. Greenland, _____ is a self-governing possession of Denmark, is the largest island
   (that / which)
   in the world.

3. The administrator _____ you were referring has resigned from the school system.
   (to whom / to which)

4. The dog _____ owners are out of town was picked up by the dogcatcher.
   (whom / whose)

5. The contestant _____ has won the most cash after five days will retire as a
   (who / which)
   champion.

6. Lines to get into the movie are supposed to be long, _____ you had better take
   (in that case / in which case)
   along a book to read.

III. ADJECTIVE CLAUSES: REVIEW AND EXPANSION

Combine each pair of sentences into one sentence with an independent clause and a dependent adjective clause. Make the second sentence the dependent clause.

1. This is the rat. The cat ate it.

   This is the rat (that) the cat ate. _____

   _____

2. São Paulo is also the largest city in South America. It is the largest city in Brazil.

   _____

   _____

3. Peter Glisson is the new assistant to the dean. We ran into him at the picnic.

   _____

   _____

4. The scholarship will likely be given to the candidate. The candidate gets the committee's recommendation.

   _____

   _____

5. The woman has agreed to keep her pets indoors. Her cats have been stealing fish from our pond.

   _____

   _____

6. The little girl is eating a lollipop. We saw her at the park.

   _____

   _____

IV. ADJECTIVE CLAUSES: REVIEW AND EXPANSION

Add commas where necessary.

1. The wheel, which was invented thousands of years ago, is one of the most significant inventions of all time.

2. The Jacksons have two sons. The son who lives on Prince Edward Island writes novels for a living.

3. The son who lives in Bermuda does genetic research.

4. Theresa Tafoya whose grandmother was also a well-known artist has a painting on exhibit in the Museum of Contemporary Art.

5. *Don Quixote* which was written by Miguel de Cervantes is considered one of the world's greatest novels.

6. The company to which Henry applied has gone out of business.

V. ADJECTIVE CLAUSES: REVIEW AND EXPANSION

In each sentence, remove the relative pronoun if it is possible to do so.

1. The composer who wrote that song has won several Grammy awards. (Pronoun cannot be removed.)
2. The woman whom we were introduced to at the office party is going to be the new boss.
3. The neighborhood that we've been living in is becoming rundown.
4. This is the dog that chased our cat.
5. The means of transportation which helped industrialize North America in the nineteenth century was the railroad.
6. The player who wins the trophy is likely to be drafted by a professional team.

VI. ADJECTIVE CLAUSES: REVIEW AND EXPANSION

Read each quotation. Then circle the letter of the quotation that is true according to the statement.

1. There is more than one red-headed woman.
   a. "The red-headed woman who is playing the piano is very talented."
   b. "The red-headed woman, who is playing the piano, is very talented."

2. The speaker has only one sister.
   a. "My sister, who participates in marathons, is in great shape."
   b. "My sister who participates in marathons is in great shape."

3. There is only one doctor.
   a. "The doctor, who just got off the phone, will see you now."
   b. "The doctor who just got off the phone will see you now."

4. Jennifer is taking more than one aerobics class.
   a. "Jennifer's aerobics class which is held Tuesday evenings is a lot of fun."
   b. "Jennifer's aerobics class, which is held Tuesday evenings, is a lot of fun."

5. All the sales representatives will receive bonuses.
   a. The sales representatives, who met company goals, will receive bonuses.
   b. The sales representatives who met company goals will receive bonuses.

VII. ADJECTIVE CLAUSES WITH QUANTIFIERS: ADJECTIVE PHRASES

Underline the adjective phrase in each sentence.

1. The woman <u>in that fresco</u> is supposed to be an ancient queen.
2. Most citizens guilty of tax evasion will eventually be caught.
3. Students interested in joining the soccer team are asked to attend tryouts this afternoon at five.
4. Certain states, including California, Washington, and Alaska, have potentially active volcanoes.
5. The man in the first row is Ken's anthropology professor.

6. *Moby Dick*, starring Gregory Peck as Captain Ahab, is based on Herman Melville's famous novel.

7. Yellowknife, located on Great Slave Lake, is the capital of the Northwest Territories.

8. Most movies directed by Federico Fellini are highly regarded by critics.

9. Monterrey, the industrial center of Mexico, is the nation's third-largest city.

10. Beginning in 1929, the Great Depression affected the entire world.

VIII. ADJECTIVE CLAUSES WITH QUANTIFIERS; ADJECTIVE PHRASES

Combine each pair of sentences into one sentence with a dependent adjective clause containing a quantifier. Make the second sentence the dependent clause.

1. Woody Allen directed *Annie Hall* and *Manhattan Murder Mystery*. Both of them are comedies.

   Woody Allen directed Annie Hall and Manhattan Murder Mystery, both of which

   are comedies.

2. *Grease, The Sound of Music,* and *My Fair Lady* have been quite financially successful. They are all musicals.

   _____

   _____

3. My broker says I have two business options. Neither of them is particularly attractive.

   _____

   _____

4. The president has vetoed many bills passed by Congress. Some of them had the overwhelming support of the electorate.

   _____

   _____

5. The Constitution guarantees to the people certain unalienable rights. Among them are life, liberty, and the pursuit of happiness.

   _____

   _____

IX. ADJECTIVE CLAUSES WITH QUANTIFIERS; ADJECTIVE PHRASES

Combine each pair of sentences into one sentence with an independent clause and an adjectival modifying phrase. Make the second sentence the adjectival modifying phrase.

1. The family dog ate the cookies. The cookies were on the platter.

   The family dog ate the cookies on the platter.

   _____

2. Venice is a charming and beautiful city to visit. It is known for its many canals.

_____

_____

3. Colombia and Panama were at one time one nation. They are connected by a narrow isthmus.

_____

_____

4. The repertory company will perform several contemporary plays this year. They include _An Inspector Calls, Equus,_ and _One Flew over the Cuckoo's Nest._

_____

_____

5. We are renting the house. The house is on Main Street.

_____

_____

6. _The Silence of the Lambs_ won the Academy Award for Best Picture in 1991. It starred Anthony Hopkins and Jodie Foster.

_____

_____

X. SYNTHESIS

Circle the most appropriate forms to complete the biography.

Winona Horowitz's parents named her after the Minnesota town (where)/ which she was born.
                                                            1.
Years later, Winona changed her last name to Ryder, <u>of which / which</u> came from a Mitch Ryder
                                                       2.
album <u>belonging / belonged</u> to her father. Winona's parents, <u>whom / whose</u> friends included Allen
       3.   **4.**
Ginsburg, <u>who / whose</u> was a Beat poet, and Timothy Leary, <u>influential / who influential</u> in the hippie
           5.   **6.**
movement, were unconventional countercultural types.

When she was seven, Winona's family moved to a commune in a small California town

<u>with whom / where</u> they lived with seven other families. Winona's mother operated a movie theater
7.
in an old barn, <u>of which / which</u> may have influenced Winona to want to become an actress. A few
                 8.
years later, Winona began to take acting classes in the American Conservatory Theater, <u>that / which</u>
                                                                                        9.
is a prestigious school in San Francisco.

Winona began to audition for and get small roles in films, most <u>of which / which</u> were not

10.

memorable. She got a big break in 1988 <u>when / where</u> she played Lydia in the movie *Beetlejuice*. In

11.

the following few years, she played teenagers in several films, <u>including / included</u> *Heathers, Great*

12.

Balls of Fire, and *Edward Scissorhands*. She got her chance to portray an adult in *Bram Stoker's*

Dracula, <u>in which / which</u> costarred Keanu Reeves. Although film critics didn't agree on the

13.

effectiveness of her performance in that film, they did like her portrayal of Mary Welland in *The Age*

of Innocence, <u>for which / of which</u> she received an Oscar nomination.

14.

Winona's other films include *Reality Bites, How to Make an American Quilt, Girl Interrupted,*

and *Little Women*. She dedicated the last film to Polly Klaas, a young girl from Ryder's hometown

<u>who / which</u> was kidnapped and murdered. At the time of the crime, Ryder offered a $200,000 reward

15.

for information <u>lead / leading</u> to the child's attacker. She continues to be a strong supporter of the

16.

Polly Klaas Foundation.

XI. SYNTHESIS

Circle the letter of the correct answer to complete each sentence.

1. That's the man _____ children live in Los Angeles.   **A B Ⓒ D**

   (A) which   (C) whose
   (B) whom   (D) who

2. People _____ mosquitoes will love this new insect repellent.   **A B C D**

   (A) whose bothered by   (C) bothered by
   (B) with whom bothered by   (D) who bothered by

3. The movie, _____ an ill-fated love affair, will bring tears to viewers' eyes.   **A B C D**

   (A) which centering on   (C) centering on
   (B) that centering on   (D) in which centers on

4. The main suspect is a man _____ has a scar on his left cheek.   **A B C D**

   (A) who   (C) whose
   (B) of whom   (D) which

5. The Basques are people _____ are from a mountainous region bordering   **A B C D**
   Spain and France.

   (A) who   (C) whose
   (B) they   (D) who they

6. Home is a place _____ you can always go. $\quad$ **A** **B** **C** **D**

(A) where $\qquad$ (C) that

(B) which $\qquad$ (D) when

7. *Falafel* is a dish from the Middle East _____ is made from crushed $\quad$ **A** **B** **C** **D**
chickpeas that are formed into balls and fried.

(A) in which $\qquad$ (C) for which

(B) of which $\qquad$ (D) which

8. I may be out of the office this afternoon, _____ you should leave a $\quad$ **A** **B** **C** **D**
message with my assistant.

(A) in which case $\qquad$ (C) in that case

(B) that $\qquad$ (D) in which

9. The Green Garden Restaurant uses fresh produce in its dishes, _____ $\quad$ **A** **B** **C** **D**
the owners grow in their own garden.

(A) much which $\qquad$ (C) much of which

(B) which of much $\qquad$ (D) which much

10. Julian looks forward to the day _____ he can retire. $\quad$ **A** **B** **C** **D**

(A) where $\qquad$ (C) which

(B) whom $\qquad$ (D) when

11. The consultant _____ the project will give a presentation this afternoon. $\quad$ **A** **B** **C** **D**

(A) that supervising $\qquad$ (C) supervising

(B) supervised $\qquad$ (D) who supervising

12. Picasso is an artist _____ work I admire. $\quad$ **A** **B** **C** **D**

(A) whom $\qquad$ (C) whose

(B) who's $\qquad$ (D) who

XII. SYNTHESIS

*Each sentence has four underlined parts or phrases. The four underlined parts of the sentence are
marked A, B, C, and D. Circle the letter of the ONE underlined part that is NOT CORRECT.*

1. The man <u>wearing</u> clothes <u>that</u> are old and torn is actually a businessman <u>who</u> $\quad$ **A** **B** **C** **Ⓓ**
        A   B   C
owns several clothing stores, <u>of which</u> surprises many people.
                                          D

2. Andy Warwick, <u>that</u> is a star athlete on a team <u>that</u> has won every game this $\quad$ **A** **B** **C** **D**
                   A   B
season, <u>is</u> also a top student, <u>which</u> is something to admire.
        C   D

3. The man <u>whom</u> we ran into <u>him</u> at the lake is a politician <u>who</u> <u>is running</u> $\quad$ **A** **B** **C** **D**
         A   B   C   D
for mayor.

4. Anyone <u>whose</u> <u>concerned</u> about the environment cannot ignore the facts
        A   B

   <u>to which</u> the speaker <u>was referring</u>.
    C   D

   A B C D

5. Vivian is a team player <u>enjoys working</u> with others and <u>who</u> can also work
                    A   B

   independently, <u>which</u> is why I think she is the person <u>we should hire</u>.
            C   D

   A B C D

6. Several famous food critics, <u>including</u> Pierre Le Chef, have written reviews
                      A

   <u>that</u> are favorable about The Brasserie and The Pickle Barrel, <u>both</u> <u>of whom</u>
   B   C   D

   are popular restaurants.

   A B C D

7. *Rain Man,* <u>starred</u> Dustin Hoffman and Tom Cruise, is a film <u>produced</u> in 1988
            A   B

   <u>depicting</u> the relationship <u>that</u> develops between an autistic savant and his
   C   D

   brother as they travel across the country together.

   A B C D

8. The company <u>with</u> I've been negotiating has decided to buy my products, <u>all</u>
             A   B

   <u>of which</u> have been very successful in markets <u>that</u> are not traditional.
   C   D

   A B C D

9. The UN Security Council, <u>which</u> purpose is to preserve peace, has fifteen
                        A

   members, <u>five of whom</u> are permanent; there are ten members <u>who</u> are not
              B   C

   permanent, <u>serving</u> two-year terms.
            D

   A B C D

10. The parking lot <u>surrounding</u> the mall, <u>which</u> is especially busy right now, may
                 A   B

    be full, <u>in that case</u> I would recommend <u>taking</u> the bus.
           C   D

    A B C D

PART V PASSIVE VOICE

I. THE PASSIVE: REVIEW AND EXPANSION

Complete each sentence with a form of the passive with be *in the correct tense.*

1. Rice ____is grown____ in hot, wet climates.
   (grow)

2. *Rashomon* and *Ran*, both very famous films, _____ by Akira Kurosawa.
   (direct)

3. The new expressway _____ until February of next year.
   (will / not / complete)

4. I'm a very light sleeper. I _____ by barking dogs and meowing cats in the
   (easily awaken)
   neighborhood.

5. *Ode to Joy* _____ by Beethoven.
   (compose)

6. In some schools, students _____ to wear uniforms.
   (require)

7. The wheel _____ thousands of years ago.
   (invent)

8. The proposal for refinancing the city's debt _____ at this week's city council
   (be going to / present)
   meeting.

II. THE PASSIVE: REVIEW AND EXPANSION

Complete each sentence with a form of the passive with get.

1. Our puppy ____got hit____ by a car, but fortunately he survived the accident.
   (hit)

2. My prediction is that the Eagles _____ by the Falcons this season.
   (be going to / beat)

3. Alice's problem in school is that she _____ by other students.
   (distracted)

4. Unfortunately, your suggestion never _____ in the final version of the proposal.
   (include)

5. John, every time we talk about this, we _____ by irrelevant issues. Let's stick
   (sidetrack)
   to the point!

6. I'm not sure how, but somehow all this work _____ by someone.
   (will / do)

III. THE PASSIVE: REVIEW AND EXPANSION

Complete each sentence with the progressive passive form of the indicated verb. Use the be-*passive if the* get-*passive is not specified.*

1. A new building ____is being constructed____ on the corner of Fauntleroy and Admiral.
   (construct)

2. The bridge _____ when the gale-force winds caused it to sink.
   (repair)

Diagnostic and Final Tests **187**

3. We've _____ for months on our phone bill! We need to call the company
   (get / overcharge)
   right away.

4. The seals _____ early today. We're trying an experiment in their feeding
   (get / fed)
   schedule.

5. People involved in the accident were taken to Madison Hospital, where they
   _____ for shock.
   (treat)

6. After Jim finishes boot camp, he'll _____ in telecommunications.
   (get / train)

IV.   THE PASSIVE: REVIEW AND EXPANSION

Complete each sentence with a passive formed with have, has, *or* had + be *or* get + *past participle. Use* be
unless get *is specified.*

1. Uh-oh. Don't buy this container of yogurt. It ___'s been opened___.
   (open)

2. I wonder why the drama department is going to put on *The Mousetrap*. It
   _____ before.
   (do)

3. Detective Sadler discovered that the evidence _____ before he saw it.
   (tamper with)

4. Ever since Miriam has been here, the work _____ on time. Let's hire her
   (get / do)
   permanently.

5. Mr. and Mrs. Houck _____ not to sell their house at this time.
   (advise)

6. By the time the rent is due, my check will _____ in the bank, so there shouldn't
   (deposit)
   be a problem.

V.   THE PASSIVE: REVIEW AND EXPANSION

Complete each sentence with the indicated modal or modal-like expression and a past participle.

1. Matter ___can be altered___ but not destroyed.
   (can / alter)

2. Small children _____ by their parents.
   (should / not / leave alone)

3. The theft _____ to the police; they're already working on the case.
   (must / have / report)

4. If a garden is going to produce, it _____ regularly.
   (have to / attend to)

5. Amanda had lost a lot of blood. She _____ to the hospital immediately.
   (should / have / take)

6. Look at the grass! It _____ every two days while we were gone. Now it's
   (be supposed to / water)
   almost dead.

VI. REPORTING IDEAS AND FACTS WITH PASSIVES

Complete each sentence with a present tense form of be + *a past participle.*

1. The wheel ____is thought____ to have been invented three or four thousand years ago.
   (think)

2. The suspects _____ to have escaped from the prison in a laundry truck.
   (believe)

3. They _____ to be armed and dangerous.
   (say)

4. Right now the Sparrows _____ the best team in professional football.
   (consider)

5. This document _____ to be a forgery.
   (allege)

6. Leondardo da Vinci _____ as one of the greatest artists of all time.
   (regard)

VII. REPORTING IDEAS AND FACTS WITH PASSIVES

Complete each sentence with the stative passive form of the indicated verb.

1. Great Slave Lake ____is located____ in the Northwest Territories in Canada.
   (locate)

2. The only diamond mine in the United States _____ in Arkansas.
   (find)

3. Samuel Clemens, a famous American novelist of the nineteenth and early twentieth centuries,
   _____ as Mark Twain.
   (more commonly know)

4. Yemen _____ by Saudi Arabia on the north and Oman on the east.
   (border)

5. The Basque language _____ structurally to any other language.
   (not relate)

6. North and South America _____ by the Isthmus of Panama.
   (connect)

VIII. REPORTING IDEAS AND FACTS WITH PASSIVES

To improve the writing style of the following narration, change each active sentence to the passive and each passive sentence to the active. In changing sentences to the passive, do not include any by *phrases.*

1. Last week a trip was taken by Mrs. Adams to New York City.

   Last week Mrs. Adams took a trip to New York City.

2. Because of a heavy rainstorm, controllers had to divert her plane to Philadelphia.

   Because of a heavy rainstorm, her plane had to be diverted to Philadelphia.

3. Controllers didn't allow her plane to land in New York until 10:00 P.M.

   _____

   _____

4. A taxi had to be taken by Mrs. Adams to her hotel.

_____

_____

5. Her hotel was arrived at by Mrs. Adams very late.

_____

_____

6. Because of her late arrival, a clerk had given away her hotel room.

_____

_____

7. A very uncomfortable night was spent by Mrs. Adams on a couch in the hotel lobby.

_____

_____

IX. SYNTHESIS

Read the article. Then read it again. Find and correct the fifteen errors in active and passive constructions.

Crop circles, small areas of crops in elaborately swirled patterns, are a modern-day mystery.

They have been ~~spotting~~ _spotted_ all over the world. One reported in England in the 1960s. More were

documenting in England and the Australian outback in the 1970s. Crop circles also appeared on a

farm in Switzerland. On this farm, the grass stalks within the circles been bent flat, but they had not

being broken. The grass continued to grow in a swirled pattern. Meanwhile, a farmer in Canada

noticed several dome-shaped aircraft in the air above his field. When the aircraft left, they had left

several crop circles in the field. More circles appeared during the next few nights.

In the 1980s, people began to research crop circles. It was proposing by one meteorologist that

they might have caused by an unusual weather phenomenon. Since strange lights or spacecraft

resembling UFOs had often been seeing around the same time these circles were form, some people

believed that these formations could have been using as landing strips for alien spacecraft.

In the 1990s, two men claimed to have created all the formations by using a plank of wood and

a piece of rope. However, they later admitted that they had lied. It then suggested that these men had

been plant by the government to cover up evidence of UFOs. The idea that crop circles had created by UFOs was becoming more widely believing, since the formations had begun to occur in even more elaborate patterns. The size of the formations had also increased. One, find in England in 1996, was 4100 feet across!

In the twenty-first century, these crop circles remain a mystery. What do you think they're cause by?

X. SYNTHESIS

Read the interview. Then read it again. Complete the sentences with passive constructions, using be *and the indicated verbs. Use the correct verb form and tense.*

INTERVIEWER: Good evening, and welcome to "In the News." Tonight, our topic is crop circles, and our guest is Dr. Roger Clampton, a science professor at Ace University who has been investigating crop circles. Dr. Clampton, over the past forty years, over 5000 crop circles ___have been reported___ all over the world. What do you think they
1. (report)
_____?
2. (cause)

CLAMPTON: Well, many theories _____ by members of the scientific
3. (propose)
community. Although the exact cause _____ for sure, today it
4. (not know)
_____ that unusual atmospheric conditions or magnetic currents
5. (believe)
may be responsible.

INTERVIEWER: Can you give us any examples of scientific theories that _____?
6. (suggest)

CLAMPTON: Certainly. There's the Whirlwind Vortex Theory, also _____ as the
7. (know)
Plasma Vortex Theory. And of course, there's the Plasma-Gravitational Theory, the Gaia Hypothesis, Earth Ley-Lines, Microwave Transient Heating, . . .

INTERVIEWER: Uh . . . OK. And can you tell us about any less scientific theories?

CLAMPTON: Of course. There have been several religious explanations. For example, in the Himalayas, crop circles _____ as a psychic phenomenon
8. (regard)
_____ when *Avatar,* which is a heavenly form of communication,
9. (create)
appear. And some people think the whole thing is a hoax. Several groups of people have claimed to have created the circles artificially using tools or machines. However, their claims _____, since they would have to have created these
10. (disprove)
circles at numerous sites _____ in vastly distant areas of the world.
11. (locate)

INTERVIEWER: In recent years, it _____ that these crop circles
13. (allege)

_____ by UFOs. What's your response to this suggestion?
13. (create)

CLAMPTON: Nonsense! Most people who believe in UFOs _____ illogical.
14. (consider)

And numerous other more rational theories _____.
15. (offer)

INTERVIEWER: So how do you explain the phenomenon?

CLAMPTON: I can't say for sure. But please rest assured that the phenomenon

_____.
16. (investigate)

XI. SYNTHESIS

Circle the letter of the correct answer to complete each sentence.

1. The murder is _____ right now.   (Ⓐ) B C D

   (A) being investigated   (C) been investigated
   (B) being investigate   (D) been investigate

2. Phil _____ when he lost the Forbes account.   A B C D

   (A) was got fired   (C) got fired
   (B) got firing   (D) got fire

3. It was too late to cancel the order because the invitations had already   A B C D

   _____.

   (A) printed   (C) print
   (B) been printed   (D) printing

4. Keep looking! I'm sure you will _____ your wallet.   A B C D

   (A) be found   (C) found
   (B) find   (D) have been found by

5. Is Jim still working? He should _____ the assignment an hour ago.   A B C D

   (A) have been finished   (C) have being finished
   (B) be finished   (D) have finished

6. The Montclair-Hilton family _____ to be very rich.   A B C D

   (A) are said   (C) are saying
   (B) is said   (D) is saying

7. I need to _____.   A B C D

   (A) be my shoes repaired   (C) get my shoes repairing
   (B) get my shoes repaired   (D) have my shoes repairing

8. Many women _____ Clark to be very handsome.　　　　**A B C D**

   (A) consider　　　　　　　　　(C) are considering

   (B) are considered　　　　　　(D) are consider

9. Little _____ about the plane crash at the moment.　　　**A B C D**

   (A) has known　　　　　　　　(C) is known

   (B) knows　　　　　　　　　　(D) is knowing

10. Did Lily _____ her hair cut at Frederick's salon?　　　**A B C D**

   (A) have　　　　　　　　　　(C) been having

   (B) having　　　　　　　　　　(D) been had

11. These floors are so dirty! They _____ in months.　　　**A B C D**

   (A) haven't been cleaned　　　(C) should have been cleaned

   (B) are being cleaned　　　　(D) should have being cleaned

12. St. Louis _____ in Missouri.　　　　　　　　　　　**A B C D**

   (A) is locate　　　　　　　　(C) is located

   (B) is locating　　　　　　　(D) located

13. The air conditioner will _____ by tomorrow afternoon.　**A B C D**

   (A) being fixed　　　　　　　(C) have being fixed

   (B) have been fixed　　　　　(D) having fixed

14. Natalie's friends _____ her "Nat" for short.　　　　　**A B C D**

   (A) calling　　　　　　　　　(C) call

   (B) is called　　　　　　　　(D) are called

15. It _____ that we will be moving to a new office.　　　**A B C D**

   (A) is rumored　　　　　　　(C) has rumored

   (B) is rumoring　　　　　　　(D) rumors

XII.　SYNTHESIS

Each sentence has four underlined words or phrases. The four underlined parts of the sentence are marked A, B, C, and D. Circle the letter of the ONE underlined part that is NOT CORRECT.

1. Most major newspapers <u>is</u> <u>published</u> every day; however, *The Weekly Blab* <u>is</u>　　Ⓐ **B C D**
              A　　　　B　　　　　　　　　　　　　　　　　　　　C

  <u>published</u> only once a week.
    D

2. The dignitaries <u>was</u> <u>being</u> <u>driven</u> to the trade talks when the limousine <u>had</u> a　　**A B C D**
           A　　　B　　　C　　　　　　　　　　　　　　　　　　　D

  flat tire.

3. The bread that <u>was put out</u> <u>for</u> the birds <u>got</u> <u>ate</u> very quickly.　　　　　**A B C D**
            A　　　　B　　　　　　　C　　D

4. The new monorail <u>will have</u> <u>been</u> <u>build</u> <u>by this time</u> next year.　　　　**A B C D**
         A　　　　B　　C　　　D

5. This table <u>is not recommended</u>. <u>It's being</u> <u>damaged</u>; one of its legs <u>is broken</u>.
              A   B   C   D   **A B C D**

6. <u>Bobby's crying</u>; he <u>got</u> <u>stinging</u> <u>by a bee</u>.   **A B C D**
     A   B   C   D

7. <u>By the time</u> the police <u>arrived</u> at the scene of the accident, the debris <u>had been</u>   **A B C D**
     A   B   C

    <u>clean up</u>.
     D

8. My son Frank <u>getting</u> <u>tutored</u> privately, so his grades <u>are</u> <u>improving</u>.   **A B C D**
                     A   B   C   D

9. The past <u>can't</u> <u>be</u> <u>change</u>; <u>don't worry</u> about it.   **A B C D**
            A   B   C   D

10. You <u>have</u> <u>been</u> <u>giving</u> a marvelous opportunity; <u>take</u> advantage of it.   **A B C D**
      A   B   C   D

PART V PASSIVE VOICE

FINAL TEST

I. THE PASSIVE: REVIEW AND EXPANSION

Complete each sentence with a form of the passive with be in the correct tense.

1. The cotton gin ___was invented___ by Eli Whitney.
   (invent)

2. In some cities, pedestrians _____ for jaywalking.
   (arrest)

3. Industrial diamonds _____ in Ireland, Zaire, Britain, and South Africa.
   (mine)

4. *Macbeth* and *Othello*, two very famous plays, _____ by William Shakespeare.
   (write)

5. The new airport _____ until July of next year.
   (will / not / finish)

6. The proposal for building a mass transit system _____ at this week's County
   (be going to / discuss)
   Council meeting.

7. I have trouble sleeping. I _____ by loud music and backfiring cars.
   (frequently bother)

8. *The Love for Three Oranges* _____ by Prokofiev.
   (compose)

II. THE PASSIVE: REVIEW AND EXPANSION

Complete each sentence with a form of the passive with get.

1. Every time we talk about selling the property, we ___get bogged down___ in unrelated issues.
   (bog down)

2. Jack's problem in school is his shyness. He _____ by other students, especially
   (intimidate)
   boisterous ones.

3. My cat _____ by a cyclist, but fortunately she escaped with minor injuries.
   (hit)

4. The way I see it, Central High _____ by only one team this year—East High.
   (be going to / defeat)

5. I don't know the specifics, but I do know that the project _____ to someone who
   (will / assign)
   can do a good job.

6. Unfortunately, your recommendations never _____ into the final version of the
   (incorporate)
   document.

III. THE PASSIVE: REVIEW AND EXPANSION

Complete each sentence with the progressive passive form of the indicated verb. Use the be*-passive if the* get*-passive is not specified.*

1. The shark habitat ___is getting cleaned___ right now, so the sharks have been put in a
   (get / clean)
   holding tank.

2. This month a new recreation center _____ on the vacant lot on Third Avenue.
   (build)

3. The highway _____ when the freak snowstorm hit—all that work for nothing.
   (resurface)

4. I can't believe this! We've _____ for months on our light bill. Do you think
   (get / undercharge)
   we'll have to make up the difference?

5. When Rolleen enrolls in graduate school, she'll _____ regularly.
   (get / counsel)

6. People rescued from the flood were taken to the Civic Center, where their condition
   _____.
   (monitor)

IV. THE PASSIVE: REVIEW AND EXPANSION

Complete each sentence with the passive formed with have, has, *or* had + be *or* get + *a past participle.*

1. The Johnsons __have been given__ an extension on their loan repayment.
   (give)

2. By the time the fire trucks got to the scene, the fire _____ by neighbors.
   (put out)

3. I don't think you should buy this medicine. It looks like the seal _____.
   (tamper with)

4. Let's not put on a historical pageant this year. That _____ a lot recently. Let's
   (do)
   think of something different.

5. By the time you move into the house, the new expressway will _____, so you
   (finish)
   should have an easy commute.

6. Ever since we hired this new janitorial service, the cleaning _____ on time.
   (get / do)
   Let's renew their contract.

V. THE PASSIVE: REVIEW AND EXPANSION

Complete each sentence with the indicated modals and modal-like expressions + be + *a past participle.*

1. All children __must be vaccinated__ before they start school.
   (must / vaccinate)

2. Dogs and cats _____ to eat junk food.
   (should / not / allow)

3. My money _____ in a mutual fund. What happened?
   (be supposed to / reinvest)

4. The injured people _____ to the hospital already. Everyone here is OK.
   (must / have / take)

5. In this dry climate, flowers _____ regularly, or they won't survive.
   (have to / water)

6. My son took a lot of unnecessary courses. I think he _____ better.
   (should / have / advise)

VI. REPORTING IDEAS AND FACTS WITH PASSIVES

Complete each sentence with a present tense form of be + *a past participle.*

1. At present the Brazilians __are considered__ the best team in international soccer.
   (consider)

2. The suspect _____ to have embezzled $5000.
   (allege)

3. Wolfgang Amadeus Mozart _____ as one of the greatest composers of all time.
   (regard)

4. The Sumerians _____ to have invented writing.
   (think)

5. Jane Bowman _____ to be contemplating a run for the presidency.
   (believe)

6. Her chances of victory _____ to be excellent.
   (say)

VII. REPORTING IDEAS AND FACTS WITH PASSIVES

Complete each sentence with the stative passive form of the indicated verb.

1. The Hungarian and Czech languages __are not related__ structurally.
   (not relate)

2. Africa and Asia _____ by the Suez Canal.
   (separate)

3. Victoria Falls _____ on the Zambezi River in Zimbabwe and Zambia.
   (locate)

4. Several productive diamond mines _____ in South Africa.
   (find)

5. Amandine Aurore Lucie Dupin, a famous French author of the nineteenth century,
   _____ as George Sand.
   (more commonly known)

6. Venezuela _____ by Colombia on the west and Guyana on the east.
   (border)

VIII. REPORTING IDEAS AND FACTS WITH PASSIVES

To improve the writing style of the following narration, change each active sentence to the passive and each passive sentence to the active. In changing sentences to the passive, do not include any by *phrases.*

1. Last summer an ocean cruise was taken by Henry and Martha Ramsey.

   Last summer Henry and Martha Ramsey took an ocean cruise.

2. Because of fear of an epidemic, officials had to quarantine their ship in Kingston harbor.

   Because of fear of an epidemic, their ship had to be quarantined in Kingston harbor.

3. Officials didn't allow the ship to leave Kingston harbor for a week.

4. To pass the time, card games were played by Henry, Martha, and the other passengers.

_____

_____

5. Many hours reading books from the ship's library were also spent by the passengers.

_____

_____

6. Fortunately, many new friends were made by Henry and Martha.

_____

_____

7. Because of the inconvenience, the cruise line gave the passengers free tickets for another cruise.

_____

_____

IX.   SYNTHESIS

Read the article. Then read it again. Find and correct the fifteen errors in active and passive constructions.

Easter Island ^is^ located more than 2000 miles west of the Chilean mainland. The island is probably best knowing for its mysterious huge stone statues that are scattering along the coastline. Calling _Te Pito O Te Henua_ or "Navel of The World" by the early settlers, the isolated island renamed Easter Island by Admiral Roggeveen, who landed there on Easter Day in 1722. Today, the land, people, and language referred to locally as _Rapanui_.

Where did the statues come from? How were they move? It was suggesting by the explorer and archaeologist Thor Heyerdahl that the people who built the statues related to the natives of Peru, since there are marked similarities between Rapanui and Incan stonework. It proposed by author Erich von Däniken that the statues could have left by extraterrestrials, since they are too large and heavy for people to move. Others thought that the island could have once been part of a lost continent. Today, it is widely believing that the island was discover by Polynesians around 400 A.D.

As the population on the island grew, the forests destroyed for agriculture, and natural resources became scarce. Later, civil war erupted and most of the statues on the coast tore down by the islanders. The population decreased even further after contact with Western peoples. Many of the inhabitants were enslave or contracted fatal diseases.

Today, Easter Island is part of Chile, but the Polynesian influence still remains. It is now a fascinating living museum in a beautiful, natural setting.

X. SYNTHESIS

Read the interview. Then read it again. Complete the sentences with passive constructions, using be *and the indicated verbs. Use the correct verb form and tense.*

INTERVIEWER: Good evening, and welcome to "Books Today." Today, we're interviewing Dr. Cynthia Adair, whose book *Easter Island: Myths and Mysteries* _____was published_____ just
1. (publish)
last month. Dr. Adair, why don't you tell us about your book?

ADAIR: Well, the book addresses some of the mysteries and theories surrounding the island. For example, how _____ the famous statues
_____ to the coastline, where there are no natural rock quarries?
2. (move)

INTERVIEWER: For those in our audience who don't know, exactly where _____
Easter Island _____?
3. (locate)

ADAIR: It's about 2000 miles west of Chile. The island _____ by Chile
4. (annex)
in 1888. It _____ that the island's isolation contributed to the
5. (believe)
development of its unique culture.

INTERVIEWER: Unique culture? In what way?

ADAIR: For one thing, a distinct form of hieroglyphics _____ as
6. (know)
Rongorongo _____ on the island. This is the only written
7. (discover)
language _____ in Oceania.
8. (find)

INTERVIEWER: _____ the hieroglyphics _____ to other
9. (relate)
hieroglyphics elsewhere in the world—for example, to those _____
10. (unearth)
in Egypt?

ADAIR: Well, some years ago, it _____ that the carvings
11. (theorize)
_____ by invaders from the east. Recently, though, it
12. (make)
_____ that the Rapanui, as the islanders _____,
13. (propose)   14. (call)

Diagnostic and Final Tests **199**

_____ to write by Spaniards who visited the island in the late
　　　15. (inspire)

1700s. However, the script's unique form _____ by the islanders
　　　　　　　　　　　　　　　　　　　　　　　16. (create)

themselves.

INTERVIEWER: That's all we have time for today. Thank you, Dr. Adair, and we look forward to

reading your book.

XI. SYNTHESIS

Circle the letter of the correct answer to complete each sentence.

1. When I was a teenager, DVD players hadn't _____ yet.   (A) B C D

   (A) been invented   (C) being invented

   (B) invented   (D) inventing

2. I'm so happy that I _____ the test!   A B C D

   (A) was passed   (C) was being passed

   (B) passed   (D) had been passed

3. Ouch! A mosquito _____ me.   A B C D

   (A) was bit   (C) bit

   (B) was bitten by   (D) ought to have bitten

4. My skirt is too long, so _____ it shortened.   A B C D

   (A) I was had   (C) I'm had

   (B) I've had   (D) I'm having

5. Where do you get your clothes _____?   A B C D

   (A) dry-cleaned   (C) are dry-cleaning

   (B) dry-cleaning   (D) are dry-cleaned

6. This sweater _____ in Nepal.   A B C D

   (A) made   (C) was made

   (B) had made   (D) was making

7. The dishes had better _____ by the time I get home!   A B C D

   (A) being washed   (C) be washing

   (B) been washed   (D) be washed

8. Scott is sad because he _____ to the party.   A B C D

   (A) didn't invited   (C) wasn't inviting

   (B) wasn't been invited   (D) wasn't invited

9. Teacher, may I _____ excused from class?   A B C D

(A) being   (C) be
(B) have   (D) have been

10. Last night, I was so tired I _____ for fourteen hours.   A B C D

(A) was slept   (C) slept
(B) was being slept   (D) was been slept

11. It _____ that dinosaurs once roamed the earth.   A B C D

(A) is believed   (C) believes
(B) is believing   (D) believed

12. When Ted didn't come to work, it _____ that he was sick.   A B C D

(A) was assumed   (C) assumed
(B) was assuming   (D) had been assumed

13. We should repaint the house. It _____ painted in a long time.   A B C D

(A) should have been   (C) should have being
(B) is being   (D) hasn't been

14. You look just like Bob Simpson! _____ to him?   A B C D

(A) Do you relate   (C) Are you related
(B) Have you related   (D) Are you relating

15. The new drug _____ unsafe by the Food and Drug Administration.   A B C D

(A) declared   (C) declaring
(B) was declared   (D) was declaring

XII. SYNTHESIS

Each sentence has four underlined words or phrases. The four underlined parts of the sentence are marked A, B, C, and D. Circle the letter of the ONE underlined part that is NOT CORRECT.

1. It was suggested that the congressman's speeches was written by a ghostwriter.   A (B) C D
    A   B   C   D

2. Don't drink the water here; it's said to have been contaminate.   A B C D
    A   B   C   D

3. Daphne got biting by the neighbor's German shepherd, so she had to get   A B C D
        A   B   C   D
stitches on her ankle.

4. Our car were being serviced at the garage when the storm hit, so we   A B C D
            A   B   C
had to take a bus.
    D

5. The recyclables that we left by the curb got picking up.   A B C D
                       A   B   C   D

6. The evidence <u>had been</u> <u>remove</u> <u>by the building janitors</u> when the
　　　　　　　　　 A 　　　　 B 　　　 C

　　investigator <u>arrived</u>.
　　　　　　　　　 D

　　　　　　　　　　　　　　　　　　　　　　　　　　　　　　　　A B C D

7. Stuart <u>getting</u> <u>trained</u> in computer programming right now, so he
　　　　　　 A 　　 B

　　<u>should be able to</u> <u>get</u> a good job.
　　　　　　 C 　　　　　 D

　　　　　　　　　　　　　　　　　　　　　　　　　　　　　　　　A B C D

8. The balance of nature <u>shouldn't disturbed</u>, but sometimes it <u>is</u> <u>affected</u>
　　　　　　　　　　　　　　　 A 　　　　　　　　　　　　　　 B 　 C

　　negatively <u>by development</u>.
　　　　　　　 D

　　　　　　　　　　　　　　　　　　　　　　　　　　　　　　　　A B C D

9. You <u>have</u> <u>been</u> <u>granting</u> three wishes; <u>use</u> them wisely.
　　　　 A 　　 B 　　 C 　　　　　　　　 D

　　　　　　　　　　　　　　　　　　　　　　　　　　　　　　　　A B C D

10. The new mall <u>will have</u> <u>been</u> <u>finish</u> <u>by this time</u> a year from now.
　　　　　　　　　 A 　　　　 B 　　 C 　　 D

　　　　　　　　　　　　　　　　　　　　　　　　　　　　　　　　A B C D

PART VI AUXILIARIES AND PHRASAL VERBS

I. AUXILIARIES

Complete the report with the correct auxiliary verbs to refer to previously mentioned information.

People get many of their beliefs about dinosaurs from science-fiction movies, thinking they must be accurate. In fact, they _____*aren't*_____. Many science-fiction movies are outdated and contain

1.
incorrect information. This report will resolve some misconceptions about dinosaurs.

It has been said that the word dinosaur means "terrible lizard." Actually, it _____.

2.
The word dinosaur comes from the Greek words *deinos* and *sauros*. *Deinos* originally meant "fearfully great," not "terrible." The word *sauros*, meaning "lizard," was used because people thought dinosaurs were lizards. In fact, they _____; rather, they represented a small percentage of reptiles

3.
that existed in the Mesozoic Era. Another misconception is that all dinosaurs were either hot-blooded or cold-blooded. Experts now say that they _____. They now think that dinosaurs

4.
were basically warm-blooded, but their metabolism changed over time. Another erroneous belief is that all dinosaurs were gigantic. In fact, many _____. Although some, such as the

5.
seisomosaurus, were as tall as 120 feet, the compsognathus was only two feet tall. Another less common belief is that dinosaurs and humans existed at the same time. They _____.

6.
The last dinosaur died out over 60 million years before the first human appeared.

What caused dinosaurs to disappear from this planet? Some say that there is evidence that mammals drove the dinosaurs into extinction by eating their eggs. In fact, there _____.

7.
Experts say that there is no proof that mammals ever ate dinosaur eggs. Others say an asteroid was responsible. Perhaps it _____. Studies show that an asteroid hit the earth at the end

8.
of the Cretaceous period, at which point the dinosaur population was already dwindling. An asteroid may have furthered the decline. But did it erase the population entirely? Most likely it

_____. It probably only contributed to the decline.

9.

Some people think that, because dinosaurs became extinct, they exemplify failure. In fact, they

_____. They ruled the earth for over 50 million years and were predecessors to many

10.
species found on this planet today.

Has this report answered your questions about dinosaurs? We hope it _____.

11.
The next time you watch a science-fiction movie about dinosaurs, you'll know which information is accurate and which isn't.

II. AUXILIARIES

Complete each tag question. Then add a short answer. Be sure to use the correct auxiliary verb and pronoun.

1. **A:** Harold is an accountant, _____*isn't he*_____?

   B: No, _____*he isn't*_____.

2. **A:** Jennifer has grown a lot taller in the past year, _____?

   B: Yes, _____.

3. **A:** George can swim, _____?

   B: No, _____.

4. **A:** You don't have change for a dollar, _____?

   B: Yes, _____.

5. **A:** Mr. Baxter will be at the meeting, _____?

   B: No, _____.

6. **A:** The Thompsons used to live around here, _____?

   B: Yes, _____.

7. **A:** Those children shouldn't be playing near that electrical fence, _____?

   B: No, _____.

III. AUXILIARIES

Complete the conversation between two coworkers. Use the correct forms from the box.

| Neither do I | So do I | so does | do too | neither is |
| is too | ~~So am I~~ | not either | does too | so do |

SANDY: I'm really glad it's Friday afternoon.

JANET: _____*So am I*_____. I really need to rest this weekend.
     <u>1.</u>

SANDY: _____. I'm tired. But I don't know what I'm going to do.
     <u>2.</u>

JANET: _____. Usually I go out of town. My husband and I like to travel, and
     <u>3.</u>

_____ my children. But this weekend, my son has things to do in town,
     <u>4.</u>

and _____ my daughter.
          <u>5.</u>

SANDY: Really? My children _____. What are your kids doing?
                    <u>6.</u>

JANET: My son has a baseball game, and my daughter has a swim meet. I honestly don't know where they get their athletic ability from. I'm not good at sports, and _____ my husband.

SANDY: I'm _____. Well, I do like to take long walks, though. Fortunately, my husband _____. Anyway, I'd better get going. My train is leaving soon.

JANET: Mine _____. Have a good weekend!

IV. AUXILIARIES

Complete each sentence with the emphatic verb form.

1. Helen doesn't have a DVD player. She _____does have_____ a VCR, though.
   (have)

2. I'm not a doctor. I _____ a nurse, though, so I'll do what I can.
   (be)

3. The Changs don't speak Mandarin. They _____ Korean, however.
   (speak)

4. She's never traveled to South America, but she _____ to Central America.
   (travel)

5. We didn't go to Norway on our trip to Europe last summer. We _____ to Sweden, though.
   (go)

6. I won't do your homework for you. I _____ your answers, though.
   (check)

7. Jack hadn't studied acting before he got his movie role, but he _____ in a few commercials.
   (act)

V. PHRASAL VERBS

Circle the letter of the synonym that best matches the underlined phrase.

1. Please <u>take my name off</u> your mailing list.
   a. add my name to
   b. remove my name from
   c. put my name at the top of

2. Many people are away today, so I'd like to <u>put off</u> this afternoon's meeting.
   a. cancel
   b. reschedule
   c. postpone

3. Zelda <u>can't do without</u> her computer.
   a. has difficulty operating
   b. doesn't know how to use
   c. has to have

4. Helen is <u>looking forward to</u> a vacation.

   a. trying to find

   b. eagerly anticipating

   c. being cautious about

5. Richard <u>gave up</u> cooking after he started a fire in his kitchen.

   a. stopped

   b. started

   c. produced

6. Ted is <u>brushing up on</u> his computer skills.

   a. saying little about

   b. trying to improve

   c. managing

7. Anthony <u>put away</u> his college textbooks.

   a. placed on the floor

   b. forgot about

   c. stored in a box or space

8. Many people are <u>concerned about</u> crime in the city.

   a. discussing

   b. worried about

   c. involved with

9. Steve is trying to <u>figure out</u> a way to make more money.

   a. discover

   b. emphasize

   c. guess

10. I'm not <u>familiar with</u> the customs of your country.

   a. knowledgable about

   b. related to

   c. ignorant of

11. The waiters <u>set aside</u> the appetizers and brought in the main course.

   a. arranged in an organized manner

   b. put to one side

   c. decided what to do with

12. Fred didn't have any power in his apartment because the electricity had been <u>cut off</u>.

   a. disconnected

   b. used completely

   c. shortened

13. The Hiltons had a lavish party because they wanted to <u>show off</u> their newly decorated living room.
    a. demonstrate
    b. try to make people admire
    c. give a tour of

14. Harriet went to the grocery store because she <u>was running out of</u> milk.
    a. had no more
    b. had very little
    c. needed

15. Paul told Alex that he would <u>think over</u> Alan's proposition.
    a. remember
    b. make guesses about
    c. consider

VI. PHRASAL VERBS

Complete the e-mail message. Use the correct phrasal verbs from the box. Change the verb tense as needed.

~~look forward to~~	show up	cut down on	figure out
run out of	be concerned about	show off	get rid of
do without	find out	put off	

Hi Jan,

I'm glad to hear that you're going to Melissa's party. I'm really __looking forward to__ it. Are you going
                                                                    1.

to bring any food? You know I don't like to _____ at a party empty-handed. I was going
                                             2.

to bring a dessert, maybe chocolate cake, but Melissa's trying to _____ calories, so
                                                                   3.

maybe that's not such a good idea.

Also, do you know what you're going to wear? I was thinking of wearing my long black dress, but

maybe that's too formal. I mean, I don't want people to think I'm _____. You know, I
                                                                  4.

really love that dress. Can you believe I was going to _____ it when I gave my old
                                                       5.

clothes to charity? Now I feel like I can't _____ it. Oh, by the way, I _____
                                           6.   **7.**

that Jeff and Kevin are going to be there. It'll be great to see them!

Anyway, I've been _____ doing my homework for long enough, so I'd better get to
                  8.

work. I have some math problems that are really hard to _____. Also, I have an essay
                                                        9.

due on Thursday, and I'm _____ time to write it. My classes are really hard this

10.

semester, and I _____ my grades.

11.

Talk to you soon,

Sue

VII. PHRASAL VERBS

Complete each conversation with a phrasal verb and a pronoun.

1. A: Have you paid Susan back yet?

   B: Yes, I ___paid her back___ a month ago.

2. A: Where can I try this dress on?

   B: You can _____ in that dressing room over there.

3. A: Why did you cut Nancy off while she was talking?

   B: Did I do that? I didn't realize I'd _____.

4. A: I'm trying to give up cigarettes.

   B: I tried to _____ last year, but I didn't have any success.

5. A: I set some cookies aside for dessert. Have you seen them?

   B: No. Where did you _____?

6. A: Have you had time to think over my proposal?

   B: No, but I'm planning to _____ this weekend.

VIII. PHRASAL VERBS

Read the short article on study skills. Then read it again. Find and correct the nine errors in phrasal verbs.

How to Perform Well on an Exam

- Get know your teachers early in the semester. You may want to ask them questions later.
  - ^to

- Don't put up studying until the last minute. Set it aside an hour each night to study for a few weeks before the exam. Brush up any materials you don't understand well.

- Show off at the examination room a few minutes early.

- Wait him or her for the teacher to give you directions before you begin.

- Think up each question before you answer it. If you can't figure it out the answer to a question, don't waste too much time thinking it about. Otherwise, you might run out for time.

IX. SYNTHESIS

Circle the letter of the correct answer to complete each sentence.

1. Sure, I can lend you some money. When do you think you can _____? A (B) C D

   (A) pay back me (C) pay up me

   (B) pay me back (D) pay me up

2. Do you remember our old high school teacher, Mrs. Adams? Well, guess what? A B C D

   Yesterday, I _____ at the mall.

   (A) ran her down (C) ran into her

   (B) ran over her (D) ran away her

3. Sam's wife doesn't like to get up early in the morning, and _____. A B C D

   (A) so does Sam (C) Sam does too

   (B) neither does Sam (D) Sam does either

4. Everybody has a different opinion about modern art. Some people love it; A B C D

   others _____.

   (A) haven't (C) won't

   (B) don't (D) aren't

5. Walter wasn't a very good student in high school. He _____ good grades A B C D

   when he went to college, however.

   (A) had gotten (C) does get

   (B) did get (D) has gotten

6. Have you heard the latest? Kirsten is _____ Dan. A B C D

   (A) going without (C) going out with

   (B) going within (D) going out

7. This assignment is due tomorrow. You can't _____ any longer! A B C D

   (A) put it on (C) put it away

   (B) put it off (D) put it back

8. Rosa's in your computer class, _____ she? A B C D

   (A) wouldn't (C) isn't

   (B) doesn't (D) hasn't

9. You used to work at Stacy's Department Store, _____ you? A B C D

   (A) didn't (C) weren't

   (B) aren't (D) haven't

10. I think that dress would look really good on you. Why don't you _____?   **A   B   C   D**

(A) try it on   (C) try them on
(B) try on it   (D) try on them

11. Some people think that cola is not addictive. However, this beverage contains   **A   B   C   D**

caffeine, so actually it _____.

(A) doesn't   (C) does
(B) don't   (D) is

12. Can you understand this telephone message? I can't _____.   **A   B   C   D**

(A) figure out it   (C) figure up it
(B) figure them out   (D) figure it out

13. I think you should apply for a job with that company. However, first you'd   **A   B   C   D**

better _____ your computer skills.

(A) brush up with   (C) brush up on
(B) brush with up   (D) brush on up

14. Anton can't speak Spanish. However, he _____ speak French.   **A   B   C   D**

(A) can   (C) doesn't
(B) can't   (D) does

15. Lynn has a cold, and _____.   **A   B   C   D**

(A) I am too   (C) so do I
(B) so am I   (D) neither do I

16. The taxi driver didn't know you could speak Chinese. I think he was surprised   **A   B   C   D**

when he found out _____.

(A) you did   (C) you could
(B) did you   (D) you couldn't

X.   SYNTHESIS

*Each sentence has four underlined parts or phrases. The four underlined parts of the sentence are marked
A, B, C, and D. Circle the letter of the ONE underlined part that is NOT CORRECT.*

1. Jerry's aunt <u>kept offering</u> him cake; finally, he <u>gave it in</u> and <u>took</u> a small piece   **A Ⓑ C   D**
          A   B   C

even though he <u>wasn't</u> hungry.
                      D

2. Bill <u>thought</u> Tricia <u>was</u> <u>looking forward to</u> retirement, but actually she <u>didn't</u>.   **A   B   C   D**
          A   B   C   D

3. In China, <u>giving</u> a clock as a present <u>means</u> that the recipient <u>is running into</u>   **A   B   C   D**
                    A   B   C

time, <u>doesn't</u> it?
          D

4. Peter <u>showed up at</u> my house late because he <u>wasn't familiar with</u> my
        A   B

   neighborhood, and <u>so</u> <u>was</u> Alex.
                        C D

   A B C D

5. I really like the idea you've <u>come up</u>, but <u>do</u> <u>run it by</u> your supervisor
                             A   B   C

   before <u>presenting it</u> at the meeting.
          D

   A B C D

6. Although I like your proposal, I <u>am concerned about</u> the expenses
                               A

   <u>related to it</u>, so <u>I'd like to</u> <u>think over it</u> for a while.
     B   C   D

   A B C D

7. <u>Look forward to</u> <u>moving</u> to the new house, Mr. Johnson <u>got rid of</u> his useless
       A   B   C

   old items and <u>so did his wife</u>.
                 D

   A B C D

8. I <u>can't</u> <u>figure out</u> these math problems, so <u>I think</u> I'll <u>set it aside</u> until later.
     A   B   C   D

   A B C D

9. <u>Don't keep asking</u> Eva to <u>pay you back</u>; I'm sure she'll <u>do it</u> when she
      A   B   C

   <u>comes up</u> the money.
     D

   A B C D

10. Ed <u>hasn't</u> <u>set aside any money</u> for his retirement, and Mark <u>hasn't</u> <u>neither</u>.
       A   B   C   D

    A B C D

11. Danielle <u>isn't</u> like to <u>show off</u>, and <u>neither</u> <u>does Mark</u>.
          A   B   C   D

    A B C D

PART VI AUXILIARIES AND PHRASAL VERBS

I. AUXILIARIES

Complete the report with the correct auxiliary verbs to refer to previously mentioned information.

Many people are unnecessarily afraid of sharks. They shouldn't _____be_____. Although sharks

              1.

can be dangerous, they are not as dangerous as most people think. This report will dispel some

rumors about sharks.

    Many people think that the shark is one distinct species. In fact, it _____. There

                                                 2.

are about 250 different species. Some people believe that sharks are random predators, killing

anybody who steps into the water. In fact, most _____. Sharks generally attack only

                              3.

the weak, sick, or dead. Some believe that sharks prefer to prey on humans. Actually, they

_____. Aside from the white shark, or *Carcharodon carcharias*, sharks usually feed on

             4.

plankton, carrion, seals, and marine animals. Some people think that humans have been victimized

by sharks for a long time. In fact, they _____. Humans have more commonly become

                          5.

victims in recent years because they've been spending a great deal of time at sea. Prior to a century

ago, they _____.

      6.

    Does this mean that sharks never attack humans? Of course it _____. However,

                                    7.

these attacks are generally caused by such factors as provocation or being mistaken for shark prey.

Do surfers and boaters have a high risk of being killed by sharks? We think they _____.

                                                         8.

In fact, they have a higher chance of being killed in a car accident.

    Some people fear that sharks will overrun the oceans. Most likely they _____.

                                              9.

Sharks have a long gestation period and do not reproduce frequently. Some think the best way to

prevent shark attacks is to kill all sharks. We think it _____. Killing sharks will most

                                    10.

probably lead to an ecological imbalance in the ocean.

    Has this report alleviated some of your fears about sharks? We hope it _____. The

                                              11.

next time you go to the ocean, just use reasonable precaution, and you should have no problem.

II. AUXILIARIES

Complete each tag question. Then add a short answer. Be sure to use the correct auxiliary verb and pronoun.

1. **A:** You've done this kind of work before, ___haven't you___?

   B: No, ___I haven't___.

2. **A:** Brian can speak Russian, _____?

   B: Yes, _____.

3. **A:** Ellen and Marie are students, _____?

   B: No, _____.

4. **A:** Ms. Jackson doesn't have a car, _____?

   B: Yes, _____.

5. **A:** You'll be at the party tonight, _____?

   B: No, _____.

6. **A:** You were in my third-grade class, _____?

   B: Yes, _____.

7. **A:** That man shouldn't be making a left turn from the right lane, _____?

   B: No, _____.

III. AUXILIARIES

Complete the conversation between two coworkers. Use the correct forms from the box.

So did I	do too	So do	Neither can I	So do I
Neither have I	does too	can't either	don't either	~~was too~~

JACK: Hi, Ben. How was your weekend?

BEN: Good. But it was much too short.

JACK: Mine ___was too___. But it was good. I watched the big football game on TV.
          _{1.}

BEN: _____. That was a great game, wasn't it? I haven't seen such a good game in
         _{2.}
a long time.

JACK: _____. I really enjoy watching football.
          _{3.}

BEN: _____. But my wife hates it.
         _{4.}

JACK: Mine _____. She says she can understand participating in sports, but she can't
                 _{5.}
understand watching sports on TV. Every time there's a game on, she goes to the gym.

BEN: I don't like to hang out at the gym.

JACK: I _____ . I think it's boring. But a lot of people in my department go there.
6.

BEN: _____ a lot of the people in my department. But I can't understand why.
7.

JACK: _____ . Well, I guess I'd better get to work. I have a lot to do today.
8.

BEN: I _____ . You know, I brought work home on Friday, but I just didn't get to it.
9.
I can never get any work done at home.

JACK: I _____ . There are too many distractions. Anyway, I hope you have a good week.
10.

BEN: You too.

IV. AUXILIARIES

Complete each sentence with the emphatic verb form.

1. Tom and Sandra don't eat red meat. They _____*do eat*_____ chicken and fish, though.
(eat)

2. I'm not an investment counselor, but I _____ an accountant, so maybe I can
(be)
help you.

3. Sheila doesn't know PowerPoint. However, she _____ Excel and basic HTML.
(know)

4. Tim hasn't directed any plays, but he _____ several. I think you should hire him.
(produce)

5. We didn't have a chance to visit Lake Titicaca when we were in South America. We
_____ it to Machu Picchu, though.
(make)

6. Burt won't call you long distance. However, he _____ you e-mail messages.
(send)

7. Fred hadn't worked as an accountant before he started this job, but he _____ as a
(work)
bookkeeper.

V. PHRASAL VERBS

Circle the letter of the synonym that best matches the underlined phrase.

1. I can't do without my cell phone.

   a. need to have

   b. don't know how to use

   c. have difficulty operating

2. Jerry isn't going out with Elaine.

   a. dating

   b. ending a relationship

   c. leaving the house

3. I don't know when the next train leaves. Why don't you <u>look it up</u>?

   a. ask someone about it

   b. search for the information

   c. study it carefully

4. Wendy can't <u>get away with</u> coming into work late every morning.

   a. go unpunished for

   b. leave by

   c. get promoted by

5. Cathy <u>tried on</u> her sister's dress.

   a. wore for a few minutes

   b. borrowed

   c. gave away

6. Before he signed the contract, Brian <u>ran it by</u> a lawyer.

   a. chased after

   b. accidentally met

   c. got the opinion of

7. Victor <u>put off</u> making hotel arrangements until a week before his trip.

   a. postponed

   b. forgot about

   c. didn't consider

8. Sally <u>insisted on</u> following her brother wherever he went.

   a. was stubborn about

   b. declined

   c. talked about

9. I'll <u>pay you back</u> Tuesday if you lend me $5 for a hamburger today.

   a. cook for you

   b. return some of the money

   c. return all of the money

10. Anne has stacks of magazines she needs to <u>get rid of</u>.

   a. read

   b. give away

   c. organize

11. Melvin's application for medical school was <u>turned down</u>.

   a. rejected

   b. accepted

   c. lost

12. Ron didn't want to <u>part with</u> his favorite old T-shirt.

    a. give away

    b. tear into pieces

    c. wear

13. George has <u>come up with</u> a plan that he'd like to share with you.

    a. thought of

    b. considered

    c. made an agreement about

14. Clark is trying to <u>cut down on</u> spending.

    a. reduce

    b. increase

    c. stop

15. The employees refused to <u>put up with</u> the terrible working conditions.

    a. tolerate

    b. complain about

    c. forget about

VI. PHRASAL VERBS

Complete the e-mail message. Use the correct phrasal verbs from the box. Change the verb tense as needed.

~~get rid of~~	run out of	run by	come up with
find out	turn down	insist on	show off
wait for	set aside	be familiar with	

Hi Mark,

How's it going? Good, I hope. I've had an interesting week. Do you remember my old car that always

needed repair? Well, I finally _____*got rid of*_____ it and bought a new one. You know, I really didn't

                                           1.

think I'd be able to _____ enough money to buy a new car. But I managed to

                                   2.

_____ a little money each month, and finally I had enough for a down payment.

                3.

    I didn't know much about current car prices or features, and I wanted to make sure I

_____ these things before I visited a dealership. So, I checked the Internet and

                4.

bought some consumer magazines. I _____ a lot about cars that I didn't know before!

                                                    5.

    When I went to the dealership, one thing I wasn't prepared for was the salesman's attitude. I told

him I wanted an inexpensive car, but he _____ showing me all these really expensive

                                                             6.

models. Finally, he showed me a car I could afford, and I made him an offer. He said it was too low,

and he had to _____ it _____ his manager. He left the showroom, and I
                                          7.

sat there for half an hour. Then he came back and told me that his manager had _____
                                                                                                              8.

my offer. I made a slightly higher offer, and he said he had to talk to his manager again. Again, he left

the showroom, and I sat there for another half hour. Finally, I _____ patience. I
                                                                                        9.

knocked on the manager's door and said, " Look, I can't _____ you all day. Do you want
                                                                                  10.

me to buy a car here, or do you want me to go to the dealership across the street?"

　　　To make a long story short, I got the car for a good price in the end. Is it OK if I drive over to

your place sometime so you can see it? I really want to _____ it _____!
                                                                                                      11.

See you soon!

Tom

VII.　PHRASAL VERBS

Complete each conversation with a phrasal verb and a pronoun.

1. **A:** Have you put away the dishes?

   B: No, I haven't __put them away__ yet.

2. **A:** I've been putting off starting my research paper for weeks.

   B: Well, you'd better not _____ any longer! It's due next Monday.

3. **A:** Come outside! Glen wants to show off his new car.

   B: Is he still _____?

4. **A:** Have you figured the directions out yet?

   B: No, I still haven't _____.

5. **A:** Should I open up these boxes now?

   B: No, you can _____ later.

6. **A:** Raymond has been trying to break Will and Grace up for a long time.

   B: Really? Why has he been trying to _____. They're a great couple!

VIII.　PHRASAL VERBS

Read the short, humorous article. Then read it again. Find and correct the nine errors in phrasal verbs.

How to Get Your Girlfriend or Boyfriend to Break Up ^with You

- Never be concerned his or her feelings.
- Never give up to him or her when making plans. Always insist for doing whatever you want to
  do. Alternatively, make plans without running it by him or her.

- Always show up dates at least half an hour late.
- Always show off of when you are in public together. Whenever he or she starts to say something, cut off him or her.
- Forget his or her birthday about.
- Start a rumor that you are going out someone else.

IX. SYNTHESIS

Circle the letter of the correct answer to complete each sentence.

1. Kyoko can't speak Korean, and _____.   **A B C (D)**

   (A) so can Jürgen   (C) Jürgen can too

   (B) Jürgen can either   (D) neither can Jürgen

2. Look at Helen in her new designer dress! She's always trying to _____.   **A B C D**

   (A) show up   (C) show forward

   (B) show off   (D) show over

3. Erkhan lives in Jones Hall, and _____.   **A B C D**

   (A) Makoto is too   (C) so does Makoto

   (B) so is Makoto   (D) neither does Makoto

4. There are a lot of difficult words in the passage, so you may have to _____ in the dictionary.   **A B C D**

   (A) look it up   (C) look them up

   (B) look up it   (D) look up them

5. Andy thinks he's not handsome, but actually he _____.   **A B C D**

   (A) does   (C) was

   (B) has   (D) is

6. Tony can't _____ his morning coffee. If he doesn't have at least two cups, he's grouchy all morning.   **A B C D**

   (A) do with   (C) do without

   (B) deal with   (D) do over

7. Linda doesn't eat chicken. However, she _____ eat fish.   **A B C D**

   (A) should   (C) does

   (B) could   (D) doesn't

8. Do you like the new president? Some people are happy with her, but others _____.   **A B C D**

   (A) do   (C) are

   (B) don't   (D) aren't

9. Susan's boss didn't think she could handle the project. However, she surprised   A B C D
him when she showed him _____.

   (A) she did   (C) could she
   (B) she could   (D) did she

10. Fred is on a diet, so he's trying to _____ fat and sugar.   A B C D

   (A) cut on   (C) cut down on
   (B) cut down in   (D) cut off

11. You were at the library on Saturday, _____ you?   A B C D

   (A) didn't   (C) weren't
   (B) wasn't   (D) haven't

12. Sharon was very shy in high school. However, she _____ more   A B C D
outgoing when she went to college.

   (A) will become   (C) did become
   (B) has become   (D) had become

13. Rebecca has a lot more space in her closet now that she's _____ her   A B C D
old clothes.

   (A) gotten rid away   (C) gotten rid of
   (B) gotten rid   (D) gotten rid off

14. Children should be taught that they can't _____ telling lies.   A B C D

   (A) get away with   (C) get across
   (B) get along with   (D) get even with

15. Class! Class! Be quiet! I will not _____ this noise any longer!   A B C D

   (A) put away   (C) put up with
   (B) put off   (D) put without

16. You'll be here when I get back, _____ you?   A B C D

   (A) shouldn't   (C) don't
   (B) aren't   (D) won't

X. SYNTHESIS

*Each sentence has four underlined parts or phrases. The four underlined parts of the sentence are marked
A, B, C, and D. Circle the letter of the ONE underlined part that is NOT CORRECT.*

1. How many pairs of shoes are you planning to try on? I'm getting tired of   A B Ⓒ D
                                                      A   **B**

    waiting you for, and so is Jennifer.
       C   **D**

2. Timothy thought his parents had forgotten about his birthday, but actually   A B C D
            A   **B**   **C**

    they didn't.
        D

3. Anne knows she should <u>get rid</u> the junk she's <u>put away</u> in the attic, but she
   A   B

   <u>doesn't want to</u> <u>part with it</u>.
   C   D
           A B C D

4. Ted found it easy to <u>cut down</u> <u>on</u> coffee and <u>give up</u> smoking, but Ed <u>hadn't</u>.
                A   B   C   D
                        A B C D

5. Jack! I won't <u>put up with</u> the mess in your room any more! I <u>want you to</u>
                  A   B

   <u>pick up your toys</u> and <u>put away them</u> immediately!
   C   D
                        A B C D

6. Educators have <u>found out</u> that many children <u>aren't familiar with</u> their
                 A   B

   country's history, and <u>neither</u> <u>do</u> their parents.
                        C   D
                        A B C D

7. After her employer <u>turned down</u> her request for a raise, Alicia became
                        A

   <u>concerned about</u> her situation. She thought that if they <u>kept refusing</u> to pay
   B   C

   her better, she wouldn't be able to <u>set inside</u> any savings.
                                 D
                        A B C D

8. Max <u>couldn't figure out</u> the chemistry homework, and Arlene <u>couldn't</u>
              A   B

   <u>figure out it</u> <u>either</u>.
   C   D
                        A B C D

9. Brenda hasn't <u>come up</u> <u>with</u> any suggestions yet, and Wanda <u>hasn't</u> <u>neither</u>.
                A   B   C   D
                        A B C D

10. Bob asked Marsha to <u>go out</u> <u>with him</u>, but she <u>turned down him</u> because
                      A   B   C

    she thought it would <u>break up</u> their friendship.
                         D
                         A B C D

11. Leona <u>wants to</u> <u>brush on</u> her Spanish, and Hank <u>does</u> <u>too</u>.
           A   B   C D
                         A B C D

PART VII GERUNDS AND INFINITIVES

DIAGNOSTIC TEST

I. GERUNDS

Complete each sentence by changing the indicated verb to a gerund.

1. My favorite hobbies are gardening, skindiving, and ___rock climbing___ .
   (rock climb)

2. The children simply have to stop _____ so much television.
   (watch)

3. _____ that dead-end job was a positive step for you to take.
   (Quit)

4. Hotdoggers give _____ a bad name. They cause a lot of accidents.
   (ski)

5. Aunt Conchita likes her retirement, but she says she's not used to _____ so much
   (have)
   free time.

6. One of the healthiest activities is _____ frequently.
   (exercise)

II. GERUNDS

Complete each sentence with the correct possessive + gerund form.

1. We appreciate ___your helping___ us in our time of need. We couldn't have made it without you.
   (you / help)

2. There's a lot that can be accomplished by _____ the problem.
   (we / sit down and discuss)

3. _____ come to the boys' defense at the right moment is what saved them.
   (John / have)

4. The man I worked with was amused at _____ so impatient with his slowness.
   (I / get)

5. The best thing in my high school education was my Spanish _____ that we speak
   (teacher / insist)
   the language. Nothing taught me more.

6. Now that she is grown up, Irene is grateful for her _____ insisted that she finish
   (parents / have)
   high school.

III. GERUNDS

Complete each sentence with the correct perfect form. Use having + past participle of the indicated verb.

1. I remember ___having run into___ Bill just before he went into the army.
   (run into)

2. In hindsight, I'd say that the boys' _____ high marks led to a positive change in
   (earn)
   their attitude toward school.

3. The entrepreneur's _____ a need and acting on it made her rich.
   (perceive)

4. I remember _____ to the Bahamas several times for family vacations when I was a
(go)
child.

5. Donna received a commendation for _____ the presence of mind to call 911
(have)
immediately.

6. Hillary, my youngest daughter, got a scholarship to college for _____ the best senior
(write)
essay.

IV. GERUNDS

Complete each sentence with the correct passive form. Use being / getting + *past participle of the
indicated verb.*

1. Anthropologist Brenda Matthews loved ___being allowed___ to participate in Navajo culture.
(be / allow)

2. _____ to study at Oxford University is the most exciting thing that has ever
(Get / accept)
happened to me.

3. Harry is ecstatic about _____ for the swim team.
(be / choose)

4. Medical personnel need to be concerned about _____ while on the job.
(get / infect)

5. Rebecca says that _____ by lightning is the most terrifying thing that's ever hap-
(get / strike)
pened to her.

6. _____ to participate in a Native American dance is a high honor indeed.
(Be / invite)

V. INFINITIVES

Complete each sentence with an infinitive, using the indicated verb.

1. Lewis's lifelong ambition was ___to become___ a lion tamer. He became one at the age of sixty.
(become)

2. Kids, I asked you _____ during the recording session. You've got to be quiet.
(not / talk)

3. _____ each moment for itself is my goal. I don't always achieve it.
(enjoy)

4. Detective Harry Sadler asked author Rolleen Laing _____ him solve the mystery.
(help)

5. _____ the Caribbean is to love it. It's the most beautiful place I've ever been.
(know)

6. One of the most important things parents can do is _____ there when their children
(be)
need them.

VI. INFINITIVES

Complete each sentence with the correct perfect form. Use to + have + *past participle of the indicated verb.*

1. You were supposed <u>to have turned in</u> your essay already. It's too late now.
   (turn in)

2. The senator is rumored _____ his resignation from Congress to accept a cabinet
   (submit)
   post.

3. You're expected _____ the basic principles of writing before you enroll in college
   (master)
   composition.

4. Homer is believed _____ both *The Iliad* and *The Odyssey*.
   (write)

5. The convicts are thought _____ from prison by digging a tunnel.
   (escape)

6. Though Nero is said _____ while Rome burned, there is little evidence to support
   (fiddle)
   this contention.

VII. INFINITIVES

Complete each sentence with the correct passive form. Use to + be / get + *past participle of the indicated verb. Use* be *unless* get *is specified.*

1. We would like <u>to be consulted</u> on this issue, even if you don't accept our recommendations.
   (consult)

2. The governor managed _____ by the slimmest of margins.
   (get / elect)

3. _____ the opportunity to visit the Forbidden City is an honor.
   (give)

4. Joe's fondest wish is _____ by a university.
   (get / hire)

5. Most individuals simply want _____ kindly and respectfully.
   (treat)

6. This proposal has its good points, but it needs _____ in plain and simple English.
   (rewrite)

VIII. INFINITIVES

Rewrite the sentence containing ellipsis, replacing to *with a full verb phrase.*

1. **A:** Let's go to the festival at the City Center.
   B: I don't want to. There'll be too many people there.
   <u>I don't want to go to the festival at the City Center.</u>

2. **A:** Is Jack finally going to go on a diet?
   B: I don't know. He certainly ought to. He weighs almost 300 pounds.

   _____

3. **A:** Melanie, did you mop the floors as I asked?
   B: I didn't have time to. It took me all day to do the vacuuming.

   _____

4. A: Didn't the Suzukis buy a new house?

    B: Not yet. They're planning to in October.

_____

5. A: Let's go camping this weekend.

    B: I'd love to. I've got to finish this report, though.

_____

6. A: Martin says he's not going to register for the selective service.

    B: He has to. It's the law.

_____

IX. SYNTHESIS

Choose the form, gerund or infinitive, that correctly completes each sentence.

1. John asked Mary ___to help___ him write his essay.
   (helping / to help)

2. What shall we do tonight? How about _____ to that concert?
   (going / to go)

3. Now that she's retired, Aunt Susan is interested in _____ a mystery novelist.
   (becoming / to become)

4. I signed up for this class _____ my Spanish grammar.
   (reviewing / to review)

5. I don't think you should wear jeans to work. The boss warned us _____ casually,
   (not dressing / not to dress)
   remember?

6. In this class, you are expected _____ prepared for each day's lesson.
   (being / to be)

7. I thought I wanted that job, but I'd have to say that not _____ it is the best thing
   (getting / to get)
   that ever happened to me.

8. My _____ a scholarship allowed me to attend college. Otherwise, I wouldn't have
   (having gotten / to have gotten)
   been able to.

X. SYNTHESIS

Complete the conversation with gerund or infinitive forms of the indicated verbs. In some cases, either form may be possible.

A: What do you want ___to do___ today?
      1. (do)

B: I'd like to _____ the day outside. How about going _____? I know you
      2. (spend)   **3. (kayak)**
enjoy _____ to the lake, so I'm sure you'll like that!
    4. (go)

A: Hmmm . . . . I don't know. Isn't _____ dangerous?
          5. (kayak)

B: Not really. You just have _____ a few easy paddling strokes. I can't claim
           6. (learn)
_____ an expert, but I can teach you how _____ a paddle, if you like.
  7. (be)   **8. (use)**

A: Well, maybe. But tell me, do you need _____ strong arms _____ the
9. (have)   10. (maneuver)

paddle?

B: I don't think you'll have any trouble _____, though your arms may get a little tired.
11. (paddle)

Personally, I don't mind _____ sore arms, since I like _____ so much.
12. (get)   13. (kayak)

A: Well , I suppose I would like _____ it at least once. Is there anything you would ad-
14. (try)

vise me _____?
15. (bring)

B: Well, I definitely recommend _____ a bathing suit, with an old T-shirt and shorts on
16. (wear)

top—clothes you aren't afraid _____ wet or dirty. It's probably going to be sunny, so
17. (get)

I also advise _____ sunblock and a sunhat, especially if you burn easily. Oh, yeah!
18. (bring)

Don't forget _____ lunch and a couple of liters of water. You'll get very thirsty!
19. (take)

A: OK. Sounds good! What time do you want _____?
20. (leave)

XI. SYNTHESIS

Circle the letter of the correct answer to complete each sentence.

1. I'd really like _____ out for dinner this evening.   **A B Ⓒ D**

   (A) to have gone   (C) to go
   (B) going   (D) to going

2. You need to practice the piano every day _____ a concert pianist.   **A B C D**

   (A) for to become   (C) to becoming
   (B) to become   (D) for becoming

3. Since Martha broke her foot, she hasn't participated in her favorite   **A B C D**

   pastime, _____.

   (A) modern dancing   (C) her modern dancing
   (B) to modern dance   (D) being modern danced

4. Alicia knows she should study for her exam, but she just doesn't _____.   **A B C D**

   (A) want to do   (C) want to
   (B) wanting to   (D) wanting

5. I'd really like _____ that movie. I've heard it's great!   **A B C D**

   (A) to have seen   (C) to see
   (B) seeing   (D) to seeing

6. Leo's idea was _____ his speech for an hour each night.   **A B C D**

   (A) practicing   (C) to practice
   (B) practice   (D) to being practiced

7. Do we have to go to the Wilsons' for dinner? I don't want to spend my evening _____ by those two. **A B C D**

(A) being bored
(B) being boring
(C) boring
(D) having been bored

8. Jennifer's husband always drives because he doesn't like _____. **A B C D**

(A) to drive
(B) she driving
(C) her driving
(D) her drive to

9. Min improved her vocabulary and increased her TOEFL score _____ a variety of articles. **A B C D**

(A) to read
(B) reading
(C) for reading
(D) by reading

10. Can I use your sewing machine _____ my pants? **A B C D**

(A) to hem
(B) for to hem
(C) for hem
(D) hemming

11. _____ smoking, Stanley thinks his health is much better. **A B C D**

(A) To quit
(B) Have to quit
(C) Having quit
(D) Quitting

12. The Longs have _____ move to Florida. **A B C D**

(A) decided to
(B) deciding to
(C) deciding
(D) to deciding

13. Rosa claims _____ her essay by herself, but I think she got help. **A B C D**

(A) to write
(B) writing
(C) to have written
(D) her writing

14. Vanessa stopped by her teacher's office _____ her a question. **A B C D**

(A) asking
(B) to ask
(C) ask
(D) to have asked

15. By the time we reached shelter, it had _____. **A B C D**

(A) stopped to rain
(B) stopping rain
(C) stopped rain
(D) stopped raining

XII. SYNTHESIS

Each sentence has four underlined parts or phrases. The four underlined parts of the sentence are marked A, B, C, and D. Circle the letter of the ONE underlined part that is NOT CORRECT.

1. I warned Bonnie <u>not lending</u> Hank any money <u>for gambling</u>, but she <u>refused</u>   Ⓐ B C D
                    A   B   C

   <u>to listen</u>.
    D

2. You <u>were told</u> <u>not touch</u> the experiment, but you <u>tampered with</u> it and now   A B C D
           A   B   C

   <u>it's ruined</u>!
    D

3. Frank's ambition <u>is become</u> a novelist, and <u>he's willing</u> <u>to work</u> hard   A B C D
                        A   B   C

   <u>to achieve</u> his goal.
    D

4. I <u>remember</u> <u>have met her</u> when we were at the recital hall, <u>waiting in line</u>   A B C D
       A   B   C

   <u>to buy</u> tickets.
    D

5. The Greenes <u>were astonished</u> at <u>I</u> <u>getting</u> a scholarship <u>to the univeristy</u>.   A B C D
               A   B C   D

6. Certain art historians <u>consider</u> Da Vinci's *Mona Lisa,* <u>his best-known work</u>   A B C D
                     A   B

   <u>hanging</u> in the Louvre, <u>be</u> a self-portrait.
    C   D

7. <u>Your</u> <u>be</u> in the right place at the right time <u>prevented</u> a serious accident   A B C D
    A B   C

   <u>from happening</u>.
    D

8. <u>My</u> <u>get nominated</u> for the office is enough; I <u>don't care</u> if I <u>win</u> or not.   A B C D
    A   B   C   D

9. According to the college's rules, instructors <u>can</u>, but <u>do not have</u>, <u>fail</u>   A B C D
                                    A   B   C

   students for <u>poor classroom attendance</u>.
              D

10. James Madison <u>is</u> <u>thought</u> <u>to having</u> <u>been</u> the principal author of *The*   A B C D
                 A   B   C   D

    Federalist Papers.

11. Rose <u>regrets</u> not <u>to learn</u> how <u>to drive</u> since she enjoys <u>traveling</u>.   A B C D
          A   B   C   D

12. After <u>having</u> <u>eating</u> dinner, we considered <u>taking</u> a walk or <u>renting</u> a video.   A B C D
           A   B   C   D

13. Jan persuaded <u>her brother</u> <u>lend</u> her the money <u>to buy</u> a computer, which she   A B C D
                  A   B   C

    expects <u>to use</u> for her schoolwork.
          D

14. While her car <u>was</u> <u>being</u> <u>repaired</u>, Mary stopped at the supermarket <u>buying</u>   A B C D
                A   B   C   D

    some groceries.

15. I don't mind <u>Jim's</u> <u>borrowing</u> my clothes, but I can't stand <u>him</u> <u>returning</u>   A B C D
             A   B   C   D

    them soiled.

16. <u>Having</u> <u>work</u> in a supervisory positions, Ms. Wade is well prepared <u>to undertake</u>   A B C D
     A   B   C

    the responsibilities that go with <u>managing</u> a department.
                                   D

Part VII Gerunds and Infinitives

I. GERUNDS

Complete each sentence by changing the indicated verb to a gerund.

1. Uncle Dal likes his new job, but he says he's not accustomed to ____having____ a private
   (have)
   secretary.

2. One key to good health is _____ at least five servings of fruits and vegetables a day.
   (eat)

3. My least favorite chores are washing windows, ironing clothes, and _____ lunches.
   (fix)

4. Harrison has simply got to stop _____ if he wants to be healthy. That's all there is to it.
   (smoke)

5. _____ the PTA was really a mistake. I can see that now. We need to get involved
   (Quit)
   with the school again.

6. _____ varies from culture to culture. Often tourists don't know how much to give.
   (Tip)

II. GERUNDS

Complete each sentence with the correct possessive + gerund form.

1. I'm in favor of ____your joining____ our team. I'm sure you can make a contribution.
   (you / join)

2. My office mate gets angry at _____ to keep the office neat.
   (I / need)

3. _____ recommended me for the position is what did the trick. I'll always be grateful
   (Mrs. Martin / have)
   to her.

4. At the time, I didn't like being told what to do, but now I appreciate my _____ in-
   (parents / have)
   sisted on our nightly curfew.

5. There's nothing to be lost and a lot to be gained by _____ to iron out their differ-
   (they / try)
   ences by themselves.

6. _____ come to your defense is what saved you. You need to thank her.
   (Doris / have)

III. GERUNDS

Complete each sentence with the correct perfect form. Use having + *past participle of the indicated verb.*

1. Sergeant Masters received special recognition for _____having gone_____ above and beyond the call
    (go)
    of duty.

2. Jamal received a scholarship to college for _____ his team to victory in the
    (lead)
    state championship three years running.

3. I remember _____ you about the problem. We talked about it very specifically.
    (warn)

4. Looking back on it all, I'd say that our _____ that contract without carefully reading
    (sign)
    it was a big mistake.

5. Christopher Columbus's _____ the right moment to petition the Spanish monarchs
    (recognize)
    contributed more than anything else to his success.

6. Molly remembers _____ a mysterious telephone call on the morning of the robbery.
    (get)

IV. GERUNDS

Complete each sentence with the correct passive form. Use being / getting + *past participle of the
indicated verb.*

1. _____Being told_____ the truth can sometimes help.
    (be / told)

2. If I were you, I'd be worried about_____ in this real estate deal. You need
    (get / cheat)
    something in writing.

3. _____ to work as a congressional page this summer is a great honor for Annette.
    (Be / select)

4. I constantly worry about my pets' _____ by a car.
    (get / hit)

5. Most students like _____ the opportunity to express their opinions.
    (be / give)

6. _____ to run for student body president was a great honor for me.
    (get / nominate)

V. INFINITIVES

Complete each sentence with an infinitive, using the indicated verb.

1. The candidate for the Senate urged the electorate _____to vote_____ for her and not against
    (vote)
    someone else.

2. _____ someone else's situation, one has to walk in that person's shoes for a while.
    (appreciate)

3. One of the best ways to learn something is _____ it relevant to our individual lives.
    (make)

4. Mrs. Goodwin, who had always wanted _____ French, finally got her chance when
    (learn)
    she was fifty.

5. Class, I warned you _____ your papers late. I can't accept them now.
    (not / turn in)

6. _____ each day to the fullest is a worthy goal but a difficult one to achieve.
    (live)

VI. INFINITIVES

Complete each sentence with the correct perfect form. Use to + have + *past participle of the indicated verb.*

1. To be considered for this position, you are required __to have worked__ for at least three years
   (work)
   for a daily newspaper.

2. The Sumerians are believed _____ the Western world's first writing system.
   (develop)

3. In the news, an earthquake is reported _____ the island of Honshu, but no confir-
   (hit)
   mation has been received.

4. Confucius is commonly believed _____, "A journey of a thousand miles must begin
   (say)
   with a single step," but it was really Lao-tzu who said this.

5. See that woman sitting alone at that table? She's supposed _____ a famous actress
   (be)
   back in the days of the big movie studios.

6. The two nations are reported _____ a peace treaty, but there's no official word on
   (sign)
   this yet.

VII. INFINITIVES

Complete each sentence with the correct passive form. Use to + be / get + *past participle of the indicated verb. Use* be *unless* get *is specified.*

1. What Anita would really like is __to get hired__ by a major theater company.
   (get / hire)

2. The vast majority of writers simply want _____ seriously.
   (take)

3. The house is structurally sound, but it needs _____ before winter.
   (reroof)

4. I'd like _____ for the position, even if I'm not hired.
   (consider)

5. Sarah is such a social climber. She even managed _____ to the Vanderdorfs' party.
   (get / invite)

6. _____ a personal tour of the mansion was beyond my wildest expectations.
   (give)

VIII. INFINITIVES

Rewrite the sentence containing ellipsis, replacing to *with a full verb phrase.*

1. **A:** Isn't Joe going to college this fall?
   B: He wants to. I'm not sure he can afford it, though.
   He wants to go to college this fall.

2. **A:** Can you come to the card party on Saturday?
   B: I'd like to. I may have to work, though. Can I let you know tomorrow?

3. A: Iris maintains that she's not going to pay child support.

    B: She has to. That's part of the agreement.

---

4. A: Let's go to the movies tonight. There's a good film playing at the Admiral.

    B: I don't want to. I'm too tired to move.

---

5. A: Is Mike really going to start working out?

    B: I don't know. He ought to. He leads such a sedentary life.

---

6. A: Frannie, did you mow the lawn?

    B: I didn't have time to. It took me all afternoon to write my English essay.

IX.   SYNTHESIS

Choose the form, gerund or infinitive, that correctly completes each sentence.

1. Grandmother asked us _____to help_____ her move the heavy furniture.
   (helping / to help)

2. What would you like to do today? How about _____ in the yard?
   (working / to work)

3. Now that he's old enough, Stanley is determined _____ into politics.
   (going / to go)

4. I made an appointment _____ my eyes checked. I've been having blurry vision.
   (getting / to get)

5. Please put out that cigarette. I asked you _____ inside the building.
   (not smoking / not to smoke)

6. To get a high-paying job, you're advised _____ prepared for a difficult interview.
   (being / to be)

7. I understand your explanation, but my not _____ a thank-you note from you really
   (getting / to get)
   hurt me.

8. My _____ my tax refund in the nick of time saved me. Otherwise, I wouldn't
   (having received / to have received)
   have been able to make my April mortgage payment.

X.   SYNTHESIS

Complete the conversation with gerund or infinitive forms of the indicated verbs. In some cases, either form may be possible.

A: Have you decided where you'd like _____to go_____ for dinner tonight?
   1. (go)

B: I'm not sure. I'm curious _____ what that new Japanese restaurant is like.
   2. (find out)

A: I really don't feel like _____ Japanese food for dinner tonight. I had it just last night.
3. (have)

B: Well, there's a new all-you-can-eat buffet on Main Street. You can choose whatever you want

_____ from the buffet.
4. (eat)

A: No way! I can't stand _____ to those places. Even if I'm determined
_5. (go)_

_____ just a small portion, I can't resist _____ some of every dish.
6. (take) _7. (sample)_

Then I find it hard to stop _____. And I'm trying _____!
8. (eat) _9. (diet)_

B: OK. Well, would you consider _____ that cafe just outside town? The food there is
10. (try)

wonderful. It is a little expensive, but I think it's worth _____ a little extra for it. And
11. (pay)

if you're on a diet, I recommend _____ a specialty salad. The salad is reasonably
12. (order)

priced, and you can ask the waiter or waitress _____ it with low-calorie dressing on
13. (serve)

the side.

A: You know, I was always afraid _____ there, since I heard the prices were so high.
_14. (go)_

But I just got a bonus, so for once I can afford _____ a little more. OK—you've con-
15. (spend)

vinced me _____. I just need _____ my clothes. I promise
_16. (go)_ _17. (change)_

_____ ready in half an hour.
_18. (be)_

B: Great! Do you want _____ my car or yours?
19. (take)

A: I'd prefer _____. Is that OK?
20. (drive)

XI. SYNTHESIS

Circle the letter of the correct answer to complete each sentence.

1. What do you want _____ this evening? (Ⓐ) B C D

   (A) to do (C) doing
   (B) to have done (D) to doing

2. "Mark, can you help me move this weekend?" A B C D

   "Sorry, I won't have time _____. You'd better ask someone else."

   (A) to (C) to doing
   (B) to do (D) to have done

3. Would you recommend _____ this course? A B C D

   (A) my taking (C) me to take
   (B) me taking (D) to take

4. I asked Stuart _____ my essay. A B C D

   (A) read (C) to read
   (B) reading (D) having read

5. Pauline's aunt and uncle plan _____ her at the airport.   A B C D

(A) meet   (C) meeting

(B) to meet   (D) to have met

6. Don't _____ the dry cleaning!   A B C D

(A) forget picking up   (C) forgetting to pick up

(B) to forget to pick up   (D) forget to pick up

7. Marco Polo is said _____ pasta to Italy.   A B C D

(A) to introduce   (C) introducing

(B) to have introduced   (D) being introduced by

8. "Do you ever _____ your last job?"   A B C D

"No way! My new job is much better."

(A) regret to leave   (C) regretted to have left

(B) regret to have left   (D) regret having left

9. These letters were supposed _____ mailed yesterday.   A B C D

Why are they still here?

(A) being   (C) have been

(B) having been   (D) to have been

10. I need to stop by the store _____ some milk.   A B C D

(A) to have gotten   (C) get

(B) to get   (D) getting

11. If your computer is too slow, you can use mine _____ on the project.   A B C D

(A) for work   (C) to work

(B) for to work   (D) to working

12. Anyone interested in _____ soccer, sign up here.   A B C D

(A) play   (C) to play

(B) playing   (D) having played

13. There's no electricity in Dave's apartment, so he can't indulge in his favorite   A B C D

activity, _____.

(A) watching TV   (C) watch TV

(B) to watch TV   (D) his watching TV

14. I really need to wash my car, but I just haven't _____.   A B C D

(A) had a chance to   (C) been having a chance

(B) had to a chance   (D) had a chance to do

15. Thanks for doing all the driving on this trip! I really enjoy _____   A B C D

around.

(A) driving   (C) being driven

(B) having driven   (D) to driving

XII. SYNTHESIS

Each sentence has four underlined parts or phrases. The four underlined parts of the sentence are marked A, B, C, and D. Circle the letter of the ONE underlined part that is NOT CORRECT.

1. I asked Jeanette <u>coming</u> <u>to the party</u>, but she <u>said</u> she <u>won't be able to</u>.   (A) B C D
         A   B   C   D

2. You <u>were advised</u> <u>not put off</u> <u>taking</u> that course; now you won't <u>be able to graduate</u>   A B C D
         A   B   C   D
   on time.

3. Ellen's ambition <u>is become</u> a fine cellist; she's <u>been practicing</u> a great deal and her   A B C D
         A   B
   teacher <u>expects</u> <u>her to do</u> well.
         C   D

4. I <u>remember</u> <u>have studied</u> algebra in high school, but I <u>don't know</u> <u>how to do</u>   A B C D
       A   B   C   D
   these problems.

5. Fred's teachers <u>are amazed</u> at <u>he</u> <u>getting</u> into college, since he <u>always got</u> poor   A B C D
         A   B   C   D
   grades in high school.

6. Most literary scholars <u>consider</u> *The Tempest,* <u>completed</u> around 1611, <u>be</u> the last   A B C D
         A   B   C
   play Shakespeare <u>wrote</u>.
         D

7. <u>Bill's try</u> <u>to save</u> the drowning girl <u>without regard for</u> his own safety <u>showed</u>   A B C D
       A   B   C   D
   great courage.

8. I <u>can't accept</u> <u>his</u> <u>get chosen</u> <u>to lead</u> the state delegation.   A B C D
       A   B   C   D

9. According to the school handbook, the headmaster <u>may</u>, but <u>is not</u> <u>required</u>,   A B C D
         A   B   C
   <u>dismiss</u> unruly students.
      D

10. Contrary <u>to earlier belief</u>, King Richard III of England <u>is</u> now <u>thought have</u>   A B C D
          A   B   C
    <u>been</u> an effective monarch.
       D

11. Throughout the city, self-help groups <u>are</u> <u>being organized</u> <u>to help</u> people quit   A B C D
          A   B   C
    <u>to take</u> drugs.
       D

12. I appreciate <u>to</u> <u>your staying late</u> <u>to help</u> me <u>clean up</u>.   A B C D
          A   B   C   D

13. After <u>have</u> <u>finished</u> <u>studying</u>, they decided <u>to see</u> a movie.   A B C D
        A   B   C   D

14. Students can <u>improve</u> their English by <u>taking</u> classes, <u>studying</u> a textbook,   A B C D
          A   B   C
    and <u>to speak</u> English as much as possible.
         D

15. <u>Having</u> <u>grown up</u> poor, some parents try <u>encouraging</u> their children <u>to pursue</u>   A B C D
       A   B   C   D
    careers that are more profitable than enjoyable.

16. Joyce enjoys <u>to volunteer</u> at the hospital because she <u>doesn't like</u> <u>to be</u> <u>bored</u>.   A B C D
          A   B   C   D

PART VIII ADVERBS

DIAGNOSTIC TEST

I. ADVERB CLAUSES

Underline the independent clauses once and the dependent clauses twice. Then write whether the dependent clause is a clause of reason, contrast, condition, time, place, comparison, or result.

time   **1.** <u>I'll be able to reimburse you</u> <u><u>as soon as I get my paycheck</u></u>.

_____   **2.** Wherever there is poverty, there is the potential for strife.

_____   **3.** Elena is such a good cook that she could get a job in a world-class restaurant.

_____   **4.** Even though you made a few mistakes in calculation, you passed the exam with a score of 88 percent.

_____   **5.** I learned more in my high school Spanish class than I did in any college course.

_____   **6.** You'll pass the course if you pass the final exam.

II. ADVERB CLAUSES

Combine each pair of sentences into one sentence with an independent clause and a dependent clause. Use the subordinating conjunction provided. Keep the two clauses in the same order as the sentence.

1. I studied very hard. I didn't do well on the test. (although)

     Although I studied very hard, I didn't do well on the test.

_____

2. Joyce has been successful in her small business. She works hard and keeps excellent records. (because)

_____

_____

3. You'll be able to reduce your mortgage payments. You make a large down payment. (if)

_____

_____

4. I ignore my inner voice. I go wrong. (whenever)

_____

_____

5. You make a payment this week. We'll have to send your account to a collection agency. (unless)

_____

_____

6. Frank did well on the advanced placement biology test. He earned college credit. (so . . . that)

_____

_____

III. ADVERBS: VIEWPOINT, FOCUS, NEGATIVE, LOCATION, AND SEQUENCE

Circle the adverb in each set of sentences. Then write whether it is a viewpoint, focus, negative, location, or sequence adverb.

__viewpoint__ **1.** I'm not worried about Dick's problem. (Frankly) it is not my concern.

_____ **2.** Have you seen my umbrella? Oh, here it is!

_____ **3.** This machine has broken down. On no account should anyone touch it.

_____ **4.** There is certainly no reason for you to worry about passing the course. You're an excellent student.

_____ **5.** I can't give you any information about the man in the photograph. I don't even know his name.

_____ **6.** Unfortunately, Minnie will not be playing soccer with us today. She sprained her ankle.

_____ **7.** When I heard the gunshot, I almost got up and called the police. However, I realized it was coming from someone's TV.

_____ **8.** I'm not asking you for a loan. I'm only asking you for financial advice.

_____ **9.** I can't believe John said that! Rarely have I been as upset as I was last night.

IV. ADVERBS: VIEWPOINT, FOCUS, NEGATIVE, LOCATION, AND SEQUENCE

Circle the most appropriate forms to complete the letter.

Dear Russell,

I was listening to your show "Sound Off" yesterday. The topics were cloning and genetic engineering.

I'm a research scientist, and I had just / (just had) to respond to Janice Stone's comments.
                                    1.

Apparently / It is apparently , Ms. Stone thinks that cloning is a new phenomenon brought on by new
        2.

technology. This at all is not / is not at all true. Actual / Actually , cloning has occurred naturally for
                      3.   **4.**

millennia. Clearly, the dictionary / The dictionary clearly defines a clone as an organism descended from
                              5.

a single organism through asexual reproduction. In nature, not only cloning occurs / does cloning occur
                                                                          6.

with small organisms such as amoebas, bacteria, and yeasts, but it also takes place with larger

creatures such as shrimp and snails. Furthermore, some organisms, such as starfish, produce new

cloned organisms if dismembered. Clones even occur / occur even naturally in humans—they're called
                                              7.

identical "twins."

So along <u>came the technology / the technology came</u> to tap into and understand one of nature's
8.
processes. The <u>thing that's only new / only thing that's new</u> is that we are now able to control and
9.
learn from it. Little <u>it is / is</u> known about what this knowledge may bring, so some people are afraid.
10.
This is understandable. However, controlled cloning research in laboratories could result in many

benefits to humanity. For example, <u>it perhaps will / perhaps it will</u> provide new clues to aging and
11.
cancer. <u>It will maybe / Maybe it will</u> assist in the development of new medications. It may
12.
<u>even / even if</u> be a way for infertile couples to reproduce.
13.

Cloning will not upset the balance of nature. Nor <u>it will / will it</u> lead to a decline in species
14.
diversity. Cloning <u>almost certainly won't / won't almost certainly</u> open up a Pandora's box, but
16.
<u>sure / surely</u> it will open up a world of opportunities.
15.

V.   DISCOURSE CONNECTORS

Circle the correct coordinating conjunction to complete each sentence.

1. The test was difficult, <u>and /but</u> most students passed.

2. Jessica doesn't like chicken, <u>nor / or</u> does she like beef.

3. Dave was tired, <u>for / so</u> he took a nap.

4. Mark made dinner, <u>and / for</u> Pat washed the dishes.

5. I have to work late, <u>yet / so</u> I can't come to your party.

VI.   DISCOURSE CONNECTORS

Choose the correct transitions from the box to complete the speech to a high school class.

| for example   second   however   also   therefore   ~~first~~ |

Kids, there are two points I want to make. _____First_____, stay in school. When I quit high
1.
school after the tenth grade, I was sure I was going to make a lot of money by going to work. That

didn't happen, _____; it took me eight months to find a job. When I finally did get one,
2.
it paid less than the minimum wage. _____, the hours were long, and the work was
3.
drudgery. _____, I don't recommend quitting school. _____, find some-
4.   **5.**
thing to do where you can help others. _____, you might volunteer to help teach some-
6.
one to read, or you might visit people in an retirement home. Whatever it is, I think you'll find that

your own life will go a lot better if you consider the welfare of others.

VII. DISCOURSE CONNECTORS

Add commas or semicolons as necessary in each sentence. Do not add words or change capitalization.

1. I have a great deal of affection for Henry but I could never see myself married to him.

2. Carolyn doesn't like green vegetables nor does she like fruit. I wonder how she stays healthy.

3. Rachel did send me a birthday card in March however, I haven't heard from her since then.

4. You passed your driving test with flying colors though you could use some practice in parallel parking.

5. We'd better have a new roof put on the house otherwise, we'll be in trouble with the first big storm.

6. Today I did all the housework and I also spaded up the plot for the garden. Where's my medal?

7. Mr. Baldwin, Hank has been absent twenty times and has missed eleven assignments therefore, he will have to repeat the course.

VIII. ADVERB PHRASES

Underline the adverb phrase in each sentence.

1. <u>Watching from her living room window</u>, Mrs. McCoy saw the accident in the street below.

2. To remember people's names, you have to focus on their names when you are introduced.

3. Scientists are searching for a vaccine for AIDS and other dread diseases, having already wiped out smallpox.

4. I learned a lot about gardening by talking with my next-door neighbor.

5. Given the choice between watching a video or going out to a theater, I'd opt for the latter.

6. I learned a great deal about the plight of the elderly while visiting a nursing home last month.

IX. ADVERB PHRASES

Combine each pair of sentences into a single sentence with an independent clause and an adverb phrase. Use the type of modifying phrase suggested in parentheses and place the subject in the independent clause.

1. Harrison felt burned out at his job. He decided to look for more satisfying work. (present participle)

   Feeling burned out at his job, Harrison decided to look for more satisfying work.

2. You can improve your English. Listen to the radio. (*by* + present participle)

3. Millie was vacationing alone in the mountains. She decided what she wanted as a career. (*while* + present participle)

_____

_____

4. Jonah earned his bachelor's degree. He was eager to enter the world of work. (*having* + past participle)

_____

_____

5. People are presented with attractive job prospects. Most people will take the one that offers long-term stability. (past participle)

_____

_____

X. SYNTHESIS

Circle the letter of the correct answer to complete each sentence.

1. Emily fell asleep _____ her head hit the pillow.   **A   B   C (D)**

   (A) as a result of   (C) as well as
   (B) although   (D) as soon as

2. Sharon's job is so easy that _____ a child could do it.   **A   B   C   D**

   (A) even though   (C) even if
   (B) even so   (D) even

3. The children had _____ a good time at the park that they didn't want to   **A   B   C   D**
   come home.

   (A) such   (C) so much
   (B) so   (D) so many

4. The meeting will take place at 3:00 P.M. on Friday, _____ everyone can attend.   **A   B   C   D**

   (A) provided that   (C) in case
   (B) unless   (D) even if

5. It's possible to take a vacation on a budget; _____, you can go camping.   **A   B   C   D**

   (A) on the contrary   (C) for instance
   (B) otherwise   (D) finally

6. There are _____ people at the festival that I don't think we'll be able to   **A   B   C   D**
   find Nicholas.

   (A) so that   (C) so many
   (B) so   (D) so much

7. I can't afford to eat at that restaurant, _____.   **A B C D**

    (A) neither can you   (C) nor can you

    (B) neither you can   (D) nor you can

8. Elmer gets good grades at school; _____, he lacks some basic life skills.   **A B C D**

    (A) moreover   (C) as a result

    (B) however   (D) in conclusion

9. Having passed all his exams with top scores, _____.   **A B C D**

    (A) Cecil was admitted to   (C) several colleges to
       several colleges   admit Cecil.

    (B) several colleges admitted Cecil. (D) Cecil admitting to several colleges

10. _____ so many people contributed so much to our cause.   **A B C D**

    (A) Never have   (C) Neither have

    (B) Have never   (D) Nor have

11. Do not open your test booklet until _____ to do so.   **A B C D**

    (A) you tell   (C) told

    (B) having told   (D) telling

12. _____ the novel, Cynthia began to write a book review.   **A B C D**

    (A) To finish   (C) Have finished

    (B) By finishing   (D) Having finished

13. _____ the language, Robert had to rely on an interpreter.   **A B C D**

    (A) His not speaking   (C) By not speaking

    (B) Not having spoken   (D) Not speaking

14. Drew has had trouble losing weight, _____ he has been dieting and exercising.   **A B C D**

    (A) almost   (C) at all

    (B) although   (D) as a matter of fact

15. _____ by his teachers and classmates, Mark decided to enter the speech   **A B C D**

contest.

    (A) Encouraging   (C) Having encouraged

    (B) Encouraged   (D) If encouraged

16. Be sure to apply plenty of sunblock before _____ out in the sun.   **A B C D**

    (A) going   (C) you going

    (B) your going   (D) having gone

XI. SYNTHESIS

Each sentence has four underlined parts or phrases. The four underlined parts of the sentence are marked A, B, C, and D. Circle the letter of the ONE underlined part that is NOT CORRECT.

1. Having <u>finish</u> college, Roberta decided that she <u>definitely</u> wanted to travel, <u>even if</u>   A (B) C   D
<u>Having</u>   B   C   D
it meant turning down some good job offers.

2. <u>After</u> <u>completed</u> this exam, you may leave the room; <u>however,</u> you must be quiet   A   B   C   D
  A   B   C
<u>so that</u> you do not disturb the other students.
  D

3. <u>Little did</u> <u>Jack realized</u> that Naomi was in love with him; <u>even if</u> he had known,   A   B   C   D
  A   B   C
he <u>certainly</u> wouldn't have divorced Amy.
    D

4. <u>As soon as</u> Rebecca got home, she turned on her computer <u>checking</u> her e-mail,   A   B   C   D
    A   B
<u>even though</u> she was <u>really</u> tired.
  C   D

5. <u>Locked</u> in the bathroom, Gertrude began to scream <u>so loudly that</u> <u>almost</u> everybody   A   B   C   D
  A   B   C
came running, <u>even though</u> her brother, who had been asleep.
         D

6. <u>Having</u> <u>already</u> <u>seeing</u> all the movies that were playing, we decided to <u>just</u>   A   B   C   D
  A   B   C   D
stay home.

7. <u>You may play outside</u> <u>provided that</u> you've finished your homework; <u>only I ask</u>   A   B   C   D
      A   B   C
that you come back in <u>as soon as</u> it gets dark.
              D

8. You can fool <u>almost all</u> of the people some of the time, <u>but</u> you can't fool <u>all</u> of   A   B   C   D
            A   B   C
the people <u>at all</u> of the time.
        D

9. <u>Seldom</u> <u>I have</u> been <u>so</u> <u>deeply</u> impressed with a performance.   A   B   C   D
  A   B   C D

10. <u>If</u> you've stopped coming to class, you <u>definitely</u> have to withdraw from the   A   B   C   D
  A   B
course <u>officially</u>; <u>or</u> you'll receive an F on your transcript.
        C   D

PART VIII ADVERBS

 FINAL TEST

I. ADVERB CLAUSES

Underline the independent clauses once and the dependent clauses twice. Then write whether the dependent clause is a clause of reason, contrast, condition, time, place, comparison, or result.

<u>condition</u> **1.** <u>Joan will forgive you</u> <u><u>if you just write her a letter of apology</u></u>.

_____ **2.** We can leave as soon as the babysitter gets here.

_____ **3.** Whenever I feel afraid, I sing a song at the top of my lungs.

_____ **4.** Esther is such a good swimmer that she could be on the Olympic team.

_____ **5.** Although Shari's Spanish accent isn't perfect, she's certainly fluent in the language.

_____ **6.** I learned more about gardening from my Uncle Joe than I ever did in my master gardener glass.

II. ADVERB CLAUSES

Combine each pair of sentences into one sentence with an independent clause and a dependent clause. Use the subordinating conjunction provided. Keep the two clauses in the same order as the sentence.

1. I have reservations about his program. He's the only viable candidate to vote for. (although)

   Although I have reservations about his program, he's the only viable candidate to vote for.

   _____

2. Melanie is a successful student. She listens in class and takes excellent notes. (because)

   _____

   _____

3. I'll be able to go on the picnic with you. I can get the afternoon off. (if)

   _____

   _____

4. I go to San Francisco. I ride the cable cars. (when)

   _____

   _____

5. The strike won't be settled anytime soon. Both sides make some concessions. (unless)

   _____

   _____

6. Kathy speaks quietly. We can't hear her. (so . . . that)

_____

_____

III. ADVERBS: VIEWPOINT, FOCUS, NEGATIVE, LOCATION, AND SEQUENCE

Circle the adverb in each set of sentences. Then write whether it is a viewpoint, focus, negative, location, or sequence adverb.

__negative__   **1.** Ashley thought her troubles were over. (Little) did she realize that Nikki was plotting her revenge.

_____   **2.** I tried to help Lena with her problem. Apparently, she didn't like any of my suggestions.

_____   **3.** There goes the last bus. Now how are we going to get home?

_____   **4.** Timothy didn't mean to break the plate. He was only trying to help you wash the dishes.

_____   **5.** Little Miss Muffet sat on a tuffet, eating her curds and whey. Along came a spider that sat down beside her and frightened Miss Muffet away.

_____   **6.** We're not asking you for permission to marry, Dad. We only want your blessing.

_____   **7.** Mark certainly seems to know what he's doing. At twenty-two, he owns his own home.

_____   **8.** I'm not surprised that so many of Fred's employees quit. Little do they realize when they're hired how demanding he can be.

_____   **9.** I was worried about Stanley and Blanche. Fortunately, they have resolved their differences.

IV. ADVERBS: VIEWPOINT, FOCUS, NEGATIVE, LOCATION, AND SEQUENCE

Circle the most appropriate forms to complete the letter.

Dear Russell,

Rarely I do / (do I) react to radio talk shows. However, as a sociologist, I total / totally disagreed with what
    1.   **2.**

Jeff Franke said on your show "Sound Off" last night, so I just had / had just to write in. His idea that
                                                   3.

there's a gene for violence is completely / completely is unfounded. Most sociologists do not attribute
                                   4.

violent behavior at all to genetic programming / to genetic programming at all; rather, they claim it is
                                   5.

the result of one's environment. It is basically / Basically, the only social effects that cloning would have
                                   6.

are detrimental. For example, consider the potential effects of cloning on the family. If cloning becomes

commonplace, a woman may need only an / an only egg and her womb in order to procreate. Men may
                                   7.

even become / become even superfluous, which will almost certainly / certainly almost lead to further
8.   **9.**

deterioration of the family as we know it. Just I / I just don't think this is right.
                                 10.

What is the purpose of cloning animals, anyway? Some people have suggested that organs from animals could be transplanted to people. However, if animals are cloned so that their organs can be used, who is to stop the cloning of people for the same purpose? Unfortunately, some / Some unfortunately individuals would find nothing wrong with this. And who
11.
would benefit? Pharmaceutical and agricultural companies would surely cash in / cash surely in.
12.
Farms might even though / even reap some financial benefits, but there would be no benefit to
13.
society as a whole. Furthermore, perhaps people will be cloned without their knowledge. Imagine someone who looks like you and has your fingerprints running around committing all sorts of crimes. This is not the society we certainly / certainly not the society we want!
14.

Not only do most / most sociologists question the effects of cloning, but also most religions
15.
believe it is wrong. Mr. Franke obviously has some strong opinions about cloning. Fortunately, they are not shared by most people. I only hope / hope only that the minority of people who are in favor
16.
of it do not take power.

V. DISCOURSE CONNECTORS

Circle the correct coordinating conjunction to complete each sentence.

1. Adrian can't swim, (nor)/ or can he ski.

2. Jennifer plays the piano, and / for Margaret plays the trombone.

3. Mike was hungry, for / so he ate a big lunch.

4. It rained during the picnic, and / but most people enjoyed themselves.

5. My parents are visiting, yet / so I can't see you this weekend.

VI. DISCOURSE CONNECTORS

Choose the correct transitions from the box to complete the speech to a parenting class.

| for instance   second   however   also   therefore   ~~first~~ |

There are two principal areas that we're going to work on in this course. _____First_____, we're
1.
going to work on listening skills. Lots of times parents think they understand what their children are going through. Research has shown, _____, that many parents often don't have a clue
2.
about what's bothering their kids, especially teenagers, and many times that's because they don't pay enough attention to them. _____, it's important for parents to learn to really listen to
3.

what their kids are telling them verbally. _____, they need to learn to read nonverbal
                                              4.
language, so we'll practice that. _____, we're going to work on developing your capacity
                                   5.
to stick by your decisions once you make them. Unfortunately, many parents today feel like apologiz-
ing to their children if they lay down the law. Suppose, _____, that you've threatened to
                                                          6.
ground your son if he breaks his curfew again. He breaks it, but you're afraid that if you ground him
he won't like you anymore. We're going to help you overcome that kind of unreasonable guilt.

VII.   DISCOURSE CONNECTORS

Add commas or semicolons as necessary in each sentence. Do not add words or change capitalization.

1. Last summer we went camping in Quebec in June, and in August we spent two weeks on Cape Cod.
2. We did not receive your rent check within the allowable period therefore, we are assessing a late fee.
3. My letter came back unopened so I'm assuming the Greenlees have moved. I wonder how we can
    contact them.
4. We'd love to have a dog and a cat but we just don't have enough space for animals right now.
5. Paul didn't get good grades in high school nor did he go out for sports. It's only recently that he's
    become interested in education.
6. Randolph does call on my birthday however, he never writes me any letters.
7. Jeremy is doing better at handing in his work on time though he stills spends a lot of time staring
    out the window.
8. We'd better leave Meredith a message on her voice mail otherwise, she won't know we had to can-
    cel the meeting.

VIII.   ADVERB PHRASES

Underline the adverb phrase in each sentence.

1. <u>To solve the problem of overpopulation</u>, governments will have to work together.
2. Gazing up at the sky on a warm August night, Robert saw the UFO.
3. Heather decided not to go with her friends to watch the movie, having already seen it three times.
4. I learned a lot about home repair by following the instructions in my *Mr. Fixit Encyclopedia*.
5. Offered the choice between rafting on the Colorado and sunbathing in Hawaii, I'd go for the rafting.
6. I learned a lot about how the school is run while talking with my son's math teacher.

IX. ADVERB PHRASES

Combine each pair of sentences into a single sentence with an independent clause and an adverb phrase. Use the type of modifying phrase suggested in parentheses and place the subject in the independent clause.

1. People are presented with the choice of several unfamiliar courses of action. Most people will opt for the one with the least risk. (past participle)

    Presented with the choice of several unfamiliar courses of action, most people will opt for the one with the least risk.

2. Johnny was digging for treasure in the backyard. He unearthed a large bone. (*while* + present participle)

3. Lily felt the need to get in touch with nature. She enrolled in an Outward Bound course. (present participle)

4. You can save money on groceries. You purchase many products in bulk. (*by* + present participle)

5. The governor was very successful at the state level. She decided to run for the presidency. (*having* + past participle)

X. SYNTHESIS

Circle the letter of the correct answer to complete each sentence.

1. James has difficulty saving money _____ he makes a good salary.

    (A) even though

    (B) even if

    (C) even

    (D) in case

    (A) B C D

2. You can watch television _____ you finish your homework.

    (A) unless

    (B) as many as

    (C) as soon as

    (D) as much as

    A B C D

3. _____ by his lack of success, Addison finally gave up his plan.　　　**A　B　C　D**

   (A) Discouraged　　　　　　　　(C) Having discouraged
   (B) Discouraging　　　　　　　(D) If discouraged

4. I am _____ hungry that I could eat a horse.　　　**A　B　C　D**

   (A) so　　　　　　　　　　　　(C) too
   (B) such　　　　　　　　　　　(D) very

5. Would you travel to another planet if _____ the opportunity?　　　**A　B　C　D**

   (A) giving　　　　　　　　　　(C) given
   (B) having given　　　　　　　(D) you had given

6. We can visit a museum, _____ you'd rather do something else.　　　**A　B　C　D**

   (A) in case　　　　　　　　　　(C) unless if
   (B) unless　　　　　　　　　　(D) if

7. Having landed at the airport, _____ to our destination.　　　**A　B　C　D**

   (A) a taxi took us　　　　　　　(C) by taking a taxi
   (B) we took a taxi　　　　　　　(D) in order to take a taxi

8. _____ Ron had a piece of cake, and he doesn't usually eat dessert.　　　**A　B　C　D**

   (A) even though　　　　　　　(C) even
   (B) even so　　　　　　　　　(D) even if

9. _____ thirty pounds, Edna has to buy new clothes.　　　**A　B　C　D**

   (A) Having lost　　　　　　　(C) To lose
   (B) Having been lost　　　　　(D) Losing

10. _____ I seen such a display of incompetence!　　　**A　B　C　D**

   (A) Have seldom　　　　　　　(C) At all
   (B) Seldom have　　　　　　　(D) Almost have

11. Bill wasn't at work yesterday, _____ come to work today.　　　**A　B　C　D**

   (A) nor did he　　　　　　　　(C) neither did he
   (B) nor he did　　　　　　　　(D) neither he did

12. I have _____ work to do that I don't know where to begin!　　　**A　B　C　D**

   (A) so　　　　　　　　　　　　(C) so much
   (B) so many　　　　　　　　　(D) so that

13. Make sure you take this medicine with water two hours after _____.　　　**A　B　C　D**

   (A) to eat　　　　　　　　　　(C) eating
   (B) you eating　　　　　　　　(D) your eating

XI. SYNTHESIS

Each sentence has four underlined parts or phrases. The four underlined parts of the sentence are marked A, B, C, and D. Circle the letter of the ONE underlined part that is NOT CORRECT.

1. Seldom I have wasted as much time as when I watched that movie.   A (B) C D
   A   B   C   D

2. Having reach childbearing age, many people have definitely decided to have only   A B C D
   A   B   C   D
   one or two children.

3. Wherever you go camping, you really should not drink any water until you are   A B C D
   A   B   C
   certain about its safety even you are very thirsty.
   D

4. The Internet definitely causes some problems in society, however it surely   A B C D
   A   B   C
   provides many benefits as well.
   D

5. Rarely does Patricia play tennis; although she generally performs well when she   A B C D
   A   B   C
   does play.
   D

6. With their adult children left home, Max and Sylvia decided to sell their house,   A B C D
   A   B
   although they really liked it.
   C   D

7. There was so good food at the banquet that I ate far too much even though   A B C D
   A   B   C   D
   I am on a diet.

8. You can get almost everyone to listen to your ideas by talk to them politely.   A B C D
   A   B   C   D

9. To think that Rick was a liar, Barbara refused even to listen to him even though   A B C D
   A   B   C
   Harriet explained that he really was telling the truth.
   D

10. Provided that safety regulations allow it, we could possibly seat more people in   A B C D
   A   B
   the auditorium by use folding chairs.
   C D

PART IX NOUN CLAUSES

I. NOUN CLAUSES: SUBJECTS AND OBJECTS

Underline the noun clause in each sentence.

1. <u>What bothers me about this job</u> is having to do so much paperwork.

2. I don't know what we're going to do to solve this problem.

3. Whatever you would like to do tonight will be fine with us.

4. Joanne obviously likes you. The fact that she returned your call says something.

5. Whoever isn't ready to go right on to college should consider national service.

6. It's essential that Mary get this message today.

7. Ask whomever you like to the party.

8. However you want to handle this problem is all right with me.

9. I think that Jim needs to take some time off from work.

10. Do you mind if I take notes during our conversation?

II. NOUN CLAUSES: SUBJECTS AND OBJECTS

Complete each sentence with the correct pronoun or expression used to introduce a noun clause.

1. _____What_____ concerns me is the fact that he's late to work so often.
    (That / What)

2. I was assigned to work with _____ needed literacy training.
    (whoever / whomever)

3. _____ you want to pay for the tickets will be fine. You can pay by credit card, check,
    (Whenever / However)
    or cash.

4. _____ is obvious that Martin thinks highly of you.
    (It / That)

5. I'm not yet sure _____ I think about her proposal.
    (what / whatever)

6. I would suggest that you tell _____ you feel comfortable with about the situation.
    (whatever / whomever)

7. I'll support _____ plan you decide to go with.
    (whichever / whoever)

8. I'm troubled by _____ you didn't report the accident sooner.
    (that / the fact that)

III. NOUN CLAUSES: SUBJECTS AND OBJECTS

Complete each sentence with a noun clause functioning as a subject or object, using the prompts given. Select the clause introducer from the words in the box.

whatever	that	the fact that	however	where	~~whoever~~

1. _____ Whoever doesn't like the rules _____ doesn't have to play the
   _(not / like / the rules)

   game.

2. Martie doesn't know _____ . She's thinking of
   _(she / will be attending / college)

   Evergreen.

3. Helen thinks _____ .
   _(you / not like / her)

4. _____ will help you get the loan.
   _(you / have / a good credit rating)

5. _____ is OK, as long I get my money.
   _(you / want / to arrange / the financing)

6. We should all do _____ to help the homeless.
   _(we / can)

IV. NOUN CLAUSES: SUBJECTS AND OBJECTS

Combine each pair of sentences into one sentence or question with an embedded noun clause. Use if or whether or not, as indicated.

1. Did she go to school today? Do you know (if)

   _____ Do you know if she went to school today? _____

   _____

2. I'm not sure. Is he coming to the party? (whether or not)

   _____

   _____

3. Did you find out? Has the plane landed yet? (if)

   _____

   _____

4. Did you decide? Is it a good idea? (whether or not)

   _____

   _____

V. NOUN CLAUSES: SUBJECT AND OBJECTS

Complete each sentence. Use a noun clause with the expression the fact that *and a simple past tense verb.*

1. I'm bothered by _____ the fact that they didn't call and say they weren't coming. _____ .
   (they / not call / and say they weren't coming)

2. _____ says a lot. It's a difficult course.
   (you / pass / the final exam)

3. What became clear was _____ .
   (I / not / be / ready for college)

4. I liked _____ . I wanted to fix it up.
   (the house / not / be / in perfect condition)

5. A hundred years ago, a major problem was _____ .
   (people / not / be / protected from most diseases)

VI. NOUN CLAUSES AND PHRASES: COMPLEMENTS

Using the prompts given, write sentences. Use noun clauses that function as adjective complements, with the pattern It + linking verb + adjective + noun clause.

1. seem / obvious / must be done / about the problem.

   _____ It seems obvious that something must be done about the problem. _____

2. be / clear / Bob / not understand / your point of view

   _____

   _____

3. appear / likely / the governor / will not support / our position

   _____

   _____

4. be / wonderful / our son / marrying / such a kind person

   _____

   _____

5. seem / possible / my daughter / will be / the class valedictorian

   _____

   _____

VII. NOUN CLAUSES AND PHRASES: COMPLEMENTS

Using the prompts given, write sentences. Use noun clauses with adjectives of urgency, necessity or advice.
Use the pattern it + be + *adjective* + that + *noun clause.*

1. essential / John / find a job / soon

   It's essential that John find a job soon.
   _____

2. advisable / Mary / be present / for the meeting?

   _____

   _____

3. important / we / attend / our daughter's wedding

   _____

   _____

4. necessary / you / make a payment / on your loan

   _____

   _____

5. crucial / the principal / have all the facts / about the incident

   _____

   _____

VIII. NOUN CLAUSES AND PHRASES: COMPLEMENTS

Using the prompts given, write sentences with noun phrases. Use the pattern it + be + *adjective* + for +
noun/object pronoun + infinitive. *Put the verb* be *in present, past, or future, as indicated.*

1. necessary / for / all students / to take this test. (present)

   It is necessary for all students to take this test.

2. difficult / for / Glen / to make friends as a child. (past)

   _____

3. mandatory / for / all passengers / to wear seat belts once this law is passed. (future)

   _____

4. unusual / for / Robin / to be late. (present)

   _____

IX. NOUN CLAUSES AND PHRASES: COMPLEMENTS

Read the following proverbs. Write paraphrases of the proverbs by using the cues to write sentences. Use the pattern noun clause with that + be + adjective. *Then match the paraphrase to the proverb by putting the correct letter before each paraphrase.*

a. Birds of a feather flock together.

b. Don't count your chickens before they hatch.

c. Look before you leap.

d. All that glitters is not gold.

e. Cross each bridge as you come to it.

f. Strike while the iron is hot.

1. __e__ _____ That people not worry about situations before they happen is advisable. ___
people / not worry / about situations / before they happen / advisable

2. ___ _____
people / choose friends / with similar interests / not uncommon

3. ___ _____
we / analyze each situation carefully / before making a decision / essential

4. ___ _____
people / take advantage / of opportunities / while they're available / necessary

5. ___ _____
we / judge things / by their real value / rather than their apparent value / desirable

6. ___ _____
people / not assume things will happen / until they happen / vital

X. SYNTHESIS

Circle the letter of the correct answer to complete each sentence.

1. This report _____ smoking is bad for your health. **A B C (D)**

(A) suggests the fact   (C) suggests what

(B) suggests the fact that   (D) suggests that

2. It is essential that _____ all students to register for classes by midnight tonight. **A B C D**

(A) that   (C) for

(B) for whom   (D) whom

3. It's uncertain _____ our neighbors will be able to sell their house. **A B C D**

(A) which   (C) whether

(B) where   (D) what

4. _____ bothers Gail about her boyfriend is that he never calls her. **A B C D**

(A) That which   (C) That

(B) Whatever   (D) What

5. We can stop for lunch _____ you feel hungry. **A B C D**

(A) what   (C) however

(B) whether   (D) whenever

6. _____ Diana's grades have improved suggest that she's been studying harder. **A B C D**

(A) However   (C) The fact that
(B) Whatever   (D) The fact which

7. Rose thought _____ the report was due today. **A B C D**

(A) what   (C) that
(B) whatever   (D) when

8. It seems _____ Frederico's latest play is sure to be an unprecedented success. **A B C D**

(A) the fact that   (C) if
(B) what   (D) that

9. The teacher said _____ finishes the test early can go home. **A B C D**

(A) whoever   (C) whomever
(B) who   (D) whom

10. I'll be home all afternoon; you can stop by _____ it's convenient. **A B C D**

(A) whenever   (C) whether
(B) however   (D) that

11. I can't decide _____ course to take. **A B C D**

(A) that   (C) when
(B) whichever   (D) which

12. Ken doesn't know _____ he can give Scott a ride to the airport. **A B C D**

(A) if   (C) what
(B) who   (D) whatever

13. It is unfortunate _____ Edna didn't pass the test. **A B C D**

(A) what   (C) the fact that
(B) whatever   (D) that

14. Can you tell me _____? **A B C D**

(A) wherever the post office is   (C) where is the post office
(B) wherever is the post office   (D) where the post office is

15. The idea _____ balance is the key to a happy life is not new. **A B C D**

(A) which   (C) that
(B) for   (D) what

XI. SYNTHESIS

Each sentence has four underlined parts or phrases. The four underlined parts of the sentence are marked A, B, C, and D. Circle the letter of the ONE underlined part that is NOT CORRECT.

1. That concerns Mildred is that her son may not graduate from high school.   (A) B C D
   A   B   C   D

2. Do that is necessary to remedy the situation.   A B C D
   A B   C   D

3. Whomever is undecided about college ought to consider what the Peace Corps   A B C D
   A   B   C   D
   can offer.

4. Tell me which you think of your new job and whether you like it better than   A B C D
   A   B   C   D
   your old one.

5. It's necessary that Howard understands that we're serious.   A B C D
   A   B   C   D

6. It became clear what Marilyn wasn't ready to leave home, although it was what   A B C D
   A   B   C
   she wanted most.
   D

7. It's mandatory that your daughter is in class every day or she won't pass.   A B C D
   A   B   C   D

8. Wherever they might live, citizens need to do however they can to help their   A B C D
   A   B   C   D
   country.

9. Have you decided wherever you are going to go for your vacation this year?   A B C D
   A   B   C D

10. Due to the fact that your credit record is excellent, whatever much money you   A B C D
    A   B   C   D
    can make as a down payment is fine.

PART IX NOUN CLAUSES

I. NOUN CLAUSES: SUBJECTS AND OBJECTS

Underline the noun clause in each sentence.

1. <u>What irritates me about this sitaution</u> is not knowing who to blame.

2. I haven't decided what we're going to do to get them to pay us.

3. Whatever you want to bring to the pot luck dinner will be fine, I'm sure.

4. Mike obviously is in your corner. The fact that he came to your defense means a lot.

5. Whoever wants to live healthily should eat five to eight servings of fruits and vegetables daily.

6. It's essential that Phil get treatment for that burn immediately.

7. Invite whomever you want to come along for the weekend.

8. However you want to arrange the sale will work—as long as we get it in writing.

9. I think that the administration should give top priority to passing health-care legislation.

10. Do you know if the mail has come yet?

II. NOUN CLAUSES: SUBJECTS AND OBJECTS

Complete each sentence with the correct pronoun or expression used to introduce a noun clause.

1. When I was a tutor, I would work with _____whoever_____ came and asked for help.
   (whoever / whomever)

2. _____ you decide to tell her will do, as long as you're clear.
   (Whoever / However)

3. _____ is amazing that Johnny has learned Swahili so quickly.
   (It / That)

4. We haven't decided _____ we're going to offer for the house.
   (what / whatever)

5. I think you ought to invite _____ you really enjoy being with.
   (whatever / whomever)

6. I'll go along with _____ proposal ends up costing the least.
   (whichever / whoever)

7. I'm impressed by _____ you kept working and didn't complain. We need more
   (that / the fact that)
   people like you.

8. _____ astonishes me is the fact that Melody can remember everybody's name so well.
   (That / What)

III. NOUN CLAUSES: SUBJECTS AND OBJECTS

Complete each sentence with a noun clause functioning as a subject or object, using the prompts given. Select the clause introducer from the words in the box.

whatever that the fact that ~~whoever~~ however where

1. _____ Whoever doesn't attend class today _____ will be dropped from the
   (not attend / class today)

   roll. There's a long waiting list to take this section.

2. James hasn't decided _____. He's thinking of
   (he / want to / work this summer)

   signing up with a fishing boat.

3. Mrs. Allbright thinks _____.
   (you / be / a bad influence / on her daughter)

4. _____ will help you get into the university.
   (you / have / excellent faculty recommendations)

5. _____ is acceptable. You can be paid weekly or biweekly.
   (you / want / me / to pay you)

6. The government should do _____ to end the conflict and bring the troops home.
   (it / can)

IV. NOUN CLAUSES: SUBJECTS AND OBJECTS

Combine each pair of sentences into one sentence or question with an embedded noun clause. Use if *or* whether or not, *as indicated.*

1. Did the owner accept our offer on the house? Do you know? (if)

   Do you know if the owner accepted our offer on the house?

   _____

2. I'm not certain. Do the Joneses plan to join us in this venture? (whether or not)

   _____

   _____

3. Did Hal find out? Has he been accepted at the university? (if)

   _____

   _____

4. Have you decided? Do you want to come along? (whether or not)

   _____

   _____

V. NOUN CLAUSES: SUBJECTS AND OBJECTS

Complete each sentence. Use a noun clause with the expression the fact that *and a simple past tense verb.*

1. I'm concerned about ___the fact that we didn't hear from them last night___. They were
   (we / not / hear / from them / last night)

   supposed to call.

2. _____ meant a lot. It was a very
   (you / go / out of your way / to help)

   unselfish thing to do.

3. What became quickly obvious was _____.
   (Sarah / not like / working here)

4. When we first got a TV set, I liked _____. There
   (there / be / only two channels)

   weren't too many choices like there are now.

5. A major advantage of life in the nineteenth century was _____.
   (most things / be / new and unspoiled)

VI. NOUN CLAUSES AND PHRASES: COMPLEMENTS

Using the prompts given, write sentences. Use noun clauses that function as adjective complements, with the pattern It + *linking verb* + *adjective* + *noun clause.*

1. seem / obvious / something / in the balance-of-power equation has changed

   ___It seems obvious that something in the balance-of-power equation has changed.___

2. be / clear / the job / not pay / enough

   _____

3. appear / likely / the senator / be going to / be reelected

   _____

4. be / wonderful / my short story / have / be / accepted for publication

   _____

5. seem / possible / the Wrights / be going to / be / our new neighbors

   _____

VII. NOUN CLAUSES AND PHRASES: COMPLEMENTS

Using the prompts given, write sentences. Use noun clauses with adjectives of urgency, necessity or advice. Use the pattern It + be + *adjective* + that + *noun clause.*

1. advisable / Edward / get / himself / a lawyer

   It's advisable that Edward get himself a lawyer.

   _____

2. important / you / listen to / your children

   _____

   _____

3. necessary / I / be / in court to testify?

   _____

   _____

4. crucial / the investigators / have / all the information on the accident

   _____

   _____

5. essential / Amanda / seek professional help

   _____

   _____

VIII. NOUN CLAUSES AND PHRASES: COMPLEMENTS

Using the prompts given, write sentences with noun phrases. Use the pattern It + be + *adjective* + for + *noun/object pronoun + infinitive. Put the verb* be *in present, past, or future, as indicated.*

1. necessary / for / you / to register your motor vehicle. (present)

   It is necessary for you to register your motor vehicle.

2. difficult / for / Ludmilla / to communicate when she first came to this country. (past)

   _____

3. mandatory / for / all employees / to submit written requests for vacation days effective January 1. (future)

   _____

4. not unusual / for Tony / to forget things. (present)

   _____

IX. NOUN CLAUSES AND PHRASES: COMPLEMENTS

Read the following proverbs. Write paraphrases of the proverbs by using the cues to write sentences. Use the pattern noun clause with that + be + *adjective. Then match the paraphrase to the proverb by putting the correct letter before each paraphrase.*

a. If wishes were horses, beggars would ride.

b. Don't cut off your nose to spite your face.

c. Don't look a gift horse in the mouth.

d. Don't make a mountain out of a molehill.

e. Use it up, wear it out, make it do, or do without.

f. When it rains, it pours.

1. __c__ ____That we accept presents graciously is advisable.____
   we / accept presents graciously / advisable

2. ____ _____
   many similar things / happen / at the same time / not uncommon

3. ____ _____
   we / not exaggerate the importance of a problem / desirable

4. ____ _____
   people / pursue dreams in order to make them come true / necessary

5. ____ _____
   we / be frugal in our use of material goods / important

6. ____ _____
   people / think carefully / about the consequences / of their actions / vital

X. SYNTHESIS

Circle the letter of the correct answer to complete each sentence.

1. I am not convinced _____ his research is conclusive.   A B Ⓒ D

   (A) what   (C) that
   (B) the fact   (D) whatever

2. You can choose _____ dessert you like.   A B C D

   (A) whenever   (C) whoever
   (B) whichever   (D) however

3. _____ Ellen has been caught lying on several occasions suggests that she   A B C D
   cannot be trusted.

   (A) The fact which   (C) Which
   (B) The fact that   (D) What

4. _____ I'd like to talk about in this presentation is how to manage your time   A B C D
   effectively.

   (A) Whatever   (C) That
   (B) What   (D) Whichever

5. It is important _____ anyone buying a used car to examine it thoroughly.　　**A　B　C　D**

(A) that

(B) whomever

(C) for whom

(D) for

6. It's obvious _____ Kelsey loves her new house.　　**A　B　C　D**

(A) what

(B) that

(C) that which

(D) which

7. Marvin can't decide _____ to apply to Harvard or Princeton.　　**A　B　C　D**

(A) whether

(B) which

(C) where

(D) whatever

8. Tell me _____ day is better for you—Saturday or Sunday?　　**A　B　C　D**

(A) when

(B) that

(C) whether

(D) which

9. Do you know _____?　　**A　B　C　D**

(A) what time is it

(B) what time it is

(C) that time is it

(D) that time it is

10. The belief _____ people should marry for love is not universal.　　**A　B　C　D**

(A) which

(B) for

(C) what

(D) that

11. You may invite _____ you'd like to the party.　　**A　B　C　D**

(A) who

(B) whom

(C) whoever

(D) whomever

12. I have no idea _____ this bus goes to San Jose.　　**A　B　C　D**

(A) where

(B) wherever

(C) whether

(D) which

13. Jim didn't know _____ he had to give you a copy of the report.　　**A　B　C　D**

(A) that

(B) what

(C) the fact which

(D) whatever

14. _____ you want to eat for dinner is fine with me.　　**A　B　C　D**

(A) Whatever

(B) Whoever

(C) Whether

(D) How

15. Mr. Jones _____ he would call you tomorrow.　　**A　B　C　D**

(A) said what

(B) said

(C) said the fact that

(D) said the fact

XI. SYNTHESIS

Each sentence has four underlined parts or phrases. The four underlined parts of the sentence are marked A, B, C, and D. Circle the letter of the ONE underlined part that is NOT CORRECT.

1. <u>Whomever</u> <u>wants</u> <u>to live</u> a long time <u>should learn</u> to handle stress effectively.   Ⓐ B C D
       A   B   C   D

2. <u>Do you</u> <u>want to know</u> <u>whatever</u> I <u>think</u> about this plan?   A B C D
        A   B   C   D

3. <u>It's necessary</u> <u>that</u> your daughter <u>understands</u> <u>why</u> she is not allowed to eat   A B C D
         A   B   C   D

   junk food.

4. <u>It became</u> <u>clear</u> to the truant officer <u>what</u> Billy <u>had not been</u> in class for weeks.   A B C D
        A   B   C   D

5. <u>It's mandatory</u> <u>that</u> your son <u>testifies</u> at the trial, <u>however</u> much he might not   A B C D
         A   B   C   D

   want to.

6. In my view, we <u>should</u> all <u>do</u> <u>however</u> we can <u>to stop</u> cruelty to animals.   A B C D
                  A   B   C   D

7. <u>Does</u> Rachel <u>know</u> <u>wherever</u> she <u>lost</u> her wallet?   A B C D
      A   B   C   D

8. <u>Whatever</u> much time you can contribute will be much appreciated, as   A B C D
        A

   <u>it is difficult</u> <u>for them</u> <u>to find</u> volunteers.
        B   C   D

9. <u>That</u> <u>is troubling</u> Dan <u>is that</u> he <u>might have to declare</u> bankruptcy.   A B C D
      A   B   C   D

10. Mr. Adams <u>did</u> <u>that</u> he <u>thought</u> <u>was</u> best for his family.   A B C D
              A   B   C   D

PART X UNREAL CONDITIONS

DIAGNOSTIC TEST

I. UNREAL CONDITIONALS AND OTHER WAYS TO EXPRESS UNREALITY

*After each sentence write **R** for real conditional sentences and **U** for unreal conditional sentences.*

1. If I were you, I'd be more careful. __U__

2. You're talking as if you know something. ____

3. Let's hope that Carrie passes the exam. ____

4. If only he takes her advice, he might be able to pull himself up by his bootstraps. ____

5. If I'd known you were coming, I would have baked a cake. ____

6. Charles acts as if he's my boss. ____

7. The lady looked as though she hadn't eaten in days. ____

8. If you hadn't helped me, I might have died. ____

9. If you follow her advice, you'll get what you want. ____

10. Had I known what would happen, I would never have authorized this experiment. ____

II. UNREAL CONDITIONALS AND OTHER WAYS TO EXPRESS UNREALITY

Write present or past unreal conditional sentences using the indicated prompts.

1. If / I / be / you / I / not spend / so much money on luxuries (present)

     If I were you, I wouldn't spend so much money on luxuries.

   _____

2. You / probably / get / the job / if / you / arrive on time / to the interview (past)

   _____

   _____

3. If / she / not / be wearing / her seat belt / she / could be / badly injured (past)

   _____

   _____

4. Mort / be / more credible / if / he / not / exaggerate / so much (present)

   _____

   _____

5. We / might / never / get to know / each other / if / we / not / go / to that party (past)

_____

_____

6. If / we / not / live / in an apartment / we / get / a dog (present)

_____

_____

7. If / Ken / be / less shy / he / go / to parties / more often (present)

_____

_____

III. UNREAL CONDITIONALS AND OTHER WAYS TO EXPRESS UNREALITY

Write conditional sentences with wish *and* hope. *Put* wish *and* hope *in the present. Put the verb in the noun clause in present, past, or future, as indicated.*

1. I / hope / it / not / rain / today (present)

   I hope that it doesn't rain today.

_____

2. Joe / wish / he / go to college (past)

_____

_____

3. I / wish / we / can / get together / more often (present)

_____

_____

4. Cynthia / hope / she / be accepted / to Columbia University (future)

_____

_____

5. Jack / wish / he / not break off / his relationship with Barbara (past)

_____

_____

6. Mike and Kelly / hope / their son / get / a good job (present)

_____

_____

7. I / wish / I / can / afford / a trip to Europe / next summer (future)

_____

_____

IV.   THE SUBJUNCTIVE: INVERTED AND IMPLIED CONDITIONALS

Change these conditional sentences into inverted conditionals.

1. If I had known you were in town, I would have invited you.

   Had I known you were in town, I would have invited you.

_____

2. If I were to offer you a job, would you take it?

_____

_____

3. If you should return before Tuesday, give me a call.

_____

_____

4. I wouldn't have invested in that company if I had known anything about its track record.

_____

_____

5. We'd need a strong indication that you could pay us back if we were to lend you the money.

_____

_____

6. Please notify the registrar in writing if you should want to drop a course.

_____

_____

V.   THE SUBJUNCTIVE: INVERTED AND IMPLIED CONDITIONALS

Choose from the items in the box to complete the sentences using implied conditionals.

if so   ~~if not~~   otherwise   with   without

1. You may or may not get the loan. _____If not_____, there's another lending company I can recommend.

2. You're already a good musician. _____ some instruction, you could easily learn the saxophone.

3. You need the support of the mayor. _____ it, you'll never get your proposal through.

4. You need to pass every test and turn in all your homework. _____, you won't make it through the course.

5. This house may have some structural problems that need to be fixed. _____, I'd recommend Harley Builders to do the work.

VI.   THE SUBJUNCTIVE: INVERTED AND IMPLIED CONDITIONALS

For each sentence, write a clause with subjunctive form after the verb or adjective of urgency. Use the pattern verb or adjective of urgency + that *+ subjunctive verb form.*

1. We / demand / the school board / meet with us / to address our concerns.

   We demand that the school board meet with us to address our concerns.

   _____

2. I / move / the motion / be / accepted

   _____

   _____

3. I / insist / Marie / be / present / at the meeting

   _____

   _____

4. My broker / is suggesting / I / sell / the property

   _____

   _____

5. We / recommend / you / consider / sending Wayne / to a private school

   _____

   _____

6. It / essential / you / fill out / this form / completely

   _____

   _____

VII. SYNTHESIS

Complete each sentence with the appropriate form of the indicated verb.

1. If I _____*had*_____ a thousand dollars, I'd buy some new furniture.
   (have)

2. What if I _____ you a secret? Could you keep it?
   (tell)

3. If I _____ you, I'd hire someone else.
   (be)

4. You looked as though you _____ seen a ghost.
   (have)

5. If only I _____ lost my temper!
   (haven't)

6. It's time we _____ started on this project. We're already behind schedule.
   (get)

7. I'd rather we _____ about that right now.
   (not talk)

8. You're acting as if _____ my boss. I'm not your slave, you know.
   (be)

VIII. SYNTHESIS

Choose the correct answers to complete the letter to the advice columnist and the columnist's response.

Dear Pamela,

Two months ago, I lent a friend some of my old essays, and now I _____*wish*_____ I hadn't. A few
1. (hope / wish)

weeks later, I was horrified to learn that he had retyped one of my essays and handed it in to his

teacher. When I demanded that he _____ the teacher the truth, he acted
2. (tell / tells)

_____ he'd done nothing wrong. Now I'm afraid that, if the teacher _____
3. (as though / if only)   **4.** (finds / found)

out he cheated, I'll be blamed. _____ I get kicked out of school? _____ I
5. (What if / If so)   **6.** (Had / Have)

known that my friend was so dishonest, I wouldn't have let him borrow my essays. I really wish he

_____ tell the teacher the truth, but I don't think he will. I'm really upset about this sit-
7. (will / would)

uation, but I do _____ we can remain friends. What should I do?
8. (hope / wish)

Distressed

Dear Distressed,

I don't know what the rules at your school are, but I suggest that you _____ with an advi-
9. (speak / had spoken)

sor. If another student _____ something wrong, you probably won't be blamed for it. And
10. (has done / will do)

if I _____ you, I'd drop that friend. _____ he tried to take advantage of
11. (was / were)   **12.** (If not / What if)

you again?

Pamela

IX. SYNTHESIS

Circle the letter of the correct answer to complete each sentence.

1. If I didn't have so much work to do today, I _____ time to meet you for lunch.　A Ⓑ C D

   (A) would have had　　　　　　(C) will have

   (B) would have　　　　　　　　(D) have

2. _____ I hadn't lost my appointment book.　A B C D

   (A) Only if　　　　　　　　　　(C) As if

   (B) If only　　　　　　　　　　(D) As only

3. I think it's time you _____ the truth about Edgar.　A B C D

   (A) should learn　　　　　　　(C) learned

   (B) would learn　　　　　　　　(D) will learn

4. It is mandatory that all students _____ an exit exam.　A B C D

   (A) take　　　　　　　　　　　(C) will take

   (B) to take　　　　　　　　　　(D) should take

5. I'm so hungry! I feel _____ I could eat a horse.　A B C D

   (A) what if　　　　　　　　　　(C) as well

   (B) as if　　　　　　　　　　　(D) if only

6. The City Health Department ordered that the restaurant _____ closed.　A B C D

   (A) be　　　　　　　　　　　　(C) was

   (B) to be　　　　　　　　　　　(D) is

7. _____ I ask Judy for a date and she laughs at me?　A B C D

   (A) As if　　　　　　　　　　　(C) What would

   (B) What if　　　　　　　　　　(D) What should

8. I _____ those children would stop yelling.　A B C D

   (A) hope　　　　　　　　　　　(C) should hope

   (B) wish　　　　　　　　　　　(D) should wish

9. If anyone _____ while I'm out, please take a message.　A B C D

   (A) should call　　　　　　　　(C) should have called

   (B) should they call　　　　　　(D) would call

10. Stella wishes she _____ that coat when it was on sale.　A B C D

    (A) bought　　　　　　　　　　(C) would have bought

    (B) had bought　　　　　　　　(D) should have bought

11. If Stanley _____ better at math, he wouldn't have to hire an accountant.　A B C D

    (A) is　　　　　　　　　　　　(C) were

    (B) would be　　　　　　　　　(D) was

12. If too many people can't come to the meeting, it _____ postponed. A B **C** D

(A) should have been   (C) would have been

(B) will be   (D) would be

13. The problem may be too complicated for the dentist to handle. _____, she A B **C** D
will refer you to a specialist.

(A) If   (C) If so

(B) If not   (D) Otherwise

14. Our neighbors insisted that we _____ for dinner this evening. A B C **D**

(A) would have come over   (C) will come over

(B) would come over   (D) come over

15. I hope the drugstore _____ open. **A** B C D

(A) is   (C) would be

(B) would have been   (D) to be

16. We'd better get tickets for the concert today. _____, they might be sold out. A B C **D**

(A) What if   (C) If so

(B) Without   (D) If not

X. SYNTHESIS

*Each sentence has four underlined parts or phrases. The four underlined parts of the sentence are marked
A, B, C, and D. Circle the letter of the* ONE *underlined part that is* NOT CORRECT.

1. If I <u>was</u> you, I <u>wouldn't</u> <u>lend</u> anyone my car, <u>even if</u> it's not new. (**A**) B C D
      A   B   C   D

2. If John <u>would have</u> <u>studied</u>, he <u>would have</u> <u>passed</u> the course. A B C D
          A   B   C   D

3. <u>If you</u> <u>hadn't</u> <u>helped</u> me, I <u>might died</u>. A B C D
  A   B   C   D

4. We <u>insist</u> <u>that</u> Kim <u>pays</u> <u>us</u> back the money immediately. A B C D
      A   B   C D

5. I wish you <u>haven't</u> <u>said</u> that, and I <u>hope</u> you <u>never say</u> anything like that again! A B C D
           A   B   C   D

6. <u>Would I have known</u> <u>you'd get</u> so upset, I <u>wouldn't have suggested</u> <u>going</u>. A B C D
        A   B   C   D

7. I <u>move</u> <u>that</u> the motion <u>is</u> <u>passed</u>. A B C D
    A   B   C D

8. We <u>hope</u> you <u>would</u> <u>come</u> to the party if <u>you're not</u> busy. A B C D
      A   B   C   D

9. Diane <u>wishes</u> she <u>can swim</u>, and she thinks it's important that children <u>be taught</u> A B C D
        A   B   C
<u>to swim</u> when they're young.
  D

10. I hear James Maxwell <u>is leaving</u> his current job. <u>If not</u>, I'd like to recommend that A B C D
                     A   B
we <u>hire</u> him if <u>he's willing</u> to relocate.
    C   D

11. <u>I had</u> <u>known</u> that it <u>would rain</u>, I <u>would have brought</u> my umbrella. A B C D
   A   B   C   D

PART X UNREAL CONDITIONS

FINAL TEST

I. UNREAL CONDITIONALS AND OTHER WAYS TO EXPRESS UNREALITY

*After each sentence write **R** for real conditional sentences and **U** for unreal conditional sentences.*

1. If I were you, I'd limit the amount of TV the kids see. __U__

2. She's acting as if she knows something we don't know. ____

3. I really hope it doesn't rain this afternoon. ____

4. If only he gets the news in time, he might be able to do something. ____

5. I would have lent you the money if you'd asked me. ____

6. Martha treats me as if I'm her slave. ____

7. The house looked as though it hadn't been cleaned in months. ____

8. He might have frozen to death if you hadn't come along when you did. ____

9. If you concentrate on talking with native speakers, you'll master the language. ____

10. Had I known you'd get so upset, I never would have suggested leaving. ____

II. UNREAL CONDITIONALS AND OTHER WAYS TO EXPRESS UNREALITY

Write present or past unreal conditional sentences, using the indicated prompts.

1. If / I / be / you / I / get / a second opinion / about the test results (present)

   If I were you, I'd get a second opinion about the test results.

   _____

2. Sally / probably / be / accept / by the university / if / she / apply / on time (past)

   _____

   _____

3. If / Josh / not / be wearing / his life preserver / he / could / drown (past)

   _____

   _____

4. Eve / be / more popular / if / she / not talk / about herself / so much (present)

   _____

   _____

5. They / might / never / get married / if / they / not / bump into / each other / on the bus (past)

_____

_____

6. If / I / not paying / so much money / on credit cards / I / can / afford / a nicer apartment (present)

_____

_____

7. If / Tom / not / be / so tired / he / go out / with us / tonight

_____

_____

III. UNREAL CONDITIONALS AND OTHER WAYS TO EXPRESS UNREALITY

Write conditional sentences with wish _and_ hope. _Put_ wish _and_ hope _in the present. Put the verb in the noun clause in present, past, or future, as indicated._

1. I / hope / it / snow / this weekend (present)

I hope that it snows this weekend.

_____

2. Chuck / wish / he / not spend / all his money (past)

_____

_____

3. I / wish / you / live / closer / to us (present)

_____

_____

4. Doug / hope / his loan / be approved (future)

_____

_____

5. Gary / wish / he / not sell / the house on Maple Street (past)

_____

_____

6. Gerry and Hilda / hope / Hugh / make / the right decision (present)

_____

_____

7. Eric / wish / Mrs. Graham / will / come back and teach his class / next year (future)

_____

_____

IV. THE SUBJUNCTIVE: INVERTED AND IMPLIED CONDITIONALS

Change these conditional sentences into inverted conditionals.

1. If we'd realized you needed help, we would have been there.

   Had we realized you needed help, we would have been there.

   _____

2. If I were to tell you something confidential, could you keep it a secret?

   _____

   _____

3. If the package should arrive before I get back, please sign for it.

   _____

   _____

4. I'd never have asked Albert to do this if I'd known he would fall apart.

   _____

   _____

5. We would need a recommendation from your former boss if we were to offer you a position.

   _____

   _____

6. Please contact our customer service department if you should have any questions.

   _____

   _____

V. THE SUBJUNCTIVE: INVERTED AND IMPLIED CONDITIONALS

Choose from the items in the box to complete the sentences using implied conditionals.

| if so   ~~if not~~   otherwise   with   without |

1. Bill may or may not be ready to go away to school. _____ If not _____, I recommend the local community college.

2. You're an excellent carpenter. _____ a little bit of training in business procedures, you could open your own shop.

3. You need approval by the city to build that fence. _____ it, you're opening yourself up for a lawsuit.

4. You've got to start exercising and eating a reasonable diet. _____, you'll never lose weight.

5. Joanie said you might be interested in changing jobs. _____, there's someone I think you should call.

VI. THE SUBJUNCTIVE: INVERTED AND IMPLIED CONDITIONALS

For each sentence, write a clause with subjunctive form after the verb or adjective of urgency. Use the pattern verb or adjective of urgency + that *+ subjunctive verb form.*

1. I / insist / my son / be allowed / to attend the meeting.

   I insist that my son be allowed to attend the meeting.

   _____

2. I / move / the motion / be tabled

   _____

   _____

3. The Illyrian government / is demanding / the Redonian government / withdraw / its troops

   _____

   _____

4. My doctor / suggest / I / exercise / three times a week

   _____

   _____

5. I / recommend / you / take / some time off from work

   _____

   _____

6. It / required / all employees / submit / to a medical examination

   _____

   _____

VII.   SYNTHESIS

Complete each sentence with the appropriate form of the indicated verb.

1. If I _____ could _____ sing, I'd join a choir.
   (can)

2. What if we _____ you a benefit package? Would you stay on the job?
   (offer)

3. I'd write a letter to the company if I _____ you.
   (be)

4. You acted as though nothing _____ happened.
   (have)

5. If only she _____ remembered to buckle her seat belt!
   (have)

6. It's time we _____. The babysitter has to be home by midnight.
   (be leaving)

7. I'd rather we _____ that subject right now. It's still too painful.
   (not go into)

8. Harold is pretty dictatorial. He acts as if he _____ the president of the world.
   (be)

VIII.   SYNTHESIS

Choose the correct answers to complete the letter to the advice columnist and the columnist's response.

Dear Pamela,

My sister and I are close, even though we live in different cities. The problem is, whenever she and

her family come to visit, they never give me any notice. I really _____ wish _____ they wouldn't do
1. (hope / wish)

this. Just three weeks ago, she and her family dropped by unexpectedly and stayed for six days.

_____ I known they were going to show up, I _____ time to clean the
2. (Have / Had)   3. (will have / would have had)

house and prepare some food. I ended up running around like crazy trying to get organized. Should I

say something to her? If I _____ to tell her that her unexpected visits cause me stress,
4. (was / were)

she might _____ insulted. I really hope you _____ help me with this
5. (feel / have felt)   6. (can / could)

problem.

Stressed Out

Dear Stressed Out,

Honey, it's time you _____ your sister your true feelings. You don't have to be rude. Just
7. (tell / told)

say, "I'd rather you _____ us before you come to visit." If your sister
8. (called / were to call)

_____ insulted, it's her problem, not yours. It's essential that you _____ to
9. (feels / felt)   10. (learn / should learn)

say no to demands that are unreasonable. _____ she tried to pull the same stunt at a
11. (What if / Otherwise)

friend's house? In fact, the next time she and her family drop by unannounced, you might want to sug-

gest that they _____ into a hotel instead.
12. (check / would check)

Pamela

IX. SYNTHESIS

Circle the letter of the correct answer to complete each sentence.

1. I hope you _____ come to our party.   (A) B C D

    (A) can   (C) would be able to
    (B) could   (D) were able to

2. The waiter suggested that we _____ the house special.   A B C D

    (A) ordered   (C) order
    (B) would order   (D) will order

3. The problem with your computer may be insufficient disk space. _____,   A B C D
   you may want to delete some old files.

    (A) If so   (C) If
    (B) If not   (D) Without it

4. You need to upgrade your computer skills. _____, you'll have a hard time   A B C D
   finding a good job.

    (A) If so   (C) What if
    (B) Without   (D) Otherwise

5. If it rains this weekend, the picnic _____ canceled.   A B C D

    (A) would be   (C) would have been
    (B) will be   (D) should have been

6. If Kevin _____ living by himself instead of with roommates, he would have   A B C D
   a lot more privacy.

    (A) is   (C) was
    (B) would   (D) were

7. The Kramers wish they _____ their home. Now they're in debt.   A B C D

    (A) didn't buy   (C) hadn't bought
    (B) wouldn't have bought   (D) weren't bought

8. You have two hours to complete this exam. _____ early, you may turn in   A B C D
   your papers and leave the room quietly.

    (A) Should you finish   (C) You should finish
    (B) Should finish   (D) Should you have finished

9. I'd rather you _____ me after 10 P.M.   A B C D

    (A) wouldn't be calling   (C) didn't call
    (B) weren't to call   (D) didn't to call

10. _____ I hadn't forgotten to lock the door.   A B C D

   (A) If   (C) If only

   (B) Only   (D) Only if

11. Dr. Whittaker prefers that his students _____ their assignments on disk.   A B C D

   (A) would submit   (C) submit

   (B) had submitted   (D) to submit

12. If you had studied for the exam, you probably _____ a better grade.   A B C D

   (A) would have gotten (C) would get

   (B) will get   (D) will have gotten

13. Lynn looks _____ she hasn't slept in days.   A B C D

   (A) as well   (C) if only

   (B) what if   (D) as if

14. The committee proposed that the president _____ suspended.   A B C D

   (A) to be   (C) were

   (B) be   (D) is

15. I _____ those people sitting in front of us would stop talking.   A B C D

   (A) wish   (C) would rather

   (B) hope   (D) should hope

16. _____ I ask my boss for a raise and he fires me?   A B C D

   (A) Should I   (C) As if

   (B) What if   (D) Would

X. SYNTHESIS

Each sentence has four underlined words or phrases. The four underlined parts of the sentence are marked A, B, C, and D. Circle the letter of the ONE underlined part that is NOT CORRECT.

1. I <u>wouldn't</u> <u>walk down</u> that dark alley if I <u>was</u> you. What if an ax murderer   A B Ⓒ D
       A   B   C

   <u>is hiding</u> there?
     D

2. If we <u>would have</u> <u>bought</u> that house then, <u>we'd</u> <u>have</u> a valuable piece of property   A B C D
          A   B   C   D

   today.

3. The cat <u>might died</u> <u>if we</u> <u>hadn't</u> <u>adopted</u> her.   A B C D
         A   B   C   D

4. I <u>insist</u> <u>that</u> my proposal <u>is</u> <u>considered</u> formally.   A B C D
     A   B   C   D

5. Phil wishes he <u>hasn't</u> <u>left</u> his wallet in the movie theater, and he hopes it <u>hasn't</u>   A B C D
            A   B   C

   <u>been stolen</u>.
     D

6. <u>Would I have</u> <u>realized</u> this was the right thing to do, I <u>would have</u> <u>done</u> it sooner. **A B C D**
     A   B   C   D

7. Mr. Baldwin <u>moved</u> <u>that</u> the rule <u>is</u> <u>voted</u> on.
              A   B   C D

8. We <u>hope</u> you <u>would</u> <u>consider</u> our offer carefully. If you <u>accept</u> it, please let us **A B C D**
    A   B   C   D

know by the end of the week.

9. The president <u>wishes</u> he <u>has</u> a little free time. <u>If so</u>, he <u>would play</u> golf. **A B C D**
               A   B   C   D

10. I understand that you <u>need</u> some financial advice. <u>If not</u>, I recommend that you **A B C D**
                         A   B

<u>contact</u> Joe Fisher if <u>he's</u> available.
  C   D

11. I <u>wouldn't</u> <u>have told</u> Anne the truth <u>had I known</u> that she <u>will get</u> so upset. **A B C D**
    A   B   C   D

NOTES

NOTES

NOTES

NOTES

NOTES